PRISON GOVERNOR'S
JOURNAL

Jeelane Kiannoort y Phryssoon

D1420041

Brendan O'Friel

Published by

Brendan O'Friel 8 High Street, Port St Mary, Isle of Man IM9 5DR
First published in the Isle of Man in 2021.

Available through

www.prisongovernorjournal.com

ISBN 978 152 62 0847 7

Produced in association with
Lexicon Bookshop, 63 Strand Street, Douglas, Isle of Man IM1 2RL

Printed by
Quine & Cubbon Printers, Athol Street, Port St Mary, Isle of Man IM9 5DS

Front cover photograph
The author opening a security gate at HM Prison Risley.

PRISON GOVERNOR'S
JOURNAL

"The mood and temper of the public in regard
to the treatment of crime and criminals
is one of the most unfailing tests of
the civilisation of any country."

Winston Churchill

Above: A typical Victorian prison cell equipped for three people.

CONTENTS

"Members of the Prison Service as a whole, against heavy odds, have managed over a number of years to contain an almost impossible situation by showing immense dedication, courage and professionalism."

(Woolf Report 1991)

PART THREE – HOPE FOR THE FUTURE?

APPENDICES

INDEX

ILLUSTRATIONS

Above: Strangeways Chief Officers together in uniform for the last time in June 1987.

INTRODUCTION

ABOUT THE BOOK

Prisons are among our oldest human institutions. Anecdotes about prisons – often scandals or disasters – are chronicled from very early times. Despite long experience, our record of running acceptable penal institutions is at best varied and at worst disastrous.

When States authorise detention, individuals lose freedoms. But detention can result in individuals suffering poor living conditions, the threat of pain and injury through violence from fellow detainees or staff and – in very extreme circumstances – death. The Nazi Concentration Camps are a stark reminder of the terrible depths to which humanity can sink when treating detainees.

Since 1946, many staff and many prisoners within the Prison Service in England and Wales have been through a torrid time. In 2020 the Covid 19 Pandemic added a new unprecedented challenge. Staff and prisoners face a very difficult future. It was this additional threat – and possible opportunity – that spurred me to complete my book.

Since I retired, many people had encouraged me to write about my years in the Prison Service of England and Wales. So this book began as a record of my experiences to help provide a reasonably accurate account of the very troubled times the Prison Service endured since 1946. There are few accounts available written by Governors. My recollections will not give a complete picture – rather how events appeared to me at the time and after reflection.

Public ignorance about the Service is hardly surprising. Locked away behind high walls, life in prisons is largely hidden from view. What emerges through the media is frequently misleading and almost always lacks balance.

The work of the Service is often caught up in wider public attitudes towards crime and offenders. Unfortunately public debate on reducing crime and making the public safer is usually woefully short on evidence and too often fuelled by dubious sound bites. Decades of prison crises have failed to enlist sufficient public support for reform.

If we are to have a Service playing a full and constructive part in our Criminal Justice System, substantial changes are needed. The starting point for change and improvement is understanding what went wrong and why. Because the book has been written over many years, I have had time to reflect on and re-examine some recent prison history. As radical improvements are urgently needed, I include suggestions for launching a programme of change.

While many diverse issues have beset the Prison Service in England and Wales, two fundamental problems stand out throughout the last seventy years.

First, the accommodation available in prisons – especially the number of cells – has been totally inadequate to house the avalanche of prisoners committed to prison by the courts. This challenge, first emerging around 1946, has never been adequately addressed. Now a chronic disorder, overcrowding has crippled the Service.

Second, and of at least equal importance, is the failure to provide adequate numbers of suitably trained and motivated staff. This omission is equally chronic and has led to decades of missed opportunities for delivering positive regimes for prisoners to reduce re-offending and better protect the public.

In my opinion, it is the combination of these two chronic failures that have led to the Service in England and Wales having such a lengthy and disturbing record of successive disasters.

In this book, as well as describing life in seven establishments, I focus on a number of key concerns impacting the Service. To assist readers, I identify those chapters most relevant to each concern. To understand these concerns, considerable detail is necessary because the task of running prisons is complex.

These are:
- Overcrowding – Chapter 14 and 35
- Staffing – Chapter 15
- Management of Prisons – Chapter 16
- Regimes – Chapters 20, 22, 26 and 31
- National Management and Leadership – Chapter 32
- Industrial Relations – Chapters 17, 24 and 36
- Contribution of the Governors Representative Organisations – Chapters 13, 25 and 34-37

The core of the book describes my experience of working with prisoners and staff in the seven establishments in which I served. This included two tours at Manchester Prison, opening the new Borstal Recall Centre at Onley; experience of Lowdham Grange, an "open" young offender Borstal; in charge of both male and female offenders at Risley Prison; working at Birmingham's Winson Green "Local" Prison and at the "Training" Prisons at Featherstone and Preston.

I begin by painting a picture of how establishments worked fifty years ago as seen through my eyes as a junior and inexperienced Assistant Governor. My career took me through several establishments as Deputy Governor – so I attempt to capture the way different establishments worked and the varied duties and challenges faced by a Deputy Governor. Then as a senior Governor during difficult times, what was it like to be taking considerable responsibility in the thick of crises – both in establishments and when holding HQ and Regional posts?

Throughout the book, there is a focus on leadership. Senior staff in the Service faced considerable ongoing challenges and some exceptionally demanding situations. I endeavour to capture the complexity of the problems of leadership and to highlight what appeared to work. This may be of interest to those currently working in prisons and perhaps in other organisations.

Being elected Chairman of the Governors' Representative Organisation from 1977 to 1984 (The Governors' Branch) and from 1990 to 1995 (The Prison Governors Association), I worked closely with many senior people in the Service and met many politicians who served as Home Secretary and as Prison Ministers. In particular, I had an unusual – perhaps unique – opportunity to see how politicians and their senior advisers dealt with some of the many crises that beset the Service between 1963 and 1996. Very little has been recorded about the work of the Governors' Representative Organisations so I shall provide some insight into how we operated and what impact – if any – we had.

There are many unanswered questions including:

- Why has prison overcrowding lasted so long and what damage has it done?
- Why did the Service suffer disaster after disaster?
- Why were acute staffing and Industrial Relations problems not tackled earlier?
- If Ministers and senior officials knew that Prison Officers did not have the right to strike, why was it kept so secret?
- Were there undisclosed factors around the decision not to try and retake Strangeways on April 2nd 1990?
- Why is the prison population in the UK so high when many of our European neighbours have much lower prison populations?

Unanswered questions are often the most interesting. Can this book shed any more light on them? Perhaps! Many of these questions require further research. Accurate analysis of past prison issues should help to provide a sound basis for developing effective and relevant future prison strategies.

ABOUT THE SERVICE

The task of the Prison Service is complex and frequently difficult. Prisons are required to contain people who do not want to be there. Few people enjoy being restricted in any way – and prisoners are no different. Much of the work of prison staff is managing a mix of inadequate, unstable, difficult and demanding people who are constantly looking for ways to get round the inevitable restrictions of being in prison.

Relationships – as Lord Justice Woolf emphasised – are crucial if stability is to be preserved in any prison. Simply applying "the rules" makes for dispirited staff and disgruntled prisoners. To achieve positive relationships, stability and continuity is required so that staff and prisoners can develop these crucial relationships. That requires considerable management attention to the use of staff, to staff training and working to achieve the greatest possible stability within the prisoner population.

To prevent prisons being – as Douglas Hurd succinctly described – "expensive places for making bad people worse", it is essential that staff are able to exert an affirmative influence. Each prison needs to provide a positive regime – a demanding programme of activity to educate, develop skills and – wherever possible – to challenge and to try and change offending behaviour. It is crucial to develop purposeful regimes within which prisoners' latent talents – and they have many – are encouraged to grow and flourish.

Why? Because positive regimes reduce the prospects of re-offending – which reduces the future risk to the public from discharged prisoners. Prisoners discharged from prison frequently re-offend. The Report of the Social Exclusion Unit "Reducing Re-offending by ex-Prisoners" 2002 reported that of the prisoners released in 1997 58% were reconvicted within two years. For young offenders the figures were worse – some 72% of 18-20-year-old males were reconvicted within two years. So there is an urgent need to reduce reconviction rates.

The alternative to staff exerting affirmative influences and providing demanding programmes is bleak. My experience was that staff can quickly retreat behind applying "the rules", disengage from prisoners and become thoroughly bored.

For prisoners, the alternative to positive regimes is deterioration. Prisons can easily become universities of crime. The old sayings about "rotten apples contaminating the whole barrel" and "the devil finding work for idle hands" are all too true. Bored prisoners rapidly seek other ways of occupying themselves and before long prisoners deteriorate, standards drop and planning future crime and criminal activities become the main focus of interest. Weaker prisoners suffer bullying; injuries and self-harm incidents multiply.

Public attention has recently focussed on how prisoners can be "radicalised" in prison. Some – perhaps many – of those involved in recent terrorist activities have been petty criminals with a string of minor convictions. Unfortunately some of these impressionable individuals have fallen victim to the influence and propaganda of extremists while in prison and have gone on to plan and sometimes execute serious terrorist attacks. This further reinforces the need to run positive programmes in prison to combat the danger of petty criminals emerging from custody likely to become more serious offenders or terrorists.

All too often, parts of the media and some politicians criticise what they describe as "lax rules and luxurious conditions" in prisons. Our new prison (2009) at Jurby in the Isle of Man is sometimes referred to as the "Jurby Hilton"! Such criticisms are rarely accurate and never balanced. Having talked to very many groups of ordinary folk over some 50 years, I find that most people recognise the need for the treatment of prisoners to be positive so that, wherever possible, it leads to a lower risk of re-offending through prisoners attending offending behaviour programmes and acquiring improved education and skills.

During my time as Governor of Risley, we opened some well-designed new cellular accommodation. Many visiting parties came round the prison: I usually met them at the end of their visit to answer questions and hear about their impressions. I often told them that we had a few spare cells if anyone fancied staying with us overnight. I never got a taker! It is one thing to talk in the abstract of new prisons as "hotels" – it is quite another to volunteer to experience what it is really like to be locked up!

Recent events may be changing public perceptions. Most people in 2020 suddenly lost some of their freedoms for months under the Covid 19 "Lockdown". Could this loss create a much greater and wider public recognition of the pain caused by loss of freedom? Has the Pandemic created a unique "window of opportunity" to revisit and review our approach to punishing offenders?

This book is divided into three parts:

Part One describes my early life and identifies factors that may have influenced me towards joining the Prison Service. This includes my Irish and Manx family background, my education at Stonyhurst College and Liverpool University and my involvement with religion. I have tried to capture some of the many connections between my early life and my subsequent career in the Service.

Part Two records some of my experiences of working in the Service – largely chronological – but as explained above, also exploring overarching issues like overcrowding, staffing, and Industrial Relations. My account covers the work of the Governors' Representative Organisations, not previously recorded.

Part Three draws together some conclusions and looking ahead suggests possible ways of achieving change and improvement for the Prison Service in England and Wales. The suggestions may be of value for other prison services facing similar problems.

Appendices include a short description of my involvement with the Irish Prison Service after retirement. While there are occasional references to my various post-retirement activities, this book is largely focussed on my experiences in the Service.

I have utilised Appendix C – "Further Reading" – to assist readers find many of the documents mentioned in the text.

Port St Mary
December 2020

PART ONE – EARLY YEARS

1. FAMILY BACKGROUND

I was born on the Isle of Man in March 1941. My father, an Irish doctor, had volunteered to serve in the Royal Navy; my mother – being from an old Manx family – sensibly returned to the Island from her career as a pharmacist in England to have her first – and as it turned out – only child. That is how I came to spend the first five years of my life on the Island at my grandparents' house on Devonshire Road in Douglas, the Island's capital.

Grandfather, Philip Ernest Cowley – known as "Ernie" – had been a Bank Manager with the Isle of Man Bank; he had run the branches at Laxey – where my mother had been born – and then at Port St Mary. Retiring in 1935, my grandfather had bought a house – the family had lived in the Bank's tied housing until then – and moved to Douglas. At the outbreak of war, he was asked to return to the Bank to fill vacancies created by men volunteering for the services. When time and weather permitted he would take me to church services at Rosemount, Kirk Braddan and All Saints. As a great treat we would sometimes watch the Steam Packet ships arriving at or departing from Douglas Harbour. I can still remember seeing a Steam Packet ship laid up at the inner harbour with her three propellers visible.

Mother, Phyllis Margaret, was the youngest of three. She was educated at Douglas High School for Girls while living in Port St Mary. She travelled to school on the steam trains – the very same trains and rolling stock which still operate on the Island – leaving Port St Mary at 07.03 for Douglas. From Douglas High, she obtained a place at Manchester University to read Chemistry and qualified as a pharmacist.

Her two older brothers went into the merchant navy and banking. Eric the eldest of the family was lost in the sinking of the SS Glenorchy on 13th August 1942 during the heroic "Pedestal" Convoy attempting to relieve Malta. When I researched his death I discovered that the engineers – of which he was one – sent all the stokers on deck while they stayed below keeping the engines going. All the engineers were lost; the stokers all survived. That was leading by example. Eric's name is engraved on the Island's War Memorials.

My branch of the Cowley family originated from Crammag, an old hill farm or "Tholtan", overlooking Sulby reservoir below Snaefell in the middle of the Island. Cowleys had lived around Crammag – which means "little hill" – since well before 1600 according to research undertaken by family members. In the nineteenth century, my ancestors had moved to Sulby village and then to Ramsey where my great-grandfather, Robert Cowley, set up a farmers' merchants business – latterly known as Corlett, Sons & Cowley, a company that still trades. He entered local politics becoming Chairman of the Ramsey

Town Local Authority. During his term of office he was involved in setting up the Mooragh Park, a remarkable reclamation of a sea marsh area adjacent to Ramsey Harbour. Elected as a Member of the House of Keys (MHK), the lower house of the Manx Parliament for the adjacent constituency of Ayre, he served for 10 years until his early death in 1906.

As a youngster I saw a little of my great-uncle Percy Cowley who had a remarkable career including becoming "First Deemster", the Chief Judge on the Island. I remember him clearly and positively as he showed great interest in whatever we were involved with. Researching his career, I was fascinated to find he played a critical role as Chair of the Island's "War Cabinet" during World War Two and led the team that purchased Ronaldsway airport – at a very good price – from the British Government. His legacy included the setting up of the Manx National Trust – now Manx National Heritage – preserving Manx history for future generations.

Above: Percy Cowley memorial at The Sound, Isle of Man.
© Manx National Heritage (PG/11134).

Grandma was born Margaret Faragher, one of three surviving children of John and Margaret Faragher. Her father had been a talented cabinet maker in Douglas.

Father's family came from Fanad in north Donegal around the townland of Ballymichael, not far from Gartan, where the O'Friels had deep historical roots. The Irish side of the family are believed to be related to the great Saint Columcille – or Columba, as he was known in English.

My Irish grandfather, Francis O'Friel, had been a member of the Royal Irish Constabulary (RIC) – a good secure career choice for him and also for one of his brothers, George. Other family members opted for the Lighthouse Service

– secure Government jobs for Catholics. In 1922, at the Partition of Ireland, he was an RIC sergeant in Belfast but decided to retire and take his pension. He told me "I wasn't acceptable to the new Royal Ulster Constabulary – because I was a Catholic; I wasn't acceptable to the new Irish Police, the Garda Siochana, in Dublin because I came from the north".

My Irish grandma was born Rose Campbell. She was a schoolteacher, the daughter of a Headmaster who – in the late nineteenth century – had run the village school in Maghery on the shores of Loch Neagh in County Antrim. Education was a high priority in the family and Rose and Francis O'Friel put their five surviving children through Queen's University Belfast, a notable achievement. The funding arrangements involved the elder children paying for their younger siblings' university fees – no student grants or loans in those days. The eldest, May, was reputed to be the first Catholic to graduate with honours in English from Queen's University. My father Arthur James, qualified as a doctor and moved to England because of the difficulty for Catholics in obtaining work in Northern Ireland.

In 1946, when the war ended, my father was demobbed and bought a medical practice in Ellesmere Port, on Merseyside. I flew across with Grandfather Cowley in a Dragon Rapide from Ronaldsway to Liverpool's Speke airport, a flight that took well over an hour. I distinctly remember that experience – very noisy and uncomfortable and nearly put me off flying for life!

We lived in the centre of Ellesmere Port from 1946 to 1958 until my parents built a house – called "Gartan Lodge" – in Little Sutton, some 3 miles away. I attended the local Catholic primary school – Our Lady's Star of the Sea – for five years and was then sent off to boarding school at Stonyhurst College in Lancashire run by the Jesuit Fathers.

2. MANX AND IRISH INFLUENCES

As I grew up I was considerably influenced by my Manx and Irish relatives. Being an only child, links with my Manx and Irish cousins were important. I saw more of my three Manx cousins, as they were close to my age, whenever I visited the Island. My eight Irish cousins were younger, the eldest, Rosaleen, being 5 years younger than me – I saw much more of them later in life as adults. I developed a particular link with cousins Anna and Kathleen who worked with the BBC as I gained experience of contributing to the media, as described in Chapter 13.

From 1947 to 1959, during most summer holidays we travelled either to the Isle of Man or Ireland – on the years when we visited Ireland, I usually visited the Island as well. We travelled overnight on the Belfast or Dublin ferry services from Liverpool, the car being craned on and off the ship: drive on/drive off car ferries was not yet generally available. Regular Irish holidays meant I visited much of Ireland. My grandparents often joined us travelling down from Belfast by train.

I developed a great interest in Ireland, especially Irish history and current affairs. This stood me in good stead in my dealings with the Northern Ireland Prison Governors over many years and later – after retirement – with my involvement with the Irish Prison Service recorded in Appendix A. When I was a youngster my Irish Grandmother presented me with the book "Twenty Years a Growing" starting me reading round Irish literature. My Auntie May – my father's sister – kept in touch by letter over many years – and she wrote an excellent letter with a memorable touch of humour. My Prison Service career interested her. Another of my father's sisters, Auntie Eileen, introduced me to the Irish Jesuit periodical "Studies" which covered a fascinating mix of Irish History, Church affairs and wider issues. My Irish cousins – Eileen's children – stayed in close touch with me, preserving my Irish connections.

When I returned to the Isle of Man I usually stayed with my cousins in Douglas and as I grew older I was allowed to cross on my own on the Steam Packet. In those days, the ships would reverse out of Douglas Harbour; the bow rudder had to be secured before they could start to move forward. The arrival of the bow thruster years later made it possible for the ships to turn around within the shelter of Douglas Harbour, a great improvement for the comfort of passengers. But on a rough day, sailing anywhere near Douglas Head can be very uncomfortable – as can be seen from the photograph below.

Above: Ben-my-Chree V, off Douglas Harbour, Isle of Man.   © Stan Basnett.

I started to appreciate how many relations I had on the Island – over 30 or so – many of whom we were expected to visit. I can recall sitting still while the adults talked! There was an exception. Great Aunt Dot Cowley, who lived above the Mooragh Park in Ramsey, greeted young visitors with a twinkle in her eye and sent us off to her special cupboard where she kept a great assortment of games and toys. Dot was also a great walker and was still walking 12 miles a day until she was eighty. Dot Cowley had the foresight to lodge an important family group photograph taken around 1890 with the Manx Museum – she had also identified each of the 20 people on the photo clearly on the back with their relationships with each other. Her initiative enabled our generation to discover more of our family history.

My links with the Island continued throughout my life. After we married and from when the children were very young, we made it a priority to have a Manx family holiday each year. For many summers we took a house at Gansey Point, close to Port St Mary's Chapel Beach. Organised activities for children such as the Port St Mary Regatta and the Scripture Union's Beach Mission provided plenty for the children to do. When they were older we acquired a flat in Port St Mary and some of them used this as a base for doing holiday jobs in the Island. Eventually we exchanged the flat for a house and settled back onto the Island full time in 2006.

I kept up my early interest in the Isle of Man Steam Packet's ferries and in 1977 – at the request of the publishers – substantially revised the book "Ships of the Isle of Man Steam Packet" by the late Fred Henry. In 1986, I completed another revision just before I took up post as Governor of Strangeways. I was fortunate to be introduced to Stan Basnett, a talented and committed photographer of ships, who kindly provided a selection of pictures of Steam Packet ships.

During my visits to the Island after I had joined the Prison Service, I occasionally visited the Isle of Man Prison at Victoria Road Douglas. This very small Victorian prison was built around 1890 to replace the cells in Castle Rushen, which had previously served as the Island's prison. An incident in the 1960s resulted in a change to the management of the prison. The person in charge had been known as the "Gaoler"; a Chief Officer from the service in England was appointed to take charge with the title "Chief Gaoler". A succession of appointments followed with varying degrees of success. When a vacancy arose around 1977, I suggested to Tom Rielly, a Principal Officer who worked for me on Staff Inspection, that he might consider applying. He was appointed and did much to improve a small overcrowded prison lacking many facilities. One of the very positive uses of prisoners from the Isle of Man Prison during the 1970s was to assist with agricultural work and at the three Manx Agricultural Shows during the summer.

Tom also succeeded in having the post regraded to take proper account of his responsibilities. So when the time came to appoint a successor, the post was advertised as the equivalent of a Governor Grade Three in England and Wales.

The Prisons Inspectorate from England and Wales was invited to inspect the prison, something I had long advocated. Isolation led to some practices being out of date and out of line with other western European services. Inspections – and the publication of Inspection Reports – helped the process of educating Manx politicians of the need for change – and in particular to recognise the need to invest in a new prison. Guernsey and Jersey had decided to build new prisons; the Isle of Man was under increasing pressure to do likewise.

Eventually the Manx Government decided to fund a new prison. Initial plans were for it to be sited near to Douglas at Braddan – adjacent to the Island's main hospital. Opposition – "not in my backyard" – drove it out to Jurby, an old World War Two disused airfield some fifteen miles from Douglas. The new prison was a huge improvement and I was pleased to visit it in 2008 just before it opened.

Above: Jurby Prison, Isle of Man, under construction.   *© Culture Vannin.*

I discovered some interesting links between the Women's internment Camp – set up in the south of the Island during World War Two – and the Prison Service. The threat of treachery – as with the Quislings in Norway – led the British Government in 1940 to intern many born in enemy countries but living in the UK. Thousands were transferred to the Island in 1940. Women and children were separated from their husbands and sent to a camp in the south of the Island living in boarding houses in Port Erin and Port St Mary.

Soon after the camp was set up, the first commandant, Dame Joanna Cruikshank, was replaced by Detective Chief Inspector Cuthbert. He was given a woman deputy, Miss Joan Wilson, who was previously Governor of the women's prison at Strangeways, Manchester – not Liverpool's Walton Prison as the Connery Chappell book "Island of Barbed Wire" records. Joining the Prison Service in 1936 Joan Wilson had served as Deputy Governor of the girls' borstal at Aylesbury, Buckinghamshire. She served for around a year on the Island and continued her career as a Governor – after the war she was appointed Governor of Hill Hall prison. I also discovered that a Mrs JD Cole had worked as a welfare officer in the internment camp – this came to light because she was a friend of the painter William Hoggatt and some of their correspondence survives. Mrs Cole later joined the Prison Service as an Assistant Governor and served at Holloway from 1955 for some 10 years.

Another Manx link was to a cousin Ken Cowley. In 1998 I wrote his obituary for "The Times". Ken had a distinguished career in Kenya in the Colonial Service. Martin Cowley, Ken's father, had been my grandfather's older brother. Martin had moved to Merseyside and set up a very successful greengrocer's chain called "Waterworths". Educated on Merseyside and at Oxford, Ken had applied to join the Colonial Service. In Kenya, he played an important part in setting up the Masai Mara Game Reserve. He told me of an occasion he remembered – as a small boy – in the First World War crossing by Steam Packet ship to Douglas when they were stopped by a German submarine but eventually were allowed to proceed unscathed.

3. STONYHURST COLLEGE 1951-1960

Situated in the Ribble Valley, to me Stonyhurst felt quite isolated. Without half term breaks, we were away from home for at least twelve weeks. It was a relief to be taken out for meals when parents visited – Stonyhurst food was not great in those days. My father drove me up to school via Preston – we usually took a route past Preston Prison's gate, probably the first time I was conscious of the existence of prisons. As I got older, I joined others on the train to Whalley Station via Blackburn with a bus completing the last leg of the journey.

As an only child, my early days at St Mary's Hall, the Stonyhurst prep school, were challenging. I learned to survive and adapt. Although I was never near the top of the class, I was usually in the top set. My favourite subject was History followed by Geography and English – unfortunately the College did not include Geography for "A" level so my third subject had to be French which was not one of my strengths or interests.

Boys at the College included youngsters from South America, the Caribbean, Malta and Gibraltar. The school was not diverse compared with today's definitions – but it was sufficiently diverse for me to develop some sensitivity to different cultures. As a single-sex boys' boarding school, the College did not offer the opportunity to develop a balanced approach to the opposite sex. I was, therefore, pleased to see Stonyhurst become co-educational some twenty years ago.

One of the strengths of Stonyhurst, which lacked the traditional Public School "house" system, was the availability and range of societies and clubs. I learned to fence through having an excellent coach, a sport I was able to continue at University. Debating and the Catholic Evidence Guild (CEG) helped to develop communication skills – as well as learning to think about issues and listen to other points of view. I took part in the Lower and Higher Line Debating Societies at Stonyhurst, being on the "Board of Six" in my last year or two, the group that took the lead in organising debates. Each speaker in the debating society had to choose a "constituency". I was always the member for "Port St Mary", building on my Manx roots. On 14th February 1960 I was the first Stonyhurst boy to appear live on TV while still at school on the "Sunday Break" programme. This happened because of my work for the CEG and Fr Vincent Whelan – adviser to ITV – organised it. The programme was live from Manchester. I was told a large group of my colleagues watched the programme in the Bayley Room at the College! Little did any of us know that some 30 years on, I would be in the international media spotlight during the Strangeways riots!

The CEG played a significant part in my life during my last 3 years at Stonyhurst and during my 3 years at Liverpool University. I was General Secretary at Stonyhurst in my final year – one initiative was running a "pitch" in Blackburn most term-time weekends. It was through this work that I got to know Fr Vincent Whelan – we kept our "platform", the stand on which speakers stood, at his youth premises.

The CEG trained boys to speak in public. Speakers were expected to describe and take questions about specific Catholic subjects – "Confession" and "Papal Infallibility" were examples. Speakers were "licensed" by the Guild – and were tested by a panel before being granted a licence. The crunch came when questions were asked by those listening – the crowd. Developing skills at answering questions – which we were trained to repeat so that the crowd knew what had been asked – was a real test of knowledge, ability to think on one's feet and to build a relationship with the crowd. Training involved working in groups to study the topic – and at Stonyhurst developing and practising our skills in public in the school playground – quite a daunting trial in front of one's peers. The CEG had around 50 boys taking part in my time at the College – and it attracted the less conventional individuals who might otherwise have had very little active involvement with their religion.

While at Stonyhurst I spoke at Manchester's Platt Fields, and at London's Tower Hill, Marble Arch and Charing Cross. I was fortunate to meet Frank Sheed and Maisie Ward, an incredible and inspiring couple who were still the driving force behind the Guild movement. They ran the publishing house of Sheed & Ward in London and New York: both were inspired writers and their books had a considerable impact on my thinking and development, laying foundations for the way my underlying philosophy developed as a Governor in the Prison Service.

I was also greatly influenced by Fr Paul Magill SJ, Chaplain to the CEG at Stonyhurst, who gave me considerable scope as General Secretary to organise and drive things forward – he was very good at motivating people. I learned much from him – which undoubtedly influenced my approach to people in the Prison Service – and other organisations – for decades to come. Looking back, Paul Magill taught me much about leadership by example. Although a big man with a considerable presence, his most effective work with me was listening to my reports of how the CEG was going and gently steering me to take good decisions.

In 1966, I was asked back to the College to give a talk. One of the older Jesuits, Fr Macadam, drew me to one side and said "Now you have joined the Prison Service Brendan, there are some old boys I think I had better tell you about!"

A year or two later this was brought home to me at Manchester Prison. An old Stonyhurst boy was sentenced to Borstal Training and briefly occupied the cell next to my office before he departed to a training borstal.

Our family connections with Stonyhurst continued. It included celebrating our silver wedding at the College in 1989 and it was the venue for the marriage of our elder son, Francis, to Claire on April 1st 1995. I was asked back to the College on a number of occasions to give talks about my work in the Prison Service.

Above: Stonyhurst College, Lancashire.

4. RELIGIOUS HERITAGE AND FRUSTRATIONS

The Catholic Faith had been an integral part of my life at Stonyhurst and continued to influence me at University and beyond. When I started my degree course at Liverpool University in October 1960, a new parish – St Saviours – had just been established in Ellesmere Port. Fr Jo O'Donnell, parish priest and close friend of my parents, asked me to set up an altar staff. I agreed and enjoyed recruiting, training and encouraging some 15 boys for the 3 years I was at University. This was the start of a long connection with altar serving!

The Prison Service caused us to frequently move – it was our seventh family house when we arrived in Sutton Coldfield in 1977. Our children coped remarkably well with a succession of primary schools but as secondary schooling approached, we needed some stability. We managed to stay in Sutton Coldfield for 9 years. The older children started at Bishop Walsh School. Our local parish was Holy Cross and St Francis at Walmley. Fr John Berry, parish priest, asked me to set up a branch of the St Stephen's Guild for altar servers. By 1986, some 30 boys were involved with the altar staff – including several who continued serving when available during their university holidays.

From the 1970s, we developed a close connection with St Columba's Church at Port Erin in the south of the Isle of Man. Fr Gerry Hurst, the long-serving parish priest, attended our silver wedding in 1989 at Stonyhurst. When we moved back to the Island in 2006, I became involved for a third time with altar servers and set up a branch of the St Stephen's Guild, this time involving both girls and boys. Another interesting challenge!

At Sutton Coldfield and again at Warrington, Barbara and I were involved in helping run courses – under the auspices of the Catholic Marriage Advisory Council – for those preparing for marriage.

From time to time I was asked by Christian groups, including Catholic organisations, to give talks about the Christian approach to crime and punishment. This was an opportunity to encourage people to see offenders for what they so often were, damaged individuals who had few of the opportunities many of us had enjoyed.

In some of these talks, I found it helpful to encourage people to reflect on the many references to prisons in the Bible going back to the successes of Joseph – perhaps the first recorded "Redband" or "trustee" prisoner. There are accounts of events in prisons in the New Testament including – in the Acts of the Apostles – some remarkable prison escapes.

For Christians and others considering their approach to offenders, the New Testament has clear messages. St Mathew's Gospel Chapter 25 includes prisoners as one of the groups for whom Christians are advised to demonstrate special care. Why? Because our care for prisoners is to be one of the tests applied to each person on Judgement Day.

What does care for prisoners mean in practice? Great work is done by many Christian – and other – organisations whose aim is to assist offenders. The Society of St Vincent de Paul (SVP), for example, works with offenders and their families. Such organisations need support. There is so much need – so much to do.

During my career, I worked with many chaplains and encouraged the religious contribution to the development, motivation and improvement of offenders. In Chapter 7, I describe trying to solve difficulties between one chaplain and his Governor. Bishops regularly visited prisons, often at Christmas, demonstrating a pastoral interest and concern for prisoners and staff.

Sustaining the work of penal establishments through prayer and spiritual support requires greater recognition. At Strangeways it was promoted through an excellent monthly "Prayer Letter" which still circulates widely. Among Barbara's wide Catholic connections was an aunt, a Carmelite nun at Dolgellau. Auntie Norah's community offered important spiritual support over many years, praying for victims, prisoners, families and staff.

Reflecting on the Christian approach to crime and punishment, I was struck by the way the odds were stacked against offenders – often because of their upbringing and lack of opportunity. So I became increasingly interested in the "Preferential Option for the Poor" partly as a result of reading what Fr Michael Campbell Johnson SJ had written. Many prisoners seemed to me to qualify as "the poor". My views were also influenced by being involved in the Working Group that produced "A Time for Justice" for the Catholic Bishops – referred to in Chapter 21.

My approach as a leader and organiser of prison staff and the wider prison community was – I hoped – grounded on Christian principles. An example was the importance of treating everyone – no matter how difficult – with respect – and working to achieve equal opportunities. Relationships were crucial to influencing prisoners and I strove to encourage staff towards making a difference. Such an approach was common to many religions not just Christianity.

In order to make a difference, staff had to know that they too were highly valued as individuals. I became heavily involved in the moves to introduce equal opportunities into the Service, especially at Manchester and Risley as described in Chapters 26 and 31.

The Pandemic of 2020 and the resulting "lockdown" gave all of us cause to reflect on the priorities that influenced our lives. During Holy Week 2020, Pope Francis delivered a powerful message about "Our Common Home" and encouraged us all to reconsider our priorities and reduce the damage we are inflicting on our world.

Among those many priorities is addressing the chronic problems of the

Prison Service in England and Wales. If there is to be fundamental change in the Prison Service, 2020 could prove to be a turning point. But it will require huge effort from the whole community to rethink our approach to offenders and reorder our priorities. How this process might develop will be discussed in Part Three.

My Christian belief does not blind me to problems within the Catholic Church. The Church's response to child sex abuse scandals, especially the response of many in positions of authority, was totally inadequate. Given the responsibilities of Bishops, is adequate training provided on appointment to ensure they are equipped to undertake their onerous duties?

Human beings need support and supervision. Some of the clergy have insufficient of either. Clergy – at all levels – have to be accountable for their actions. Some clergy appear to have had very limited training about running organisations and about inter-personal relationships. Feedback is sometimes not encouraged, expected or accepted.

Consulting the laity is a critical issue. Machinery – such as Parish and Pastoral Councils – is needed – as many parish issues need careful consideration and discussion. Final decision should take account of the views of lay people. Financial resources are largely donated by the laity – lay expertise should be more fully utilised through parish Finance Committees.

The apparent inability of the Church to take forward the issue of ordaining married priests is very discouraging. So too is the lack of involvement of women in Church ministry. I fear that one motivation for resistance to change – often cloaked in obscure theological and biblical arguments – is underlying male attitudes within a closed male organisation finding it extremely difficult to reform and modernise. It sometimes feels not unlike the opposition I faced years ago to introducing women officers into male prisons.

5. PRISON SERVICE VIA LIVERPOOL UNIVERSITY

When I was considering applying to University, my preference was to train to be a teacher and to study history. My father, coming from a family of teachers, regarded teaching as not suitable for a male – his sisters were all teachers – and pressed me to study another subject. We compromised on Law and I started in 1960 at Liverpool University's Law Faculty under Professors Seaborne Davies and Dennis Browne.

Going to Liverpool turned out to be a very sensible move. After 9 years away at boarding school, I needed to become grounded in real life. Walking up to the University each day was part of that process, passing very poor children and very poor housing. The University was full of challenging ideas and my continuing work with the CEG brought me into contact with a very wide cross-section of people.

Living at home, I travelled on the train from Little Sutton station, changing to the Mersey Electrics at Rockferry for Liverpool Central. The service from Little Sutton to Rockferry changed from steam to diesel during my time as a student commuter, an experience I was to remember when I became Chair of the North West Rail Passengers Committee nearly 40 years later.

At Liverpool University I regularly took part in the Student Guild debates, and won the Law Faculty's "Dean's Debating Cup" – set up by Professor Seaborne Davies – in my first year. I also joined the University Fencing Club, building on my experience at Stonyhurst, and regularly represented the University, gaining my University colours.

I found my degree course a rather mixed experience. Roman law – with a very poor lecturer – was dreadful; Criminal law, with Seaborne Davies, was interesting. I was uncertain about a career in law, but continued on, becoming Secretary to the Faculty's Law Society. The Faculty attracted a significant Welsh contingent – not surprising with Seaborne Davies' influence – but I found the approach of a few of the Welsh students unfriendly as they would switch to Welsh if they didn't want you to know what they were speaking about. A useful lesson in what not to do to win friends!

Another new experience at University was being exposed – for the first time – to disability issues. We had a mature student in our year – Frank – who had lost his sight and was retraining as a lawyer. Frank depended on a guide dog "Queenie" who generally did an excellent job as Frank came in on the underground trains from the Wirral and then walked up Mount Pleasant to the Law Faculty. For me with little previous experience of disability, this was a valuable learning experience as I often walked up to the University with Frank.

At University, I joined the Liverpool branch of the CEG and became an experienced speaker at Liverpool Pierhead. In my third year at Liverpool University, I qualified as a CEG Chairman, which authorised me to run meetings in public as well as to speak in public. There had to be a Chairman in charge of every public meeting so I had greater responsibility. More importantly, I was exposed to a huge variety of views and a great cross-section of people through regularly speaking at Liverpool Pierhead; experiences which undoubtedly influenced me in my work in the Prison Service. We had regular hecklers, who included communists, a wide selection of Christians – from right-wing Catholics to fundamental Protestants – as well as atheists and agnostics. All were interesting and had knowledge and experience they were ready to share with me. Much discussion went on after completing speaking and taking questions, so I got to know a far wider range of people – some on the margins of society – than I had previously been exposed to in the relatively restricted and sheltered world of Stonyhurst.

One of the best learning experiences I had was during one miserable damp day down at the Pierhead. The Chairman, an unassuming Catholic of considerable experience as a speaker, opened the meeting – I was next up.

A large rather inebriated Orangeman appeared and proceeded to berate our Chairman quite unpleasantly. Suddenly he was stopped in his tracks. A small fury appeared before him – and I recognised the little old lady who sold flowers close by. She told the Orangeman his fortune and added about the Chairman "I have listened to this man week after week. He is a gentleman and you will not speak to him like that." The Orangeman departed tail between his legs. The interesting thing was that it was not so much what the Chairman had said as his politeness and concern that had impressed the flower seller. Actions speak louder than words. That was a lesson to ponder and absorb.

I helped organise the CEG National Conference – held in Liverpool – in 1962 where we arranged for an Anglican vicar to speak to us – a first for the Guild. It was at Liverpool CEG that I first met Dick Atherton, Chaplain to the Guild, later to become Mgr Dick Atherton, Senior RC Chaplain to the Prison Service.

So how did I become interested in the Prison Service? Although I became a student at Gray's Inn, I was still not keen on a career as a lawyer, either as a barrister or a solicitor. By my second year at Liverpool, I was starting to revisit my interest in teaching. Teaching experience was not generally available during university holidays, but I discovered that Home Office Approved Schools were open throughout the year. I managed to arrange visits to several of these Approved Schools in my last two years at University, including – with other students – some teaching experience at one school. I was horrified at what I saw in some of the Approved Schools – and with the idealism of youth wanted to change what I thought to be wrong to make the world a better place! Little did I know that some of the approved school boys I first met in 1962 and 1963 would appear as "old lags" in adult prisons that I governed between 1980 and 1995. Or that I would occasionally come across former offenders when I eventually retired to the Isle of Man, not all of whom appeared to be following a law abiding path.

The Home Office advert seeking Assistant Governors in the Prison Service caught my eye in the summer of 1963 – this seemed a better career opportunity for someone wanting to work with offenders than the Home Office Approved Schools – so I applied. Selection was by interview in Horseferry House in London. The panel consisted of senior Prison Service people. They included the remarkable Lady Charity Taylor, who had been promoted from Medical Officer at Holloway to Governor. She was – in 1963 – an Assistant Commissioner of Prisons. Lady Charity, whose obituary I was to write decades later, was probably the first woman Governor to combine a Prison Service career with raising a family.

The outcome of the interviews was announced by sending out a list of the successful candidates adding – "if your name is not on the list, you have not been successful". At least I had a list of people with whom I would be working and living for the coming six months and perhaps for years in the Prison Service.

PART TWO – PRISON SERVICE

6. PRISON SERVICE STAFF COLLEGE 1963-1964

The Course

Assistant Governors were recruited annually by the Prison Service through public advertisements: usually between 20 and 30 were appointed. They included promoted prison officers, mature people with experience of working overseas especially in the Colonial Police and Prison Services, some young graduates and others from very diverse backgrounds. We were joined by a small group appointed by the Scottish Service. Three women arrived – destined for the women's service which – in those days – was quite separate. A decade later the first woman Assistant Governor was posted to a male young offender establishment.

The Prison Service recruited people with a range of degrees including theology, geography and social science. My law degree proved helpful and relevant as the work of the service was heavily influenced by the Prison Act and the accompanying statutory regulations such as the Prison and Borstal Rules.

In late September 1963, we assembled at the Prison Service Staff College at Wakefield for a six month training course. We were the "Twentieth Staff Course" as we followed a fairly well-established programme by which the Prison Service aimed to prepare us for the challenging task of working with offenders. The College – in Love Lane – was opposite Wakefield Prison and sandwiched between the prison and the main Leeds to London railway line.

Our training began with a week's attachment to a penal establishment. Four of us went to Everthorpe near Hull, a new "closed" i.e. secure borstal. The plan

Above: 20th Staff Course – Autumn 1963.

was to give us a very brief taste of officer duties so we shadowed the borstal staff from early in the morning until late at night. A key learning moment was when I went off with an experienced officer and a party of ten lads to pick carrots on the borstal farm. The officer settled us down to work; then said he was off to see two other lads working in an adjacent field. I was left with the rest of the party and had to face the reality of being on my own with offenders who – not surprisingly – wanted to talk rather than work. This early experience brought home to me how difficult it can be for an officer working with offenders – especially for an inexperienced officer.

The Staff College course was residential. Some of us had not fully appreciated the standards expected – two of us turned up for a lecture without our jackets and were promptly told to go and put them on before the lecture commenced. To prepare us for the duty days expected of Assistant Governors, we worked alternate weekends. We had academic input on offenders; we started to learn about the service we had joined; we had occasional visiting speakers from HQ to give us their views of what we should seek to achieve as Assistant Governors.

We were allocated to one of three tutors who were experienced Assistant Governors and were able to share their recent knowledge of working in prison establishments. My tutor was AW (Bill) Driscoll who went on to become Governor of Liverpool's Walton Prison and Regional Director in the North Region. Bill was to be involved in resolving a hostage incident at Liverpool in which he was stabbed by the perpetrator. His braveness was acknowledged by him receiving the Queen's Gallantry Medal, the only Governor to do so in recent history. I became friendly with Bill and stayed in close touch with him. In 1989, he retired close to Lancaster and we continued to meet periodically to discuss the past and to mull over news of our many colleagues and friends from the Service. Another tutor was Brian Emes. I was to come across him again from time to time and at a crucial moment in April 1990.

Prisons in 1963 – and before

In September 1963, the Service was locking up some 28,000 prisoners. The Prison Commission had been abolished on 31st March 1963 and the Prison Service was now a department of the Home Office. The Death Penalty was still in place although executions were increasingly rare and soon to be suspended. Some of our mature course members had extensive experience of overseas prison services including executions.

Prison history was important. Centuries earlier, prisons were places for those awaiting trial, transportation or execution. As one historian had remarked, "Newgate was the antechamber for the New World or the Next." It was the ending of transportation – when the colonies refused to continue to take UK prisoners – that led to the prison building boom in the mid nineteenth century. Before that time, the prison system consisted of a large collection of "local" prisons run by the local authorities around the country. Many were very small and quite inadequate. Fortunately we have very graphic accounts of the state of the prisons in the eighteenth century from the great prison reformer, John Howard, so that we know in some detail what conditions were like – usually grim. The local prisons served the local courts holding those on remand, awaiting trial and also prisoners serving shorter sentences.

We learned about the major Victorian prison building programme. Pentonville was built in 1842 and a further 54 new prisons on the same model were built by 1848 providing 11,000 separate cells. Many of us were destined to work in these Victorian establishments for much of our service.

In addition to the many "local" prisons, there was the "convict prisons" system, a collection of larger prisons such as Dartmoor, Portland and Parkhurst, run and funded centrally, which from 1850 came under the Directors of the Convict Prisons. These prisons held the longer sentenced prisoners and the most serious offenders.

In 1878, the patchwork of small, outdated and often inadequate local prisons was nationalised and brought under the newly formed Prison Commission. The cost of running the prisons was transferred from local taxation – the rates – to central taxation. On April 2nd 1878 – vesting day – there were 20,442 prisoners in local prisons. Adding in the 8843 males and 1251 female prisoners held in the convict prisons gives a total population of just over 30,000. The total accommodation available was over 37,000 places in the 113 local and the 9 convict prisons. More places than prisoners.

The Directors of the Prison Commission were the same people as the Directors of the Convict Prisons so in practice the two systems were under unified control.

During the first few years of nationalisation, the local prisons were reduced from 113 to 59 with major savings in running costs. The prison population fell to around 20,000 at the beginning of the twentieth century.

One early change during the first years of a national prison service was the imposition of a rigid uniformity into the regime of prisons. This had advantages in sweeping away past very poor practice but imposed great rigidity into prisons that made innovation difficult. Sir Edmund Du Cane first Chairman of the Prison Commissioners was reported to have told an international Conference that he knew exactly what was happening in any prison at any time. The "routine" or the "timetable", a central instruction of precisely when any prison activity would occur, was the tool for implementing this rigidity. Interestingly, Paterson, the great reformer of the interwar years, remarked "Prison routine, however carefully thought out and intelligently applied, will not change the course of a man's life".

At the end of the First World War there was a further remarkable and sustained decline in the prison population. Throughout the 1920s and 1930s there were between 10,000 and 13,000 in prison. The inevitable happened and the Government instituted another major programme of prison closures which was only partly offset by the opening of several open borstals and one open prison. By 1935 the prison system had 16,000 places and about 11,000 prisoners.

I remember my astonishment at being told by an old Chief Officer who had joined the service at Wakefield not long before World War Two that there were no prisoners located in cells on the top landing – the "fours". Why not? Because there were fewer prisoners than cells and it made good sense to keep them located on the lower landings. For those of us who were to face the need to place two or three prisoners together in a single cell, this was a world we could scarcely envisage. I will return to the issues around population in Chapters 14 and 35 on overcrowding.

Purpose and delivery of imprisonment

We were encouraged to discuss fundamental questions about the purpose of imprisonment, especially punishment and rehabilitation. Were the two compatible?

Our tutors introduced us to the various government reviews of penal policy from the Gladstone Committee of 1895 to the 1959 White Paper "Penal Practice in a Changing Society". We studied the Prison Act of 1952 and the various statutory instruments deriving from the Act. The Prison Rules set out that the Service had a duty with convicted offenders:

"The purpose of training and treatment of convicted prisoners shall be to establish in them the will to lead a good and useful life on discharge and to fit them to do so" (section 6).

But what did this mean in practice for those running prison establishments?

We were told that three primary tasks should concern us:

First – Custody – to prevent escapes.

Second – to provide acceptable living conditions for those in custody.

Third – to encourage rehabilitation in order to reduce re-offending on release.

We started to learn more of how prisons operated. A few visits were organised: some to penal establishments; others to external organisations to study how organisations ran. We started to learn the curious language of the service – such terms as "landings" – the different levels within cell blocks; "recesses" – the toilet facilities – especially on the landings of cell blocks; the "segregation unit" – where prisoners were kept apart either for their own safety; or because they were deemed a threat or while they were undergoing a period of punishment. Then there were endless abbreviations, initials – CNA – "Certified Normal Accommodation"; CC – "Cellular Confinement" and "E" List for "Escape" List.

A critical part of the security routine of any penal establishment was checking the prisoner "numbers" or "roll". The numbers of prisoners in custody had to be verified several times a day by the staff physically counting prisoners. Staff were not allowed off duty until the numbers of prisoners were agreed with the "Orderly Officer", often the Principal Officer in control of the establishment's routine. What complicated an apparently simple routine was that the total numbers in custody was constantly varying – for example by new arrivals or by prisoners being discharged. In training establishments this was not a frequent occurrence but in large local prisons and remand centres dozens of prisoners would be arriving and departing daily. The difficulties this could cause in practice became apparent when we were posted to establishments.

Learning about offenders

Lectures about offenders were delivered by academics and by our tutors. For many of us this was the beginning of a long learning curve as we tried to draw together theory and practice. Learning about offenders would continue throughout our career as additional research became available and our own experience of working with offenders accumulated. The College offered us no clear direction about what might prevent re-offending. We were told about the possible value of group work and case work; we gathered that education and skill training had a part to play in rehabilitation. But this was long before programmes to address offending behaviour were developed for prisoners.

Little discussion took place about research and re-offending. This was partly because of the difficulty of conducting such research. We were told that there was feedback available on young offenders through the Borstal Aftercare Organisation but this was patchy and not sufficiently systematic to be able to rely on it. We were introduced – in the broadest terms – to some of the difficulties of interpreting national crime figures.

Offenders are not understood by many people. This is in part because the media tends to sensationalise crime and encourage a highly oversimplified, negative and stereotypical view of offenders. This is compounded when politicians play the "tough on crime" card to improve their electoral prospects. It takes courage and fortitude to display a balanced attitude to offenders in the public arena and to be prepared to explain the complex problems society faces in reducing re-offending.

For a number of decades, the Prison Reform Trust has performed a very valuable public service by regularly publishing facts about offenders in a series known as "Bromley Briefings". These briefings provide the public with a snapshot of offenders and their backgrounds, compared with the general population. For instance:

The social characteristics of prisoners:

	General Population	Prison Population
Ran away from home as a child	11%	50%
Taken into care as a child	2%	27%
Regularly truanted from school	3%	30%
Excluded from school	2%	49%
No qualifications	15%	52% men; 71% women
Homeless	1%	32%
Suffers from 2 or more mental disorders	5%	72%
Drugs use in the previous year	13%	68%
Hazardous drinking	38% men/ 15% women	63% men/ 39% women

This was the background of the people we were going to be responsible for. Statistics conceal the real people: there was a great deal more for us to learn, as individual offenders are as diverse as the rest of society, each with their own unique story, often one of multiple deprivations. Especially concerning was the exceptionally high incidence of mental illness, coupled with drug and alcohol abuse.

We were to learn how many prisoners had appalling experiences of relationships with parents, teachers, employers and authority figures generally. So they were often slow to make relationships and suspicious of authority. Couple this with poor communication skills and it will be apparent that many prisoners were without some of the basic life skills many of us take for granted.

An example of the inability to relate and communicate was often demonstrated when released prisoners tried to access services like the Health Service or Social Security. The requirement to queue and to wait for attention was not something they could easily cope with, and often a failure to access a service was because they had left a health facility or an office having lost their temper because they were frustrated. These were issues that prisons and other agencies needed to address with prisoners.

Many prisoners – we also learned – had very poor health records and appalling dental records. This was brought home to me time and again over the years when I came across an individual offender I had first known early in my service. Almost invariably I was astonished at how greatly they had aged – often appearing to be old men (I had no experience with women offenders in my early years) and how afflicted they were by disease or disability. Further health issues were to emerge over the following decades including the arrival and spread of HIV and the return of tuberculosis.

Repeat offenders were of particular interest. We were told about the many prisoners who repeatedly appeared in prison – some over 20 times. So much for the alleged deterrent effect of prison – a point much emphasised by those in favour of harsher sentences and regimes. But most first offenders did not reoffend. The recidivist – the offender who returns time and again – was to challenge us throughout our service as we saw them age and deteriorate but continue to offend and return to our establishments. Many recidivists also came from families with a history of offending – a sad reflection on our inability to break the "cycle of re-offending" that blights the life of many offenders as well as the lives of their victims.

Terence and Pauline Morris had just published their important research "Pentonville – a sociological study of an English Prison." This started to expose the realities of one of the large Victorian prisons and made both fascinating and sobering reading.

The College taught us much about the way prisoners were treated and organised. In 1963, the Service partly depended on the use of selected prisoners as "Trustees" – virtually auxiliary staff. Prisoners were chosen to be "Red Bands" and "Blue Bands". Red Bands were prisoners who operated with little staff supervision often in trusted posts like the Prison Library or the Prison Chapel.

Blue Bands were prisoners who could supervise other prisoners – for example taking them from one part of the prison to another. Blue Bands did not survive the security changes of the Mountbatten Report; Red Bands continued to be used in differing ways in some prisons. Both had to display their coloured bands – on their arms – at all times to demonstrate their status. As new Assistant Governors we saw the system of Blue Bands and Red Bands in operation at Wakefield Prison especially on our weekly visits to interview prisoners as part of our training programme.

The use of prisoners to play a part in the organisation and running of prisons is a very interesting issue and one that – if deliverable in an ethical way – may be part of the answer to keeping the cost of running prisons within bounds. It is a subject that deserves further research and consideration. There may be considerable scope for prisoners assisting each other in the quest for rehabilitation and perhaps gaining qualifications which would assist their ultimate resettlement. Years later I was to experience the use of prisoners in assisting their peers through the adult literacy scheme and through the "Listeners" scheme introduced through the Samaritans as part of our efforts to reduce suicides. Both initiatives were successful.

Prisoners also provided the workforce for penal establishments. It was prisoners who worked in the kitchens and laundries and who kept the establishments clean. The co-operation of the prisoners was vital to running our prisons.

Preparing us to work with young offenders – and many of us were destined to be posted to young offender establishments – meant learning about borstal training. The name "borstal" originated from the Kent village where the old convict prison near Rochester was located. This was turned into a borstal just after 1900 as part of the move to develop more constructive approaches to young offenders. Those sentenced to Borstal Training – an indeterminate sentence from 9 months to 3 years – in my time shortened to 6 months to 2 years – were known as "Borstal Boys" – hence the title of Brendan Behan's book about his experiences at Hollesley Bay Colony, near Ipswich, as a young offender. Borstal boys were known as "lads" in day to day discussions in borstals. The word "trainee" was also brought in later to try and avoid the term "boy" or "lad".

Borstals developed their own culture and organisation in the interwar years. Lowdham Grange was opened in May 1930 as the first "open" borstal following a march by staff and young offenders from Feltham borstal in London. On 31st May 1935 – after a march of 110 miles from Stafford Prison – North Sea Camp near Boston in Lincolnshire opened with 20 lads and 6 staff. The housemasters, recruited to try and reform the young offenders, were expected to spend a very large part of their days, evenings and nights supervising and influencing the young men. At North Sea Camp where the work was extremely hard, reclaiming ground from the sea, hearing accounts of the life former housemasters lived in the thirties was fascinating – and perhaps rather horrifying! Alan Bainton, who was in 1963 Governor of Wakefield Prison, provided our Staff Course with such an account. We were glad times had changed! But the efforts of staff and lads over 50 years meant that almost 1000 acres of land was reclaimed – all excellent for farming. A considerable and little known achievement.

Prison Officers and Governors

The Second World War caused divisions between staff. When war broke out some staff volunteered to join the armed services, older staff were asked to continue in service to ensure prisons could function. Many prisons were closed; some suffered bomb damage – Hull, Liverpool and Portland for example, with prisoner and staff fatalities – so more cellular accommodation was lost. Fortunately prison numbers stayed exceptionally low for much of the war. When peace arrived, some older staff were allowed to retire, as many new recruits were available from those who had fought. But some of those who had remained to run the prisons were pacifists and we heard stories about tensions between some senior Governors and their newly acquired ex-military staff.

Governors were an interesting and diverse group of people. Some were from Christian – especially Quaker – backgrounds; some with experience of command in the Armed Services and other – usually Colonial – Police and Prison Services. While many Governors had similar views about practical issues over the treatment of prisoners and the running of prisons, there were sometimes tensions because of the different backgrounds and philosophies of the two groups.

We were taught very little about the way prison officers were organised to cover the work of an establishment. It would be a decade later before I started to grapple with shift systems, how staff were deployed and the importance of many of the detailed rules about meal breaks and lengths of shifts. Such "technical" deployment skills could make a huge difference to ensuring continuity of staff – a vital factor in prisons. This lack of training about staff deployment was a serious omission.

Nor did we focus on prison management systems, delegation and supporting communication systems. There was practically no discussion about Industrial Relations, an issue that was to dominate our lives at times. Leadership learning came largely through listening to serving Governors reflecting on their careers. There was no systematic attempt to look at management style and its potential impact on the culture, effectiveness and health of establishments. There was a reluctance to discuss what might be the most effective style of leadership.

We discussed how good staff role models had an impact on prisoners. I was to witness many staff – in countless different ways – make a positive impression on prisoners. This also applied to senior staff – time and again I saw the positive impact that good senior staff could have on less experienced staff. I also saw some very poor examples given to junior staff by senior staff who should have known much better.

One critical area in which we received no training was the use of force by staff. From time to time prisoners would assault other prisoners and would fight among themselves. Occasionally staff would be assaulted by prisoners. Officers were expected to intervene quickly and effectively when an alarm bell was sounded. But how this was to be controlled and documented was not – at that time – on the College's agenda. Nor was there sufficient discussion of the dangers of staff abusing their position of power over prisoners. These would be issues that we faced in establishments in the years ahead.

In the three weeks leading up to Christmas 1963 we were attached to an establishment to work closely with an Assistant Governor. I was sent to Lowdham Grange, the original open borstal near Nottingham. This was a valuable learning experience as the work we would find ourselves doing became clearer – especially day to day dealings with staff and young offenders. The six months of the course passed uneventfully but by March 1964 the priority for most of us was to know where we were being posted to.

Towards the end of the course, a TV programme was made about Assistant Governor Training in which several of us took part, the second time I had been involved in appearing on television.

In March 1964, I was interviewed by the Director of Borstal Administration who informed me I was to be posted to Lowdham Grange – where I had been working for my three week attachment before Christmas. This was an ideal location as I was by then engaged to Barbara Poole, a primary school teacher, who lived in Nottingham. I had met Barbara at a meeting of the Nottingham CEG during my Christmas attachment to Lowdham and we saw a great deal of each other over the next few months.

7. LOWDHAM GRANGE 1964-1966

Lowdham Grange was situated some 10 miles east of Nottingham, not far from the River Trent, less than 2 miles from Lowdham village. The borstal was built between two farms, situated part way up a hill. Staff quarters were close to the establishment. As few staff had cars, Lowdham felt quite remote and staff and visitors had plenty of walking to reach the nearest bus stop. For many of the young men sent to Lowdham it was a completely different experience from the city or urban life most had been born into.

Above: Lowdham Grange.

Life as an Assistant Governor – or Housemaster – at Lowdham Grange in 1964 was also very different from any of my previous life experiences. Governor Bill Noall, an ex-naval commander with substantial war service, ran the institution in an unusual – perhaps unique – way, spending a high proportion of his working week going around the establishment – often on a motor scooter – visiting and talking to staff and young offenders as they worked. He appeared to regard new young Assistant Governors as something akin to midshipmen – new, wet behind the ears and not to be taken too seriously! Luckily I arrived at

Lowdham with a colleague from the Staff Course, Reg Withers, a mature and experienced ex-PEI officer, who had a helpful sense of perspective when my frustrations about the Governor were getting the better of me. Reg went on to become a senior Governor and retired from Brixton.

Hugh Klare of the Howard League had written that "a good Assistant Governor should always feel rather frustrated". Klare was absolutely right – and I often thought – even when a senior Governor – that the comment still applied decades later to both senior and Assistant Governors.

On arrival at Lowdham I followed in the footsteps of many other bachelor Assistant Governors and lived in a room adjacent to the boys' dormitories. To get to my room at night, I had to contact the Night Patrol Officer to gain access. Occasionally I would be awoken by some misbehaviour but by and large the young offenders were reasonably well behaved. Fortunately new bachelor quarters were under construction when I arrived and I was soon able to occupy my own room a short distance away from the institution.

Despite the frustrations, I learned a great deal from Governor Bill Noall, especially the value of knowing in detail what was really happening in an establishment – but his management technique with his senior team did not always bring out the best in us! In those days, Governors dealt with a daily round of adjudications and applications – deciding on the guilt of offenders charged with internal disciplinary offences and awarding punishment on those found guilty – and listening to individuals who had issues they wanted to raise. Governors were also required to deal with a range of staff matters including authorising staff overtime – a function often left to the Chief Officer

Above: Borstal boys milking.

– dealing with staff disciplinary issues, complaints about staff quarters – most staff lived in tied housing close to the establishment. Cheques had to be signed, security keys checked, specialist staff such as doctors and chaplains dealt with. Governors were required to write an annual report about the state of their establishments and in earlier years extracts from Governors reports were included in the Prison Commissioners' Annual Report. Once a year the boundaries of the establishment had to be walked to check their integrity. At Lowdham, this was a task usually delegated to young Assistant Governors and one year I accompanied the Deputy Governor on a considerable hike – there were 2 farms and over 600 acres on the Lowdham Estate.

Following their march of 132 miles from Feltham in May 1930, borstal boys and staff had built Lowdham Grange, the first "open" establishment in England. By "open" is meant without a perimeter wall or security fence, although some open establishments had fences to mark their boundary. The old borstal is now demolished and a new private prison built on the site.

Lowdham Grange in the early nineteen sixties still retained traces of the influence of Alexander Paterson, the Prison Commissioner and reformer who had an immense influence on the development of the prison system – and especially the borstal system – from the nineteen twenties to the nineteen forties. His mantra "You cannot train men for freedom in conditions of captivity" was the underlying justification for open establishments. "Stickability" – the phrase describing one of the virtues we were trying to encourage in our youngsters at Lowdham – was also attributed to him. While his book "Paterson on Prisons" now seems decidedly dated – nonetheless I am sure he would have strongly supported the principles underlying the Woolf Report of 1991. Paterson also understood the vital importance of staff. He appears to have had considerable success in encouraging staff involvement and ownership of the new positive approach to prisoners and young offenders. It was a great loss that his approach to staff had not continued and further developed under Sir Lionel Fox.

Lowdham had 4 accommodation blocks or borstal "houses" as they were known, each named after someone who had contributed to the development of the establishment – Paterson, Malone, Warner and Stansfield. I was given responsibility for Paterson House. Each house had 5 dormitories for a total of 60 young men, and there were showers and baths, recreation rooms and a dining hall. Food was prepared centrally and brought out to each house by trolley. The Governor was always pleased if his housemasters were around at meal times keeping an eye on the service of food, a useful experience for new Assistant Governors as food was always a potentially tricky issue in penal establishments.

The borstal system was designed to encourage the "lads" to progress towards discharge by hard work and achievement. The sentence of Borstal

Training was an indeterminate sentence of 6 months to 2 years. There was a series of stages from new arrivals to "Training Grade" "Senior Training Grade" and finally "Discharge". The grades were marked by the colour of the ties the lads wore. To progress from one stage to another, there were monthly boards at both house and institution level at which progress was assessed. I was soon involved in this process – chairing the board at house level and then pleading the cause of individuals at the institution board. Because the Governor spent much of his time around the borstal, he knew a great deal about the lads and was quick to challenge any exaggerated plea for promotion to the next grade. It was a good lesson for Housemasters – they needed to know the individuals in their care. The lads from Lowdham generally served around 15 months – the shortest time around 12 months and for some over 20 months. However, those who misbehaved seriously – for example by absconding – were usually sent to a secure or "closed" borstal for the rest of their time.

When a lad was discharged, he was placed on licence to Borstal Aftercare. The licence required him to report as required to his probation officer and not to change his address without permission. A failure to adhere to these conditions could result in a recall to one of the Borstal Recall Centres. Housemasters were encouraged to visit Borstal Aftercare's offices in London once a year to follow up on the progress of their lads.

Lowdham employed lads on our two Farms, on a Forestry party and a Gardens party. Several Vocational Training courses, some full time education, and the usual domestic services – laundry, kitchen, orderlies and cleaners – completed the range of occupations. There was adequate work for the young men to keep them busy and hopefully to learn new skills and improved work habits. It was, however, debatable if any of them were likely to be able to use their experience of farm work when they returned to their home areas.

One unusual and very positive scheme operating at Lowdham was the "Miner's Scheme". This was an agreement between the Prison Service and the National Coal Board to allow any suitable trainee – who had previous connections with the industry – to work for the NCB at a nearby colliery on "proper" wages while still serving his sentence. This meant that when he was discharged he had a job to continue in; he had savings, because the money he earned – after a deduction for board and lodging to the borstal – went into a savings account for when he was discharged. This appeared an excellent scheme – demonstrating how rehabilitation can be successfully put into practice.

At the weekend there was sport largely led by the PEIs although the Governor was always keen to see his Housemasters playing their part. Canoeing and camping trips for staff and lads were also quite frequently organised. The weekend activities included church services. There was usually a weekly inspection of dormitories by the Housemasters after the staff had encouraged the lads to square up their kit and clean up the dormitories. Inspections were common in young offender establishments at this time. They played a part in trying to ensure communal living standards were reasonable and reflected something of the old military or naval traditions that many ex-service Governors and staff brought with them.

The ex-service tradition was also evident in the way the lads were marched around from activity to activity. On Sundays, the Church of England trainees marched a mile or so down to one of the local churches. During the week, parading the lads in work parties also allowed for a numbers check to be carried out – an important part of ensuring that the roll of the establishment – the number of lads we were responsible for – was correct.

Our lads were also encouraged to become involved in socially useful activity while serving their sentences. I found myself running a project whereby selected lads went down to Lowdham village and helped pensioners with their gardens. In return they got a cup of tea – and a piece of cake. As with most of these projects, some gained considerably from the experience; some did not. The old folk got some help with their gardens – but many of our lads didn't have much natural aptitude or interest in gardening. But for some of the lads building up a positive relationship with the pensioners was very valuable.

There was good continuity of staff so that the lads were known by name by staff members and responded better as a result. There were less experienced members of staff who needed support – even from a young inexperienced Assistant Governor like me – especially if they were on their own supervising a full house of 60 lads. There were a few female members of staff; borstal matrons who had responsibility for kit and were perhaps seen as a "mother" figure for some of the young offenders. These ladies tended to be mature and were paid as "Principal Officers". Other female staff members worked as teachers, social workers and in the administration offices.

Borstal officers came from a very wide variety of backgrounds. At Lowdham we had a number who had been miners, reflecting the local economy in Nottinghamshire. There were also ex-military staff including some who had been prisoners of war. By and large they were positive and constructive and contributed considerably to assisting their charges.

Assistant Governors had largely derived from the borstal "Housemaster" based on the public school model brought in by Paterson to work with young offenders in the early part of the twentieth century. The management structure was unclear; uniformed staff came under the Chief Officer and the responsibilities of the Assistant Governors varied greatly from one institution to another. This is an issue I shall return to in Chapter 16.

Housemasters were involved in a number of routine duties in their houses. We adjudicated on "Minor Reports" – minor infringements of the rules – with the power to fine offenders. We paid out the weekly "wage" to the lads – performed shop keeping duties by running the house canteen – sweets and tobacco being the main purchases – and running the "bank" for those who wanted to save their wages. We were expected to censor and record the mail and to take appropriate action when for example a letter to a lad contained bad news that might lead to an abscond. We also issued "Visiting Orders" – permission for relatives to visit. Both visits and letters were generally very important both to the families and to the young offenders.

Housemasters were expected to make contact with families when they visited. I found this helpful as the range of visiting parents, relatives and families provided some insight into home circumstances. I was struck by the number of grandparents visiting who had brought up a young offender and were often especially anxious to speak with Housemasters about how their grandsons were progressing.

One very clear responsibility for the staff was to reduce absconding. Housemasters often took the lead, spending time trying to involve individuals in positive activity – as boredom could be a factor in triggering an abscond. Barbara and I spent much of my first Christmas Eve at Lowdham with one young Blackburn lad named Martin, involving him in helping prepare the RC Chapel for the celebrations the next day. Some Housemasters had unfortunate experiences – one of my colleagues in another borstal took a group of offenders for a walk and returned without two of them. He was christened "Two away Toby" for the next few days!

When we became aware that a lad had absconded, there were local contingency plans to try and find him. Without communication equipment, these plans were rather haphazard but at least we did our best.

Trying to work effectively with offenders was a constant challenge. The extent of the deprivation experienced by many lads was staggering. One Irish lad from Cork was so illiterate he was not able to read the numbers on the front of the Cork buses. I received a report from a Probation Officer about the home circumstances of a youngster from the north-east we were considering sending on Home leave. "I was more fortunate than the social worker who visited the house last week," wrote our Probation Officer, "as the lady is now in hospital having been assaulted by the mother. Mother is awaiting a Court Appearance on the assault charge; father is serving 3 years in Durham Prison; elder brother is in borstal; elder sister is believed to be 'on the game.' The other children may be taken into care in the next few days." This example illustrates the reality of a "cycle of re-offending" reaching across generations. Where do you start to try and tackle such ingrained difficulties?

A colleague at Lowdham had a particularly loud mouthed young man to whom the use of foul language was routine. To try and encourage change, my colleague invited him into the office, sat him down and after a few exchanges

said to this lad "What would your mother say if you asked her to pass the F......
salt when you were having a meal?" The lad responded immediately "She
would say – pass it your F....self!" Some of our assumptions about what families
regarded as acceptable behaviour were quickly put in their place!

I had not appreciated when I joined the Service that Prisons Board members
were looking for some new Assistant Governors from different religious
backgrounds who could ensure offenders' religious needs were being
adequately met.

This was brought home to me when I was posted to Lowdham Grange in
1964. The Director of Borstal Administration drew me quietly to one side. "One
of the reasons we are sending you to Lowdham Grange is because we need a
Roman Catholic Housemaster to work with the Roman Catholic boys. There
are difficulties at present between the RC Chaplain and the Governor." So my
first posting to a penal establishment in 1964 had a distinctly religious purpose!

I quickly found out about the "difficulties" between the RC Chaplain and the
Governor. Both were strong characters; the Governor having been a wartime
naval commander was used to getting his own way; the Chaplain was a busy
parish priest and regarded the Chaplaincy to the borstal as something of a
distraction. The Chaplain demanded that the Governor provide transport to
bring him the several miles from the parish to the borstal chapel for Sunday
Mass; this was difficult to arrange, so one Sunday, the Governor sent the milk
lorry: the Chaplain was not amused and communication had virtually ceased
between Chaplain and Governor.

I was able to persuade the parish priest to let his curate take on the borstal work;
we found an organist and gradually started to improve participation in worship
by the 70 odd teenage RCs. Prisoners, both young and old, were compelled to
attend church in those days. Barbara and I took several enthusiasts among the
boys to a nearby RC Seminary – a Centre for Training potential priests – for the
Easter Vigil and we also arranged for groups of Seminarians to come into the
borstal to work with the lads. Seminarians made a real impact, being generally
only slightly older than the lads yet having quite different values. One mature
Jesuit novice of Hungarian background – a very strong man – was a great hit
with the lads because he joined their work parties – including coal shovelling
– and was able to relate remarkably well with our deprived youngsters. They
would sit round and listen to him in a way they would never be able to listen
to our chaplains.

On 3rd October 1964, Barbara and I were married at St Barnabas Cathedral
in Nottingham. We honeymooned in the Lake District, beginning a love of
the Lakes that has lasted all our married lives. On the way up to the Lakes we
drove past a party of prisoners working on the roadside – a project run by the
Open Prison at Bela River, Milnthorpe. The prison closed some years later as
the Service realised it was oversupplied with open establishments.

In 1964, most of the staff lived in "quarters", tied housing often next to the penal establishment. As a newly married couple in the autumn of 1964, we moved into a large four-bedroomed house on the Green at Lowdham, a short walk from the establishment. It could be very cold as heating was by open fires and we quickly learned the advantages and disadvantages of quarters' life. Our first child, Mary, was born the following summer so we were soon having to cope with the needs of a baby in a house that was far from "user friendly".

This early experience of quarters, later reinforced by living in quarters at Manchester and at Onley, led me to volunteer to serve on the Governors' Representative Committee to try and achieve higher standards for staff quarters. This was the start of a long involvement with what was effectively the Governors Trade Union – which I discuss in Chapter 13. The crucial issue in the 1960s in quarters was to try and get a programme of installing central heating agreed with the Home Office – as it was I had to wait until we were able to buy our first owner occupied house at Preston in 1972 before we experienced our first centrally heated house.

The provision of quarters was part of a network of services provided for staff. In the years before the Second World War; the prison doctor often looked after the staff families; the prison kitchen's bakery provided bread for staff families while the prison chaplain provided spiritual direction and comfort.

The experience of living on quarters estates had an interesting impact on the social and professional lives of many staff in the Prison Service. It created links between many families that were to last into retirement.

After two years at Lowdham, the Director of Borstal Administration interviewed me and explained he had selected me to help open a new Borstal Allocation Centre in Manchester's Strangeways Prison.

So what had I learned at Lowdham? I had accumulated useful experience of working with young offenders and was starting to understand the problems they presented to staff and to wider society. The complexity of running a penal establishment with the wide range of staff issues that Governors had to address was also becoming clearer – although I had no answers to the many intractable problems.

8. MANCHESTER PRISON 1966-1968

In spring 1966, I transferred to Manchester Prison to help open the new Borstal Allocation Unit in the former women's prison. Manchester Strangeways has two radial accommodation blocks within its walls; the smaller was originally designed and used for women prisoners. The women prisoners were moved out to the newly opened Styal Prison in Cheshire, leaving the accommodation in Strangeways available for young offender use. The name

"Strangeways" was said to be taken from the area around the prison – Lord Strange had property to the north of the prison site and the "ways" – or paths – led across the prison site to his estate. Further details about the prison will also be found in Chapter 26 recounting the years when I was Governor from 1986 to 1990.

Before I moved, I spent a week at Wormwood Scrubs Prison in London. Borstal Allocation was conducted from Wormwood Scrubs at that time and Manchester was being opened to relieve the pressure on the "Scrubs". I found that the young offenders were located in "B" Hall, one of four large accommodation blocks within the perimeter wall. I gained some insight into the allocation procedures at Wormwood Scrubs and met a number of Governor Grades including Alan Rayfield who was also moving to Manchester. We were to remain colleagues and friends for many years.

Barbara and I moved the family from Lowdham to Chorlton-cum-Hardy, south Manchester, renting a modern terraced house for a year before a prison quarter was purchased in Prestwich, north Manchester, for us. The allowances on offer from the Prison Service did not fully cover the rent so I took on some evening lecturing in Social Administration at the Manchester College of Commerce. This kept me in touch with academic work and I lectured at Keele and Nottingham Universities later in my career.

In 1967, when we moved to Prestwich, we lived in a very Jewish area; we arrived in the middle of the Six Day War so it was an interesting and very different cultural experience with quiet descending on Friday nights and shops being open on Sundays. But it was a reasonable area to bring up our growing family as two further girls, Helen and Anne, were born during this time. We continued to lament the lack of central heating in the Prestwich quarter!

Strangeways was a fascinating experience as I worked with several very senior Governors, all very different in their approach to the task. It was a great opportunity to learn about different styles of leadership and different approaches to management. All the senior Governors I worked with at Manchester were very different from Bill Noall. When I arrived, Arthur Coomes was in charge, a man who had started as a prison officer and was rightly very proud of his achievement in being promoted to Governor Class One. He made a considerable impression on his staff. Arthur left on retirement after a year. He was replaced by Norman Golding, a flamboyant character, larger than life, who drove expensive cars and didn't appear to spend much time in the prison. I had limited opportunities to see him in operation. After a year, Norman was posted to Dartmoor – a move he had wanted. He was replaced by Captain W.I. (Lynn) Davies, a dapper Welshman with a background of substantial army service from the War. He was an effective Governor, one who drew his own security keys and went around the establishment, often with one of his dogs at his heels. Bringing dogs into secure prisons soon became too difficult as the

Above: Strangeways handler and dog.

Prison Dogs Section held sway and pets could no longer be tolerated.

When I arrived, the Deputy Governor was Norman Brown who went on to be Governor of Strangeways in the 1980s and featured in Rex Bloomstein's BBC TV series on Strangeways. Norman had suffered serious war wounds in Italy in 1944 with 80% burns to his whole body; his face was heavily scarred. His father had been Governor of Dartmoor. He told me the story of how when he was posted to Eastchurch Prison on the Isle of Sheppey as Deputy Governor, he had awarded a punishment to an elderly prisoner for some offence: the prisoner looked at him in astonishment and said "and to think I used to push your pram around at Dartmoor when you were a baby".

Another unusual member of the Governor team at Strangeways was C.C. Farmer-Wright – Assistant Governor Class One in the main prison. Born in 1900 Farmer had a considerable career in the Indian Prison Service. He applied for the Service in England and Wales in 1946 but was rejected as "too old"; spent the next few years working in Germany with those guarding Nazi War Criminals; re-applied in 1950 and was accepted. He claimed when he finally retired in 1967 to be the oldest serving Governor – possibly of all time.

Manchester Borstal Allocation Centre was to be run by D.R.N. Maxwell, an experienced Governor well used to working with young offenders. He was a Governor Class Three. His move to Manchester from being in charge of a small young offender establishment in the south was regarded as something of a demotion as he was now working under a Governor Class One. The management structure was very ill-defined. Governor Maxwell certainly regarded himself as independent from the rest of the prison although in practice he was entirely dependent on the Governor One for all the services including providing all the uniformed staff. To reinforce the confusion about lines of accountability, the Borstal Allocation Centre reported to a Borstal Assistant Director; the Prison to a Prison Assistant Director.

The management situation was further complicated by the setting up in the north-west of the first experimental Regional Office – situated in old prefabricated buildings almost opposite Strangeways. It would not be until the HQ re-organisation of 1969 that the line management arrangements above establishments would be clarified.

Governor Maxwell also had significant health problems which meant he had to have periodic implants. After an implant he was quite energetic but rather like a spring he gradually wound down and we would see less and less of him. He would phone in frequently to say that he would not be in today and we would carry on without him. His spasmodic attendance was reported to the Regional Director by the Governor One; there was a difficult meeting in the Governor One's office where the gate book – the official record of the times staff had entered and left the prison – was examined. Governor Maxwell's attendance improved somewhat thereafter.

Governor Maxwell decided we should go and see the newly opened Risley Remand Centre near Warrington as he knew the Governor in charge of the women's prison. We had a tour around the women's section of the remand centre. Little did I know that I would be back to take charge many years later – see Chapter 31.

The main task of the two Assistant Governors was to interview the borstal trainees and allocate them to one of the various borstals. The first issue was whether an individual could cope with open conditions; then how close to home we could place them. The geographical position of borstals in the north had been very uneven; there was only Hindley closed borstal west of the Pennines – all the others were to the east – hardly handy for our many Liverpudlian trainees. But the experience of allocating young offenders was interesting – there was some discretion over what decision to take and occasionally it was possible to persuade a Borstal Governor to take a borderline case where it appeared that allocation should be of benefit to the individual concerned.

I saw and interviewed a large number of young offenders during the two and a half years I was at Manchester. We received young men from a much wider range of backgrounds than I had come across at Lowdham; young offenders from Wales and Scotland as well as England – even the occasional Manx youngster. There were a wider range of ethnic minorities and a troubling number of very disturbed young men who required medical oversight.

In 1966 HQ had organised an experiment using three small open borstals at Pollington in east Yorkshire, Hewell Grange near Birmingham and Morton Hall in Lincolnshire to test out the relative effectiveness of Group Work, Casework and the traditional borstal regime. We were asked to allocate those borstal boys who fitted the criteria for the experiment on a random basis between the three establishments.

The results of this experiment – released years later – were apparently not significant. But far more should have been done to establish what were the most effective programmes and regimes to prevent re-offending. This was a serious weakness of the Service – an inability to learn lessons from hard earned experience and from research findings.

To address the shortage of places in borstals, in early 1966 just as the Manchester Borstal Allocation Centre opened, the new prison at Stoke Heath in Shropshire was changed over to be a borstal. This gave us a greater range of outlets for young offenders requiring closed conditions. I learned from the Deputy Governor there that because Stoke Heath Prison had commercial contracts to deliver work for a private sector firm, it was decided to gradually employ young offenders alongside the adults to train them in the necessary skills. Although this only lasted for a short period and was not researched, the Deputy Governor was convinced that the presence of the older men had a very positive impact on the behaviour of the young offenders. Segregating young offenders from adults may not always have been sensible and it would be worth conducting some controlled experiments on whether selectively mixing some young offenders with adult offenders had beneficial results.

As I learned over the years, the Prison Service used the device of "reclassifying" young prisoners to be adults as a method of managing some of the more difficult ones. However, little if any research has been done on this practice – and such research should be considered so that we have better information about the impact of mixing groups of prisoners.

Despite the opening of Stoke Heath, the pressure of rising numbers continued and we were told to start placing our young offenders three in a cell. I quickly learned that this change had many disadvantages. We were not equipped to manage the additional youngsters; they often fell out with each other in multiple occupied cells and we had one incident when two of them tried to hang the third on the basis that they would make it look like suicide and would – they thought – qualify for release because they had had such a dreadful experience. In fact there was a police investigation and the two assailants ended up with additional sentences. I was learning that prisoners could be immensely cruel to each other and that we had a duty to try and prevent this – very difficult to achieve in a very overcrowded Victorian prison.

Another consequence of overcrowding was a rise in the amount of vandalism and damage to equipment and property. When borstal boys were in single cells, there was a reasonable chance that the staff could monitor the state of cell equipment. Once overcrowding started this was much more difficult. Damage and loss was all too frequent and it was very difficult to prevent. The environment of the establishment deteriorated further. Faeces were thrown out of windows; toilets were deliberately blocked, equipment disappeared and quality of life for both young offenders and staff grew worse.

Cell windows were a particular problem. Efforts to reduce the amount of rubbish thrown out included the fitting of grills – this was unsightly, reduced the airflow to cells and was not always effective. But damage to cell windows became a constant problem. They were often broken during hot weather to try and improve ventilation – and then blocked up with cardboard when the weather turned colder. Repairing cell windows became a low priority and the appearance and state of cells became worse.

I shall consider the impact of overcrowding further in Chapter 14.

We were also responsible for a Young Prisoner wing with some 50 young prisoners serving sentences. This group was rather neglected as the emphasis was on the borstal trainees. We also occasionally received a fourteen-year-old young offender serving a very unusual sentence such as "Detention during Her Majesty's Pleasure" or a fixed term of ten years or more. The crimes involved were usually horrendous – but often the offender turned out to be rather inadequate and pathetic.

The young offenders – both borstal trainees and young prisoners – at Manchester had some activity; there were limited workshops providing very basic and repetitive work together with some education and cleaning jobs. Exercise was provided daily – weather permitting – on the old exercise yards and there was a little access to the gym. For the borstal trainees, their stay at Manchester was relatively short so organising a positive regime was not easy – but less relevant. We should have been trying to provide much more for the young prisoners as they were spending a considerable time at Strangeways. But we lacked space for activities as well as staff to organise and supervise them.

The fact that the Borstal Allocation Centre had previously been a women's prison was brought home to me when one of our officers brought to me a piece of incoming mail for a borstal trainee. It was the lad's birth certificate – and on it was the address where he had been born – 1, Southall Street, the address of the prison. The lad's mother had delivered him in custody in the former women's prison – and he was now back where he had been born awaiting allocation to a borstal. We made sure that when the post was delivered, the lad was given some support – although we got the impression he knew the story from other sources. At least all pregnant prisoners deliver their children in NHS hospitals now – recognition of the importance of trying to give these children a better start in life.

This was my first experience of a very big prison with a very large number of staff and a wide spread of specialist staff. The staff had little previous experience of young Assistant Governors: it was something of a shock when coming into the prison through the main gate to be greeted by the Principal Officer in charge with a salute and informing me of the numbers locked up – usually around 1500; it certainly brought it home to me that this was quite different from life at Lowdham Grange where the numbers were around 240 young offenders.

Manchester Prison was also responsible for an attendance centre, one of the few penal establishments running a non-custodial option for offenders. Staff from the prison ran the centre close to a central Manchester police station and appeared to be doing an excellent job with the boys.

Our full time Catholic Chaplain, Fr Aspinal, an experienced Lancashire priest ministered effectively to both prisoners and staff. For Sunday Mass there would almost always be a number of Catholic staff on duty. Prisoners generally responded much better to the example of staff taking part in services rather than just adopting a custodial approach or opting out altogether. Fr Aspinal was later replaced by Fr Joe Barrett, a Jesuit, who worked in the Prison Service for many years before retiring to a post in Rome. Fr Barrett was later credited with preventing a difficult situation in the streets in Rome deteriorating into a riot by addressing the potential disturbers of the peace in an authoritive voice and declaiming a prayer in Latin – probably the "Grace before Meals". This apparently had the desired effect and disorder was prevented! This intervention was – of course – quickly attributed to Fr Barrett's prison experience.

In 1968, Strangeways reached its centenary and we organised a staff photograph to mark the occasion. I was delighted to find copies still on display when I returned to govern the prison in 1986.

9. MOUNTBATTEN REPORTS – SECURITY IS GIVEN PRIORITY

While growing prisoner numbers and overcrowding were a constant worry, security issues began to dominate the prisons agenda from 1965. The thirty year prison sentences imposed on the Great Train Robbers in 1964 were the catalyst for prison escapes attracting considerable public interest and concern.

The breakouts began with two of the Great Train Robbers – Charlie Wilson from Birmingham's Winson Green on 12th August 1964 and Ronnie Biggs from Wandsworth on 8th July 1965. Some extraordinary measures were taken by the Prison Service in response – at Durham Prison the military were used to guard the perimeter at the end of 1965 because of the perceived threat of armed attempts to free prisoners. So concerned were some of the public authorities about attempts to "spring" prisoners from secure prisons that the then Chief Constable of Durham hinted darkly that some of those wishing to attack prisons might use "tactical nuclear weapons". I suspect this was hyperbole to encourage the use of the army for perimeter security – and it probably helped the civil authorities to get the military help they sought. So while the soldiers were confined to providing perimeter security, their presence was a reminder that the military can be used to support the civil power – and would be used again in the nineteen eighties to cope with different prison emergencies arising from industrial action.

In Ireland, because of the threat of armed attack by terrorist groups during the "Troubles", the Irish Army was brought in to guard the perimeter of Portlaoise Prison, a duty they were still performing thirty years later. In Northern Ireland, there was also a long period of using the military to guard the perimeter of the most secure prisons during the "Troubles" as well as the use of a naval ship in Belfast docks as a temporary prison.

Over many years, the Service had developed systems for identifying and managing those regarded as presenting a high risk of escaping. The "E" (Escape) list system was devised whereby high risk potential escapees were required to wear "patches" – yellow patches on their prison uniform which immediately and clearly identified them as high risk. The "E" list prisoners were closely supervised; had to put all their clothes outside their cells at night and were subject to other constraints. But the system was found wanting as security was breached far too often.

On 22nd October 1966, the spy George Blake – serving 42 years – escaped from Wormwood Scrubs Prison. There was a huge political and public outcry. The Home Secretary, Roy Jenkins, and the Prime Minister, Harold Wilson, agreed that drastic measures were needed. On 24th October 1966, Lord Mountbatten was appointed to conduct an Inquiry. He reported in December 1966 – perhaps a record for the speed of conducting an Inquiry and producing a report – declaring that "there is really no secure prison in existence in the country". The Prison Service was confronted with a demanding and radical programme of change to improve security and much else besides.

Investment in security followed and prison perimeters of top security prisons were strengthened. Closed circuit cameras were installed to monitor what was happening and to enable staff to raise the alarm – a move expected to save staff patrols around the walls. At Wakefield Prison this cost some £200,000 and the Deputy Governor expressed his reservations to a Parliamentary committee as follows:

"How much is this going to relieve the officers' duties and how much is it going to stop us seeing no more than a clean pair of heels going over the wall".

Subsequent experience, when CCTV operators were carefully conditioned by determined prisoners and consequently failed to notice prisoner behaviour leading to escapes, justified the Deputy Governor's reservations.

Mountbatten also recommended the introduction of a Prison Dogs Service to provide an intervention force to foil escape attempts. At Manchester, we borrowed police dogs for a period before the Prison Service acquired and trained our own dog sections. But weaknesses in physical security were not properly tackled at Manchester – and many other prisons – as I discovered when I returned 20 years later.

The Mountbatten Report examined the escapes of the Train Robbers from Birmingham's Winson Green Prison and from Wandsworth. Wilson's escape from Winson Green followed an intrusion during the night raising questions about whether any of the night staff had been involved in colluding and facilitating the escape. The Biggs' escape from Wandsworth – in broad daylight from an exercise yard with the use of a furniture van externally, some outside intervention and the threat of firearms – all highlighted the weakness of what had previously been regarded as "top security" perimeters.

Above: Security improvements included anti-climb device – the gander.

Perhaps the most visible change to security over the next ten years was the installation of the anti-climbing device – the "gander" – at the top of many prison walls. A number of new prisons had been built with only high wire fences as the perimeter – these proved too vulnerable to being breached with wire cutters and similar tools – and a programme of "gunniting" begun. This involved spraying the fences with concrete and creating a solid impenetrable wall which was then topped with a gander.

Within prisons, it also became apparent over the next decade that cell windows were relatively easy to cut through with the right tools. So new designs and new materials were tried and a huge programme of installing better cell windows in high security prisons began.

The Mountbatten Report addressed some staffing issues, recommending the introduction of a new grade of "Senior Officer" and reducing the dependence of night security on the relatively untrained and less well paid night patrol officers. Night Orderly Officers who previously were expected to sleep for much of the night were turned into "live" duties offering a speedier response to any emergency in the middle of the night. These additional duties – introduced without matching staffing increases – were one of the factors destined to complicate staffing and Industrial Relations for years to come as discussed in Chapter 15 (Staffing) and Chapter 17 (Industrial Relations).

There were casualties following the Mountbatten Report – the Governor of Wormwood Scrubs took early retirement. The Director of Prison Administration, Hugh Kenyon, was another casualty.

Kenyon was an interesting man, with Manx ancestry. His career illustrates the culture that dominated the Service in the interwar years. Attracted by the magnetism of Alexander Paterson's personality and by Paterson's belief that borstals and open prisons could reform offenders, Kenyon had joined the Prison Commission in April 1934 as a Borstal Housemaster and in 1936 he was appointed to North Sea Camp, a new open borstal, in Lincolnshire. The challenges of working there have already been described in Chapter 6.

In 1946, Kenyon was appointed Governor of Lowdham Grange Borstal. He was promoted to govern Portland Borstal in 1950. The borstal occupied the buildings of the old convict prison, which had been damaged by German bombing during the war. Portland was expected to train the more difficult young offenders and when Kenyon arrived there had been a number of disturbances causing some damage. He was faced with the loss of electric power on a dark evening in one of the borstal's houses – with some 80 young men going on the rampage. Going into the house with a very powerful torch Kenyon prevented further damage as the young offenders scuttled back to their cells.

In 1953 he was again promoted – this time to Governor Class One – and took charge of Birmingham's Winson Green Prison. This was in very sharp contrast to his work with young offenders – the task of governing an old overcrowded Victorian prison serving the courts demanded different skills and offered fewer opportunities to influence prisoners. After several years at Birmingham, he was further promoted to Assistant Director of Prisons, responsible for oversight of a large group of adult establishments, supporting Governors and encouraging improvements.

In 1964, Kenyon was promoted to Director of Prison Administration with a seat on the Prisons Board. In 1966, he found himself having to deal with implementing the Mountbatten Report changes, completely different priorities to those that motivated him during much of his service. For nine months, he did what he could to start the process of adapting the prisons to the new security and other requirements. In September 1967, amid considerable media speculation, he decided that he could do no more and resigned. A sad end to a considerable career.

One of the lasting legacies of Mountbatten was the decision to divide all prisoners into four security categories – A being the highest, D the lowest. Prisons were increasingly described by their security category – the open prisons became "Category D" establishments.

As part of the implementation process of the Mountbatten recommendations, a number of "Special Wings" were established with extra security to hold the most dangerous prisoners.

While the Special Security Wings provided an immediate response to the security crises, the Prison Service had to decide what the longer term solution should be. Mountbatten had recommended that a new maximum security prison – he suggested it be called "Vectis" – should be built on the Isle of Wight. As Mountbatten was the Governor of the Isle of Wight, he knew the Island well and appreciated the advantages that it offered as the potential home for a new prison. Interestingly he had also examined the possible use of the Calf of Man, a small Island just off the coast of the Isle of Man, and regarded it as the next best option.

Above: Calf of Man, Isle of Man – Mountbatten's reserve site for a maximum security prison.

In February 1967, the Home Secretary asked the Advisory Council on the Penal System to consider the regime for long term prisoners detained in conditions of maximum security and to make recommendations. The Council's report – published in 1968 – came down against concentrating all the most difficult prisoners in one prison and suggested that they be "Dispersed" among a small number of top security establishments. This led to the creation of the "Dispersal System" with a small number of prisons being fitted out with improved security. These included Gartree – a new prison under construction near Market Harborough; and several existing older prisons – Hull and Parkhurst being two. The new prison planned at Long Lartin, near Worcester, was earmarked to join the Dispersal System and in due course other new prisons at Frankland (Durham) and Full Sutton (Yorkshire) were also added.

Practical experience of running the Dispersal System revealed a variety of weaknesses and many improvements had to be added as resources permitted. Unfortunately some establishments were never fully brought up to the standard required as we were to experience over the perimeter at Parkhurst in 1995 – see Chapter 37.

In addition to the Dispersal System, some of the "special wings" were upgraded and retitled as Special Security Units (SSUs) – prisons within prisons. These were units for small numbers of very difficult prisoners. One unit was at Leicester; another at Parkhurst.

The IRA organised the escape of three of their members from Mountjoy Prison in Dublin in October 1973 by using a helicopter. This event caused many prison services to review their plans to prevent this method of escape being repeated. In England, the SSUs included exercise yards with mesh roofs to prevent escapes by helicopter. However, there was a successful escape by helicopter from Gartree Prison in December 1987 when two criminals serving long sentences were lifted out of the prison. The helicopter had been hijacked.

10. ONLEY BORSTAL RECALL CENTRE 1968-1971

Location

Towards the end of 1968 I was posted to Onley, a newly built secure young offender establishment for 300 near Rugby on the Northants/Warwickshire border. Built on surplus Ministry of Defence land transferred to the Home Office, the borstal had a high wire perimeter fence enclosing 5 units, each with 60 cells.

We moved onto a new quarters' estate – Onley was built on an old army camp site called Barby Camp named after a nearby village. While it was good to move into a new four bedroomed house, the lack of central heating – especially as we had 3 very young children – was disappointing. Developing a new staff community was all part of the learning experience. Disputes at work could spill into the quarters' community and vice versa. Staff and families came from many different establishments. We found ourselves living on a building site for the early months; people quickly got to know each other and learned to work together. Barbara was soon involved with developing a playgroup for the numerous young children on the estate.

An example of the way we lived and worked very closely together was that I often found myself in my dressing gown first thing in the morning bringing in a bottle of milk from the doorstep to be greeted with. "Good morning Sir" by the Chief Officer out walking his dog.

Onley was quite an isolated establishment, with poor public transport connections. This made it challenging for staff families living on the quarters' estate and very difficult for the families and friends of our young offenders wishing to visit. We found in the winter that the link road from the A45 to the establishment could easily be closed by snow so working parties from the borstal had to be pressed into service.

Above: Borstal boys entering workshop.

Opening a new establishment

Opening a new establishment was challenging and different. We had to quickly develop work systems sometimes without essential equipment – we operated without internal telephones for the first few weeks. Checking the roll required staff to take the numbers for each wing, following their roll calls, down to the Orderly Room by foot rather than phoning in the numbers.

Our first receptions arrived very quickly before systems were adequately tested. Several trainees breached our security in the first few weeks as they quickly discovered weaknesses in the physical security – deficiencies left by contractors. We were full with 300 trainees by February 1969, just two months after opening. Headquarters – because of the pressure on local prisons with substantial overcrowding – had instructed us to receive trainees as quickly as possible. After my experience of overcrowding in the Manchester Borstal Allocation Centre, I understood the need to fill our places very quickly – so we did our best.

Establishing a routine and finding sufficient activities for the trainees were early priorities. Partly because of the speed with which we opened, we were short of work and we had to improvise. Education was given particular attention and our energetic Education Officer helped to provide additional activity places. We started each day's work on a parade ground with a roll call and the work parties marched off smartly thanks to a good proportion of staff, often with experience from the services, with the ability to encourage and control organised movement. I was not to see that way of moving young offenders around after Onley as the tradition of marching and parades faded away other than in detention centres.

Borstal Recall

Borstal Recall Centres were designed to take those young offenders who had completed their borstal training, been released on licence and then either re-offended or broken the conditions of their licence. These youngsters were returned to us for only a few months so Onley had a very high turnover of offenders. I was in charge of A Wing housing 60 young offenders. We saw a good deal of the organisation charged with providing and co-ordinating Borstal Aftercare which was interesting and often salutary. We learned a good deal about why offenders re-offended on release, often at least partly caused by a lack of accommodation or work. I shall return to those factors in Chapter 39 dealing with the reduction of re-offending. Frank Foster, a diminutive figure but with a strong personality, who was Head of Borstal Aftercare, visited frequently to interview those recalled for breach of the conditions of their release licence. I sat in on many of these interviews and learned a good deal.

Among the interesting innovations at Onley was an industrial unit which worked on KD packing cases for Fords of Dagenham. Unfortunately when Fords had a national strike our work dried up and we still had our young offenders to occupy. This was a useful early lesson in the limitations of relying on the private sector to occupy prisoners!

After working at Lowdham and Manchester, two very different establishments but both very traditionally run, Onley opened my eyes to different ways of operating. This experience was the start of learning how to blend good ideas from different traditions and being open to quite new ways of tackling problems. By now, I was starting to develop my own views on offenders and on the way to operate to become an effective Governor. The bedrock of my education and Catholic philosophy was becoming more integrated into the realities of the challenges offenders posed. Onley gave me opportunities to test out ideas about how to get the best out of staff and through them to have positive influences on offenders.

Chaplaincy

We developed a very positive Chaplaincy team. We appointed an enthusiastic part-time RC Chaplain. We were fortunate to be joined by Frank Davies as a mature, but newly appointed, Assistant Governor who had a background in entertainment having sung with the great Val Doonican. He introduced a fresh and relevant collection of hymns, taught the lads how to sing and got a very good response. We were also able to attract the services of a talented organist, Mary Woodward, who had been at the teacher training College at Newbold Revel, located between Coventry and Rugby, at the same time as Barbara.

The requirement to attend church services was under review so we introduced a two-part service – compulsory attendance up to and including the sermon and then voluntary attendance for the rest of the mass which emphasised the historical purpose of the first part of mass for teaching new Christians about the Faith. This was an example of how change and improvement could be introduced at local level – and it worked well.

At Lowdham and at Onley and later on at Featherstone and Risley, there were opportunities for staff families to join in at Sunday Mass – several of our children made their first communion in the borstal chapel at Onley. While we were at Onley, our first boy Francis was born and was baptised in the borstal chapel.

Management responsibilities

Onley also broadened my management experience as I was the senior Assistant Governor, the person who took on the Deputy Governor's role in his absence or when he was acting as Governor. Among other duties I was introduced to the requirement for the Governor to perform periodic "cash checks", part of the role of a "sub accounting officer" in the public service. Then there was the need for occasional "key checks" to be sure that the security keys – a vital part of the security of the establishment – were all accounted for.

Among a wide range of duties, Governor Grades were expected to visit their establishment in the evening and at night. The reason behind this requirement was to ensure that the establishment was running in accordance with the rules at all times. So throughout my career, it was normal practice to be in the establishment at least one evening a week – in borstal it was often every evening on duty days – and to visit at night on a rota to ensure that a night visit was paid every week. These practices if followed conscientiously had considerable advantages – senior people knew what was happening and the staff – by and large – were pleased to see senior staff on duty and offering them support when they were working at inconvenient times. When I joined, most governing Governors worked alternate weekends – over the years that reduced to one weekend in three or to Monday to Friday working with occasional weekend visits. Deputy Governors generally worked alternate weekends.

During the Staff Course, we had been introduced to the Prisons Act 1952 and other parts of the framework of rules within which the Prison Service operated. I was now starting to learn how this worked in practice. When a new prison opened, the Home Secretary had to sign a certificate that the site and buildings were now a prison. Seeing that happen at Onley brought home to me how knowledge of the law was relevant to being a Governor. More detailed statutory requirements were contained in the subordinate regulations "Prison Rules" and "Borstal Rules". These covered some of the duties and the powers of Governors.

The Prison Service also operated under large numbers of written instructions. There were sets of Standing Orders; Circular instructions to Governors as well as Home Office instructions about wider civil service matters. After 1970, Headquarters also introduced confidential Memorandum to Governors which enabled HQ to advise or instruct Governors about more sensitive issues. Examples were the instructions for handling hostage incidents; procedures to be followed in the event of a disturbance and many instructions about the handling of industrial disputes.

Our Governor was Roland Adams, an experienced Borstal Governor good with both staff and inmates, a man of great integrity and an able leader. In 1970, I was fortunate to be promoted in post to Deputy Governor. Roland was transferred to take charge of Gartree dispersal prison in 1971, his first experience of dealing with adult offenders, and I was to catch up with him there the following year. Leslie Oxford, another experienced Governor, took over and had a very different style of working. This was another good learning experience for me as I was involved in the "handover" between Governors and saw different ways of achieving results and the impact on staff and trainees of different styles of leadership. At that time there was no formal laid-down procedure for handing over command between Governors so, as with so many aspects of being a Governor, we learned by watching how experienced Governors performed.

On promotion to Assistant Governor Class One, those selected for promotion were expected to attend a two week course at the Prison Service College to assist us in taking on additional responsibilities. This was the only time I attended formal additional training – an indication of how little "development" training was available for Governors at this time.

On being promoted to Deputy Governor, I started to take a closer interest in staffing matters. There was a lack of clarity about the respective roles of the Chief Officer and the various Governor grades in respect of staff matters. The theory was that the Chief Officer was responsible for the uniformed staff – that included borstal officers who were not in uniform. Most Chief Officers had a wealth of experience to draw on and many were both committed and conscientious. But the rules around the staff attendance systems and about overtime payments were negotiated centrally between HQ and the POA and were complex and often far from clear. Keeping a proper balance between staff and prisoner interests was a continuing challenge. The more junior Governor grades were concerned to get the best out of the staff allocated to their houses; issues like continuity and decisions about which staff worked in which locations were important but largely in the Chief Officer's hands. It was an uneasy arrangement that would not be properly clarified until "Fresh Start" was introduced in 1987. I shall examine these issues further in Chapters 15 and 16.

Deputy Governor responsibilities included organising work for offenders: problems revolved around finding sufficient work and dealing with a few individuals who were difficult to place and who provided staff with particular challenges. The Staff Training Committee was also chaired by the Deputy Governor as was the Security Committee.

Being Deputy Governor meant that you were regularly the "in charge" Governor. This happened every other weekend and in the absence of the Governor on leave or attending meetings. I started to make entries in the "Governor's Journal", a large bound book, providing a record of information about the establishment. Many Governors were content to only record some very limited and basic information – the numbers of prisoners/trainees unlocked; numbers discharged and received; the number of adjudications for the day. Serious incidents were recorded – including escapes, disorder, and deaths. Handing over "in charge" responsibility was formally noted. Some Governors added details of significant duties performed. Important visitors and unusual events might be listed. Some Governors also recorded current difficulties and concerns.

The "Governor's Journal" had been in use for decades. The Governor of Dartmoor in 1870 let it be known that he saw the Governor's Journal as "a record for the information of the visiting Director". I don't recall ever seeing a visiting Director look at the Governor's Journal in my time. But Governor's Journals remain an interesting potential source of information for researchers.

The "in charge" Governor was expected to do a "Governor's Round" each day. Usually accompanied by the Chief Officer, this varied greatly in my experience. Some Governors would try and get around much of their establishment – others would be content to visit the punishment block and the kitchen. A sample meal and the menu book was provided in the kitchen – given the importance of food, tasting the meal was a sensible routine.

Acceptable Conditions

In 1969, the Government published a White Paper "People in Prison". This spelt out in sharper terms the tasks of the service – Custody, Providing Acceptable Conditions and Rehabilitation. By now, I had sufficient experience to start to appreciate the challenge of trying to work towards all these aims. Providing "acceptable conditions" was especially challenging given overcrowding.

I began to realise the changing nature of providing "acceptable conditions". Conditions were improving in society at large so such improvements gradually impacted on penal establishments. When I joined there was little provision for prisoners to watch TV. This rapidly changed and most establishments – except the most overcrowded – had some arrangements for prisoners to watch TV if they wanted for part of the evening. We quickly noticed that the TV could be as useful as an extra officer because it provided an occupation for quite a large group. But over the years, TVs changed – colour TV came in generally in society and before long we were coming under pressure to provide colour TV in penal establishments. Where did we draw the line? How did we assess what was reasonable and was not reasonable? This challenge of providing "acceptable conditions" was, and no doubt continues to be, a subject of debate, controversy and ultimately judgement for Governors.

An article on "Overcrowding" that I wrote for the Prison Service Journal in April 1971 attracted some wider media interest – the beginnings of my long association with the media in relation to prisons. This article drew on my experience at Manchester where

Above: Governor Rowland Adams with author – served together at both Onley and Preston.

I have already described, in Chapter 8, the impact of overcrowding on both prisoners and staff. I shall return to the underlying problem of overcrowding in Chapters 14 and 35.

Onley had provided reasonable conditions for the trainees; we had tried to run a regime which would improve their prospects of avoiding re-offending on release. I had been able to absorb more valuable experience about running young offender establishments – but it was time to move on.

11. PRESTON PRISON 1972-1974

I was posted to Preston Prison as Deputy Governor in late 1971 to give me experience of working with adult prisoners. Having driven past the prison many times on my way to Stonyhurst as a youngster, I had never dreamed that I would spend nearly three years there. It was an excellent move for the family as it enabled us to purchase our first house in Fulwood, north Preston, to enjoy the friendly community and parish and to take advantage of the good schooling for our four young children.

Preston Prison in 1972

The Governor, Major Geoffrey Nash, had served in the Indian Army and followed an unusual routine of arriving at 0700, having a short siesta around noon and departing by 1600. He had governed Preston for over 10 years, an exceptionally long period. He had a firm grip on the details of his establishment and of his staff: the only Governor I knew who had two boards in his office – one with the details of every cell in the prison; the other with a list of the key staff posts and the current post holders. Skilful with staff and prisoners, he taught me a good deal in the few months I served with him before his retirement.

A training prison for medium security prisoners, Preston was very overcrowded with some 700 prisoners in a prison designed for 400. It was built in the late eighteenth century with radial wings, quite similar to many of the Victorian prisons. Preston had been closed in the 1920s as the prison population fell and fewer prisons were required. Used by the military during World War Two, it was brought back into use as a civil prison around 1948.

There were an amazing number of long serving staff; most of the senior officer grade had been promoted in post. Effecting change was not easy as many were very set in their ways. Staff were well accepted by local people and often went out of the prison in uniform for shopping at lunchtime without any concerns. It was not like that at many inner city establishments – the Morris's book on Pentonville detailed the difficulties for staff living and working in the area around their prison.

Preston had reasonable and sufficient workshops so prisoners spent much of their day out of cell. Major Nash recognised the value of a positive regime and even when there was a shortage of work he encouraged staff to take prisoners to the workshops with the injunction that they write letters home, read their library books, play board games and talk quietly among themselves. Quite a contrast to some other establishments where prisoners stayed in cells if there was a shortage of work. One workshop was sewing and repairing mailbags. This was favoured by some of the older prisoners, probably because they were used to the work and they knew and liked the experienced instructors. I was fascinated to find the instructors move the whole shop out doors in the summer so that the men could enjoy some sun – to carry a chair and their work outside was not a great hardship and made a welcome change. I was learning how flexible and creative prison staff could be in unpromising situations – especially if encouraged.

At the beginning of 1972, shortly after my arrival, the impact of the miners' strike led to a 3 day week as steps had to be taken to save power. Major Nash insisted that all the prisoners went to the workshops during the day and took books, letters or games so that they had time out of their cells. The local POA committee were not happy but the Governor insisted and this move helped to keep the prison running smoothly despite the impact of the national difficulties.

Working with adults

I quickly adapted to working with adult prisoners. Most of the men in Preston were serving short to medium length sentences. They included my first Manx adult prisoner, whom I met years later apparently doing well back on the Island.

There was an interesting attempt to run prisoner groups led by staff during some evenings. I found myself with a group of old recidivists who tried it on with a very new and young Deputy Governor! Once I had the measure of them, they settled down and provided a valuable source of information and views about how the prisoners saw the Prison Service. One old prisoner asked me about the progress of the former Governor of Strangeways, Captain W.I. Davies – whom I had served with. I explained that he was now a Prisons Inspector. "He used to be my housemaster at Feltham Borstal" explained the prisoner, "and now he is Inspector of Prisons – and look where I am!"

Above: Governor Davies, after retirement.

Introducing change

Preston lacked a segregation unit. Prisoners awaiting adjudications stayed in their own cells; if the Governor awarded a punishment of cellular confinement – which Major Nash rarely did – the prisoner served his punishment in his own cell. Major Nash also tried to deal with any adjudication remarkably speedily – almost within minutes of staff members putting the prisoner on report.

The lack of a segregation unit also meant that if a prisoner requested "protection" we were in no position to provide proper segregation. Prisoners who had committed a sexual offence were often at risk of being attacked by other prisoners. So too were those prisoners suspected of giving information to the police or prison authorities. Such prisoners applied to the Governor for protection – and under the Prison Rules the Governor could segregate. These prisoners came to be titled "Vulnerable Prisoners" in years to come – and keeping them safe was a priority.

We needed a proper segregation unit. After much discussion with staff, I was able to reach a local agreement on subdividing C1 landing and setting up Preston's first segregation unit. I was starting to learn how to introduce change into an old prison.

One of the more unusual tasks I took on at Preston was reorganising the car parking for staff. It appeared that the situation in 1972 had changed little since the prison re-opened in 1948 with very junior, but long serving, staff having acquired all the best car parking spaces. After several meetings, much negotiation with vested interests, a solution emerged and was implemented. It was another good learning experience for me – how long standing practices could be changed for the better with attention to detail, much consultation and determination.

Parking some staff cars inside establishments continued for many years. We were still parking cars within the walls of Strangeways in 1990. This partly reflected the lack of proper parking facilities outside prisons, especially our nineteenth century urban prisons.

After Major Nash's retirement, Jack Beaumont arrived as Governor in 1972 for a year; he was then transferred to Gartree while Roland Adams came to Preston. Jack was a very different Governor to Major Nash. He had started as a Prison Officer and had been the "representative officer" or Secretary of the POA at Manchester. Unfortunately he was a heavy smoker and I had to spend many meetings with him in a smoked filled office. Fortunately changes to the rules about smoking were eventually to come about but many of us non-smokers suffered, largely in silence, in those far off days. I was delighted when Roland Adams arrived at Preston in 1973 as I always found him easy to work with.

The 1972 disturbance

I found myself in charge of Preston – Governor Jack Beaumont being on leave – at the time that the prisoner organisation PROP called for demonstrations in the summer of 1972. On August 4th many prisoners across the country demonstrated but during the morning Preston's prisoners were well behaved. Returning after lunch however, I learned from our gate staff that the main exercise yard was full of demonstrating prisoners – some 400 or so. Fortunately the Principal Officer in charge of the exercise yard was a great character, a Pole who had flown Spitfires during the war. He was not at all concerned by the demonstration and when some of the older men asked for permission to leave the yard he sent them in and about half the prisoners followed them off the yard and returned to their cells. It was well into the evening, however, before we got the remainder of the prisoners back to their cells. This was my first experience of a major act of indiscipline by large numbers of prisoners. It was also an opportunity to experience the approach of Regional and Head Office. I was constantly being asked by Regional Office to count how many prisoners were left on the yard – a virtually impossible task as the prisoners were not going to stand still and be counted! There was no suggestion any prisoners were missing; the priority was to persuade them to come in and resume normal routine. Headquarters probably wanted exact figures so they could brief the Minister – rather than focussing on restoring order.

Staffing issues

At Preston, I continued to take a close interest in staffing matters. Onley Borstal had operated to a staff working system called Functional Group Working (FGW). At Preston, I quickly learned about the other staff working system known as "Scheme V". Preston, as a training prison, should have been using FGW which was the working system designed for training establishments. Unfortunately Preston staff was working to Scheme V and changing working systems was virtually impossible because of resistance to change led by the local POA branch. FGW provided a higher proportion of staff in the evening allowing a wider range of evening activities. Because the staff were working Scheme V, there were fewer available in the evening, restricting evening activities for the prisoners.

We had two Chief Officers, a Chief Officer Class One and a Chief Officer Class Two. As with Deputy Governors, the junior Chief Officer seemed to be there primarily to cover the days when the senior Chief Officer was off duty or on leave. I recognised the need to give middle managers discrete areas of work, something I was able to develop better at Winson Green Prison, Birmingham, a few years later. But the uncertainty over responsibilities for proper use of staff hindered our efforts at Preston to make improvements.

While at Preston, I visited my former staff College tutor, Bill Driscoll, who was then Governor of Lancaster Prison. It was a fascinating experience going around the oldest prison in the country where the Lancashire Witches had been held centuries earlier and a number of Catholic priests had been incarcerated before they were executed. The establishment was an extraordinary combination of castle and prison, close to the railway station and the city.

Castles were often used to contain prisoners centuries ago. Castle Rushen, in the Isle of Man, was another example as illustrated on the back cover of this book.

Lancaster Castle had been re-opened as a prison in the 1950s and years later, the Retired Governors Newsletter published Major George Bride's account of bringing it back into commission. Lancaster also had acquired a farm which some of the prisoners worked. The farm was to become the young offenders' establishment adjacent to the M6 motorway, later called "Lancaster Farms".

Towards the end of my time at Preston, our second son Michael was born. There were difficulties with his birth and for some time we were concerned that there could be lasting consequences... Fortunately that turned out not to be the case and in years to come I was to spend much time cheering him – and his elder brother Francis – while they played rugby.

In 1974, I was successful on the promotion Board to Governor Class Three. A vacancy arose in the new Manpower Management project as team leader and I agreed to take the post. Although London based, this involved staff inspection in prisons all around the country so we decided to move to Rugby and I would commute daily when in London.

12. LOSING CONTROL: PRISON RIOTS

An important part of running a penal establishment is that the authorities retain control. The old radial prisons were ideal for that purpose with very good sight lines enabling staff to view what was taking place and quickly intervene when necessary. When the Prison Service started a programme of building new establishments in the 1950s, after a gap of almost 50 years, the Prisons Board began to experiment with different designs. The first at Everthorpe near Hull retained the open wings with good visibility but departed from the radial design. But the next few establishments, of which Onley was one, departed from the tradition of "open" wings with good visibility. Staff and management quickly learned that this provided many opportunities for prisoners' misbehaviour to go unseen so more bullying and assaults resulted. Perhaps the worst of the new designs were the new remand centres built in the 1960s, of which Risley was a particularly bad example. Sight lines in the original wings at Risley were horrendous and with a population of remand prisoners about whom we knew little, staff had to be very careful about their

Above: Typical riot damage.

own safety let alone being able to properly supervise, and where required protect, the prisoners in their care.

It was not until the 1980s that the Prison Service returned to what most Governors regarded as sensible designs of "open" wings. Consequently the Service had to continue to operate a number of establishments from the early post-war building programme which had built-in control problems.

Disturbances in prisons have a long history. In England in 1930, there was a violent and destructive riot at Dartmoor Prison followed by an inquiry and court action against the rioters. In October 1969 there was a violent disturbance at Parkhurst Prison on the Isle of Wight with allegations of staff brutality emerging afterwards.

Gartree riot 1972

My first experience of a riot was in December 1972. Prisoners at the Gartree Dispersal High Security Prison in Leicestershire rioted and caused substantial damage to the prison. I was asked to temporarily replace, for several weeks, the Deputy Governor at Gartree. I had previously worked with Governor Roland Adams who needed support in trying to restore some normality. On arrival I found that all the prisoners were locked up and the staff were suffering from an understandable loss of confidence. Over the next three weeks we edged the prison back towards the beginnings of a proper regime, although much still remained to be done when I headed back for Preston.

I spent much time at Gartree just talking to everyone I could to assess the issues and to try and work out where we had room to move forward. This was stressful work, as none of us knew if the prisoners might cause further trouble so every move we made to restore the normal regime was fraught with uncertainties. But doing nothing was not an option as the prisoners would only become more and more frustrated at being locked up and deprived of all activity. So progress was very gradual – and every change had to be thrashed out with the POA who reflected the loss of confidence of the staff.

This was a challenging experience. The prisoners had been on the rampage for a number of hours and had reduced parts of the prison buildings internally to rubble and smashed huge quantities of fixtures and fittings. Seeing the extent of the destruction; the damage to staff inmate relationships; the loss of confidence by the staff and the practical difficulties of trying to start to normalise the regime were all valuable learning experiences to help prepare me for some of the problems I was to face in years to come

The prison population usually contained a few individuals ready to cause trouble but the majority of prisoners wanted a quiet life. However, incidents between staff and prisoners badly handled could unsettle the balance and provide the troublemakers with a cause to whip up support among other prisoners. Moreover any long term prison had prisoners who had been in and out of the system for decades and sometimes had old grievances festering from long ago. The abolition of the death sentence brought increasing numbers of life sentence prisoners into the system; very long sentences – such as those imposed on the train robbers in the sixties – were also becoming more common. This was the seed ground from which riots could develop.

I have already referred to the lack of discussion about handling violence during our initial training on the Staff Course. Prison Services have always had to deal with situations where prisoners assaulted staff or became involved in violence towards other prisoners. Incidents also occurred when staff used unjustified force upon prisoners. Use of force by staff could be a flash point resulting in a wider more serious disturbance.

While the Prison Service had written rules to deter staff from using force gratuitously, little attention had been given to training staff in the use of force, of ensuring that force was properly authorised and that any use of force was properly recorded and reviewed. In Chapter 21 I shall explain how this situation was eventually tackled and procedures gradually improved.

Hull Prison riot 1976

The riot at Hull Prison in 1976 had similarities – although on a much smaller scale – with the Strangeways riot of 1990. The disturbance lasted 4 days; a great deal of damage was caused – some £750,000 at 1976 prices; the prison was put out of action for a year; the prisoners seized the roof and used slates and other missiles to impede the staff taking counter measures; the use of water as a control device was not straightforward; command and control issues emerged as the riot went on. After the riot was over, the behaviour of some staff towards some of the rioters who had surrendered was unacceptable – it led to a police investigation and to some staff being charged with offences against the prisoners. My involvement with this is discussed in Chapter 13 about the Governors Branch.

The then Chief Inspector of Prisons, Gordon Fowler, was asked to investigate the riot. His report provided a valuable record of what happened although how far the lessons emerging from the experience were learned by the Service is another matter.

There were further significant disturbances at Gartree in 1976 and at Wormwood Scrubs in 1979. There was also a major fire at Chelmsford Prison in 1978, resulting in the closure of the prison for a period for extensive rebuilding. While not riot related this was a reminder of how disaster could close a prison overnight, worsening overcrowding across the whole prison system. The Chelmsford fire was handled very well by Deputy Governor and staff, avoiding any significant casualties.

Passive demonstrations

In 1972 an organisation was founded for the Preservation of the Rights of Prisoners – known as PROP. Throughout 1972, this organisation caused considerable difficulties for Governors through a series of passive demonstrations. On August 4th 1972, a considerable number of prisons experienced passive demonstrations – Chapter 11 explains how this impacted Preston Prison. At first, Headquarters were uncertain how to deal with passive demonstrations, but gradually a response was agreed; some sanctions were applied to prisoners who refused to follow the normal prison routine. Placing large numbers of prisoners on report to the Governor and conducting many adjudications was a time consuming and tedious experience – the outcome was usually a relatively minor sanction.

The feeling among staff was that they had lost the control they once had. This encouraged many officers to turn to their trade union for a lead. It may also have increased staff willingness to take industrial action. Yet one of the factors that could increase instability in prisons was industrial action by staff. This was to become a major concern in the next decade and will be examined in Chapters 17 and 24.

13. GOVERNORS' BRANCH 1968-1984

Background

How did Prison Governors become involved in the trade union movement?

We know that the representation of Prison Governors dates back to May 1920 – one hundred years ago – when the "Superior Officers' Representative Board" (SORB) was first introduced under Captain R.H. D'Aeth, then Governor of Parkhurst. The SORB covered Governors, Medical Officers and Chaplains. It was set up following the establishment of the "Prison Officers Representative Board" in 1919. Little information is available about the workings of this board but it gave evidence to the Stanhope Committee in 1923. We do know that some, perhaps many, Governors felt that it was unable to deliver effective representation.

According to the Prison Commissioners Annual Reports, the SORB was disbanded in 1948 and the senior staff were encouraged to join conventional civil service trade unions. Chaplains and Medical Officers joined the Institute of Professional Civil Servants; Governors formed the Prison and Borstal Governors Branch of the Society of Civil Servants (SCS). But representing Governors through a major civil service union was not popular with some Governors. The SCS represented thousands of civil servants whose priorities did not coincide with those of a few hundred Prison and Borstal Governors.

In 1972, the SCS affiliated to the TUC. There was growing dissatisfaction among some Governors that the SCS was too "political" and did not focus sufficiently on Governors' interests. Matters became especially difficult when industrial action was taken by the union. Most Governors considered it difficult to reconcile running prisons safely with taking industrial action and feared that industrial action, in prisons, risked considerable danger to life and property.

For some thirty years, the Governors' Branch did not attempt to develop any public profile. Representatives of the Branch gave evidence to the 1958 Wynn-Parry Committee investigating the pay and conditions of service of prison Governors and prison officers. On 23rd January 1967, probably for the first time, representatives of the Branch gave evidence to a Parliamentary committee – the "Estimates Committee" – the full record of the proceedings being published in January 1968.

During the 1960s the Branch developed position papers on penal policy usually responding to issues under review by the Government. While the Branch position was conveyed to Prisons HQ there was no attempt at influencing wider debate by publishing Governor's views in the media. Consequently, our influence was negligible – a fact that caused growing frustration and considerable debate at Governors Conferences.

In the 1970s, there were around 500 Governor Grades in England and Wales. The Governors Branch represented the five grades of Governors working in adult and young offender establishments in England and Wales. Most of the Governor Grades were Assistant Governors Class Two working as borstal housemasters, in charge of wings in adult prisons and as Deputy Governors in small establishments. Assistant Governors Class One were generally Deputy Governors or third in charge of very large prisons. Governors Class Three were in charge of small establishments or Deputy Governors of the largest prisons; Governors Class Two were in charge of the medium sized establishments and the 15 or so largest prisons were in the charge of Governors Class One. Above the prisons were a number of posts filled by promotion from the Governor Grades. These senior posts were involved with deciding or advising on policy and operations and providing support and supervision to the field.

Branch Committee

When I joined the Branch Committee in 1968, we met every two months using the offices of the Society or the facilities in one of the prisons. When David Hewlings was Branch Chairman, we met at Wormwood Scrubs Prison where he was the Governor. David Hewlings had a reputation for being a great listener and for always consulting staff and colleagues. However, I also learned that he could be very decisive when needed – a useful pointer to the need to develop different styles of leadership for different situations within prisons. Being on the Governors Committee meant opportunities to meet and learn from a much wider range of Governors and to see how some of the senior Governors functioned as Committee Chairmen and officers.

Meetings with members took place during Annual Conferences. Introduced in the 1920s, these were an important part of the support, briefing and communication structures of the Service. Governing Governors met once a year – generally in the autumn. The Assistant Governors were split into two Conferences – all those working in borstals attended one; all those working in prisons the other. The Governors' Branch had a "domestic session" during each Conference: committee members reported back to the wider membership and listened to members' opinions.

I became involved with raising standards in prison quarters, especially the installation of central heating, and wrote an article for the Prison Service Journal in 1970 "Living with the Job". I was part of discussions and negotiations that led to the introduction of 5 day week working for Governors – previously we had worked for 12 days every fortnight with alternate weekends off. This pattern of attendance was relatively recent as previously Governors were allowed only one weekend off a month, including when 5 weekends fell in a particular month, and a day off each week.

Both HQ and Governors had to grapple with the fundamental questions of what the tasks and responsibilities of Governors were – and how these responsibilities were to be covered in their absence. In September 1972, the Branch Committee met with a very senior civil servant, Mr AR Bunker, the

Principal Establishment Officer at the Home Office – probably the first time such a meeting had occurred in the history of the Branch. The new conditions of service, giving Governors 4 days off each fortnight, were agreed and introduced in April 1973 – years after prison officers had started working a 5 day week!

Governors' pensions lacked the enhanced pension arrangements of Prison Officers – every year they worked after 20 counted as two for pension purposes – "Two for One" as it was known. Many Governors, particularly late joiners, felt they were disadvantaged by being unable to earn a full pension. This issue was never resolved. However, under the Fresh Start changes of 1987, new entrant prison officers lost the "Two for One".

In 1969 a review of "fast stream" graduate entry was set up by Home Secretary, Jim Callaghan. Following the review and considerable lobbying, a new system was introduced for young – under 25 year old – graduates to gain two years prison officer experience before attending the staff course and being appointed to the Governor Grade. The Committee monitored the changes and the new system appeared to work reasonably well.

By the early 1970s the POA was threatening or taking industrial action in prisons with increasing frequency. This development reinforced Governors' views that taking industrial action in prisons was very dangerous especially the risks of prisoner reaction leading to a loss of control. Governors pressed the Branch Committee to seek a solution.

Branch officers and changing tactics

John Wheeler, an Assistant Governor at Wandsworth Prison, was seconded to the Society of Civil Servants as a full time official. His brief included dealing with Governors Branch issues. However, John decided on a change of career and left both the Society and the Service to take up a post representing part of the private security industry. He was selected for a constituency and became a London MP. He was a valuable contact for the Governors Branch and became Chair of the Home Affairs Committee – before which we gave evidence. He later became Sir John Wheeler and was a junior Government Minister in the Northern Ireland Office.

In 1975, the Branch negotiated a new agreement with the Prison Service to allow the Branch Secretary to be seconded on "Facility Time" to Branch work. Before that, the Branch had had to rely on Committee members working in their own time. Jim Hayes an experienced Assistant Governor became the first full time Branch Secretary.

In 1976, following growing concerns among Governors about the increased overcrowding of prisons, the Branch took a radical step and arranged a Special Conference entitled "Methods of Reducing the Prison Population". This took place from 25th to 27th February 1977 and was followed by a Press Conference at the offices of the Society in London on 28th February. It attracted much publicity. For the first time the Branch Chairman Barry Wigginton, Governor of Brixton Prison, appeared on national TV news. This was a complete departure from previous practice as the Branch Committee had been very uncertain about how far it could make media statements without being in breach of the Official Secrets Act.

Thus began a process of engagement between the Branch and the media. Unfortunately, Barry Wigginton died unexpectedly shortly after the Conference, one of three senior Governors to die "in harness" in the same year – perhaps an indication of the growing stresses being experienced by senior Governors. In the subsequent election for Chairman, I was elected, the first relatively junior Governor – then a Governor Class Three, Deputy Governor of Birmingham Prison, to hold the Chairman's post. Previously, the Chairman had always been a senior Governor so this was a radical culture change for the organisation!

About this time, the Committee started to introduce changes that were eventually to lead to the setting up of an independent trade union. An early step was to change our image – we started to use the motto "Sui Generis" together with a rather striking crest on our notepaper – a term lifted from the 1958 Wynn-Parry Report. This is what Wynn-Parry had to say:

"It must we think be recognised that the Prison Service, although part of the Civil Service, is sui generis." (Paragraph 7).

The Latin tag "sui generis" is generally taken to mean "unique" or "in a class or group on its own".

As newly elected Chairman, I led a Branch delegation to meet the Home Secretary, Merlyn Rees, in September 1977. The meeting discussed issues around overcrowding and we advocated ways of reducing the prison population. This was the start on a steep learning curve about how to influence our political leaders.

Meetings with the Home Secretary became part of the normal work of the Committee. Over the next twenty years, I led delegations to meet Merlyn Rees, Willie Whitelaw, Douglas Hurd, David Waddington, Kenneth Baker, Ken Clarke, and Michael Howard. We also regularly met with junior Ministers given special responsibility for prisons.

We were invited to give evidence to the House of Commons Expenditure Committee – which had decided to inquire into "The Reduction of pressure on the Prison System". We had to draft evidence for the Committee and then appear to give oral evidence. Preparing the written evidence was a lengthy task – largely undertaken in the evenings and weekends. This was followed in 1979 by another appearance – this time before the House of Commons Education Arts and Home Office subcommittee. It was a daunting experience leading a team of Governors before a group of MPs – no matter how much preparation had been done.

In evidence to the 1978 Expenditure Committee, we stressed the extent that prisons were being overwhelmed by the rising numbers of prisoners against declining resources. We suggested that there should be restrictions on the powers of the courts to commit to prison without first finding a vacancy.

In 1978, the deteriorating industrial relations within the Service led to the Governors taking further action which triggered the setting up of the May Inquiry. This development is covered in Chapter 17 – Industrial Relations.

The Branch tried to educate the politicians and the public to the realities of life in our prisons. We considered that the root of our problems was that the tasks and resources of the Prison Service were out of balance. We argued that either the politicians should take steps to reduce the pressure on prisons by restricting the numbers coming in, or the Service should be given greater resources. Given the age and conditions of many of our old establishments we argued that additional resources were also needed to bring old establishments up to an acceptable standard.

Prisons were the only institutions in the country that had to accept whoever and how many are sent. We stressed that the costs of this "Open Door" policy should be shared with other organisations – such as the NHS and the Immigration Service – whose clients the Prison Service was expected to accommodate without financial recompense.

We also explained that rising standards in society raised expectations among staff and prisoners about improving conditions. Thus the deteriorating conditions in prisons were doubly dangerous – both in themselves and because they ran contrary to the rising expectations. The impact of deteriorating conditions will be explored in Chapter 14 on "Overcrowding".

Governors were also increasingly concerned at growing difficulties around staffing. These difficulties probably originated before 1960. But when the Prison Commission was abolished in 1964, responsibility for prison staffing moved to a division of the Home Office "Establishments" – which appeared to be quite disconnected from the line management of the Service. In response the Prison Service had to set up its own "Staffing Division" – P6 – to which I was attached for 3 years from 1974 and 1977. So the Governors Branch advocated a radical change of structure so that prison staffing came under the control of the Prisons Board. The difficulties over staffing are explored further in Chapter 15.

The Committee contacted opposition politicians as we appreciated that any new incoming Government, of whatever party, following the 1979 General Election, should be briefed about the difficulties they faced in the prisons. The approach of Willie Whitelaw, then Conservative lead on prison Issues, was encouraging as he showed an unusual interest in prisons and quickly developed considerable knowledge about our problems. Briefing opposition politicians was to yield positive results when the Conservatives formed a new administration in 1979.

We also built up our contacts with the various pressure groups that were concerned with criminal justice matters. I had regular contact with Stephen Shaw, then Director of the recently formed Prison Reform Trust. We worked together where our views coincided.

Media work and handling disasters

From 1977, as newly elected Chair of the Governors' Branch I was asked to appear regularly on national media, both TV and Radio to comment on prison issues. The first Governors' Branch Press Release had been in February 1977 following the Overcrowding Conference. I instituted regular press releases updating the media on our work.

Handling disasters was a constant concern. Within months of becoming Chairman, I discovered that police inquiries were going on into the behaviour of staff at HMP Hull after the serious disturbance there as recounted in the last chapter. A relatively junior Assistant Governor was being investigated for not preventing possible misbehaviour by staff. We had difficulties persuading the Society of Civil Servants that if a charge was laid, our member needed legal support. Initially we were told that the legal aid scheme operated by the Society specifically excluded cases where members were involved in police proceedings. After much discussion, we achieved the necessary legal support for our member, but the difficulty of persuading the Society left the Committee concerned that we might not be able to protect members in the future. It was another step towards Governors realising that they needed their own representative organisation.

On 16th December 1980, three high security prisoners escaped from HM Prison Brixton. There was an inquiry into the escape by the Deputy Director General of Prisons, Gordon Fowler, and his report was published on 27th July 1981. The Governor of Brixton was moved to a post in South East Regional Office. I had the difficult task of ensuring that the Governor's side of what happened was represented in the media and had to face searching questions during media interviews which filled the headlines of BBC TV News.

Perhaps the most challenging interview I had to give was in the aftermath of the serious disturbance at Wormwood Scrubs on 31st August 1979 where the staff re-established control but prisoners and staff were injured.

Allegations of brutality were being made in the media: it was the first night of BBC's new "Newsnight" programme and the Prison Service would not put up a spokesperson. If only the allegations were to be heard on the BBC, the public would draw its own conclusions. I agreed to appear and a large team descended on my house in Birmingham to arrange to beam a live interview to the studios. While it was not possible to answer some of the allegations, I was able to give another view of the issues involved that night and the public – hopefully – gained a broader view of the complexity of what took place. Official public statements about the Wormwood Scrubs disturbance were only made in the House of Commons on 23rd February 1982 following the Prison Service's Inquiry led by Keith Gibson, Regional Director South East.

Governors were increasingly concerned at how many disasters had shaken the Prison Service over the past two decades. The serious escapes of Wilson, Biggs and Blake had led to the Mountbatten Inquiry. The escape of Hughes from a Leicester Prison escort in 1977 – followed by dreadful murders – had resulted in a further inquiry. Escapes of top security prisoners from Brixton Prison had caused yet another inquiry. Disturbances at Parkhurst, two at Gartree, at Hull and at Wormwood Scrubs, increased Governors' concerns. The PROP demonstrations of 1972, although passive, had created further instability. Industrial action by prison officers was becoming more frequent and despite the May Inquiry of 1979, we feared the potential for industrial action to trigger yet more prisoner disturbances.

Meanwhile the prisoner population continued to rise; there were an increasing number of life sentence prisoners; terrorist, particularly but not exclusively with Irish connections, threatened more escapes or disturbances and the conditions in prisons were increasingly bleak. The rising number of very dangerous prisoners – including terrorists – serving very long sentences also had unwelcome consequences. Threats to staff have probably always been a factor in prisons but the increase in the readiness to issue credible threats to Governors was a new concern. As we were to witness, our colleagues in Northern Ireland faced the real possibility of death when at home or travelling to work. A few Governors in England and Wales mentioned to me that they had received death threats from terrorist inmates and had reported these threats to the police. It was becoming apparent that governing prisons was increasingly demanding and dangerous and very different from the work of many other public servants.

On a more positive note, in 1978, to mark the centenary of the nationalisation of the prisons, the Queen visited the Service. As Chairman of the Governors Branch, my wife and I were invited to join the anniversary lunch at Leyhill in Gloucestershire and to be introduced to the Queen, along with many others

During the years from 1979, I had considerable informal contact with the Director General, Denis Trevelyan and the Director of Personnel and Resources

John Chilcott. John Chilcott went on to develop a remarkable career as a civil servant finishing up as Permanent Secretary in Northern Ireland. He went on to take up the challenge of investigating the Iraq War, the work for which he will be most remembered. These informal meetings enabled me to alert senior management to the realities of the issues faced by Governors – something that helped to pave the way for the many improvements that the Service achieved in the next decade or so.

The Governors' Branch also developed closer ties with our colleagues in Scotland and Northern Ireland. At the May Inquiry of 1979, the three organisations representing Governors from the different parts of the UK gave evidence together.

Growing concerns about representation

Throughout the seventies, internal discussions continued, spasmodically, about the desirability of having an "independent" organisation to represent Governors. Behind the discussion of setting up an independent organisation was another important issue. Members were becoming increasingly interested in having a representative organisation that could speak out on "professional issues". So the question arose as to whether the trade union could balance its traditional "conditions of service" work with "professional work". Members' growing interest in professional issues was an understandable response to growing public attention to prison matters. The setting up of a number of inquiries into the Prison Service; the growing media interest and the consequent political interest in penal policy created an atmosphere where many different interest groups and pressure groups started to speak out on prison issues. Prison Governors wanted to have their views expressed clearly and publicly. The danger was that if this could not be achieved, Governors would lose their ability to influence penal policy.

This growing expectation among Governors that our professional views should be developed and promulgated created considerable problems for the Governors' Branch Committee which was made up of people with full-time management jobs; the limited time they had available for the work of the Branch made it extremely difficult to deal adequately with the growing workload on both trade union and professional issues.

Despite the success of the 1977 overcrowding conference, there was growing frustration over the adequacy of the professional representation of Governors by the Governors Branch. This led some Governors to set up the "British Association of Prison Governors" (BAPG) in order to provide "professional" representation for Governors. Support was forthcoming from Governors in both Scotland and England and the BAPG soon acquired around 150 members – most of whom were also members of the Governors Branch. At this time the Governors Branch in England and Wales had around 500 members against a potential some 600. After a short life, BAPG closed but only after the Governors Branch undertook to give more time and effort to "professional" issues. Interestingly, BAPG survived in Scotland as a separate "professional" organisation.

However, the difficulty of trying to develop professional policy as well as dealing with the traditional "trade union" representative work was considerable and we had neither the time nor the resources to do the work justice. We looked with envy on the arrangements for developing policy which the senior police had acquired – but their structure was quite different and was not a model we could hope to follow.

A significant influence on the Governors' Branch throughout the sixties and seventies was Peter Timms who became Governor of Glen Parva Young Offenders establishment in Leicester and then Governor of Maidstone Prison. Peter was to retire and become a Methodist Minister and play an important role under the guidance of David Astor in the establishment of a number of prison charities including the Prison Video Trust and the Prison Charity Shops.

I continued to be Chairman of the Governors' Branch when I moved to Featherstone in 1980 and when I moved to HQ – P5 Division in 1982. One of the unexpected and difficult issues that emerged in 1983 was that of capital punishment. The Branch Committee were reluctant to take a position on this highly controversial issue, but under pressure from members decided it could not be avoided. After a membership survey at which 200 members were consulted the Committee agreed a letter to the Home Secretary and a media release. The overwhelming membership view was abolitionist but a small minority were strongly in favour of retention. The Committee suggested that if capital punishment were retained it should be separated from the prison system and special facilities for executions created away from prisons. Despite the strong opinions on both sides of the capital punishment debate, only three members resigned, one of whom subsequently re-joined.

In 1984 on moving to Midland Regional Office in Birmingham as Deputy Regional Director, I stood down as Chairman to avoid any conflict of interest as I was expected to be on the Official Side in any negotiations. However, I was asked by colleagues to provide informal advice from time to time, especially as the momentum developed to set up our own independent trade union – the Prison Governors Association. This development is described in Chapter 25. I was to return to the Branch Committee in the run up to the setting up of the Prison Governors Association in 1987.

14. OVERCROWDING – IMPORTANCE, IMPACT AND CAUSES

Overcrowding of prisons is both a historical and current problem, found in many parts of the world. Overcrowding of cells in the prisons of England and Wales in the second half of the twentieth century dominated the life of prisoners and staff for decades. How did this come about? What was the impact of overcrowding? Why was overcrowding not abolished? Let us start by considering the legislation and rules under which the Prison Service operated and how this legal framework was put into practice.

Statutory and regulatory framework

The Prisons Act 1952 is the statutory basis under which the Prison Service operates. When a new prison opens, the Home Secretary signs a certificate that the site and buildings are a prison. All the cells have to be certified, a safeguard against any room being used as a cell without authority. To be certified, cells have to be suitable for the confinement of a prisoner and to have the means for a prisoner to call staff. Certificates were required for hospital accommodation and for segregation units including "Special" cells. These were cells devoid of furniture and specially strengthened for confining a violent prisoner. Each cell has to be identified by a mark, usually a number. Dormitories and other rooms used for sleeping prisoners required certification including the maximum numbers allowed for each unit of accommodation.

The total number of prisoners who could be held in a prison was also controlled – although the controls were not as effective as they might have been. Cell certificates had to specify how many prisoners could be confined to a cell – usually cells were certified for single occupancy or for either two or three prisoners. There was no requirement to certify that cells had access to sanitation or any laid down standards of cell sizes. Older prisons often had a variety of cell sizes. Cell certificates had to be signed by HQ or Regional officials but as there was no written guidance – it was entirely at their discretion. In practice, most cell certificates submitted by a Governor were signed without question.

John Howard in "The State of the Prisons", published in 1777, had this to say about cell sharing:

"I wish to have so many small rooms or cabins that each criminal may sleep alone. If it be difficult to prevent their being together in the daytime, they should be [sic] all means be separated at night".

Elizabeth Fry took a similar view in the early nineteenth century.

The Victorians, in drawing up rules for cell occupation, envisaged cells being occupied by only one prisoner. However, the 1865 regulations had a measure of flexibility:

"Every such prisoner will sleep in a cell by himself, or under special circumstances in a separate bed in a cell containing not fewer than two other male prisoners."

By 1949 the Regulations had changed to:

"Where sleeping accommodation is in separate cells, each prisoner shall occupy a cell by himself. Provided that where it is necessary for special reasons the Commissioners may authorise the accommodating of not more than three prisoners to a cell."

Totalling up the number of certified places available gave an establishment a "Certified Normal Accommodation" or "CNA". But this gave no scope for overcrowding. So each establishment had a "maximum capacity" – this figure was usually negotiated between the Governor, Regional Offices, and HQ and when disputes arose – after discussions with the POA. In setting the maximum capacity, little account was taken of supporting services such as whether the establishment had adequate space for activities, bathing and visits facilities. These "maximum capacity" figures, arrived at by negotiation, were the result of years of overcrowding and population pressures.

Overcrowding in practice

Overcrowding probably occurred in some of the local prisons before nationalisation in 1878. But the first few decades of the new national Prison Service saw drastic rationalisation of accommodation and a programme of closure of unsuitable older and smaller prisons. There were around 20,000 in prison by the outbreak of World War One. The outbreak of war produced a sharp fall in the prison population with early release emergency measures.

There appears to have been no overcrowding of prisons or of cells in the interwar years as the numbers of prisoners contracted to some 10,000 - 13,000 and 14 prisons were closed. I have already referred to the astonishing flexibility available at this time when prisoners were not located in the top landings of prisons for convenience because there were many spare cells available. The reason for the dramatic decrease in numbers in prison between 1918 and 1939 deserves greater research, especially given the stresses within the country including very high unemployment.

The outbreak of World War Two saw a sharp reduction in the population as emergency early releases and an increase in remission were authorised. From 1942, the prisoner population began rising and soon exceeded the pre-war total. From 1946, Governors of local prisons started to run out of cell spaces and from 1947 were forced to overcrowd their establishments by placing some prisoners three in a cell.

During some of the worst years of overcrowding in the local prisons, prisoners were occasionally required to sleep in the reception area, in uncertified rooms and even on landings. This was especially likely if a court sat well beyond the normal finishing time resulting in prisoners being received into the prison unexpectedly late into the evening. Staff had to use initiative and ingenuity to ensure everyone had somewhere to sleep for the night.

Terry Weiler, retired Prisons Board member, researched and published an account (See Appendix C) of the origins of placing three prisoners in a cell. He was unable to find a management or political decision authorising the change, or even a Ministerial or Parliamentary announcement that it had occurred. The news crept out in references in the Prison Commission Annual Reports and other documents. So while there was a remarkable effort to house the growing numbers – almost anywhere and anyhow – overcrowding cells, and its impact on prisoners and staff, was never properly authorised. The regulations about "special reasons" for justifying placing more than one prisoner in a cell were ignored as the number of prisoners sleeping three to a cell rose to over 5600 in 1952 and over 8000 in 1961.

There was little effective Parliamentary scrutiny of cell overcrowding. Perhaps the lack of scrutiny was partly because the Chairman of the Prison Commission throughout this period was Sir Lionel Fox whose reputation was considerable. Politicians may have felt that they could safely leave prisons to Sir Lionel.

The efforts made to house the population were exceptional, with old military camps quickly converted to prisons and prison establishments, shut down during the interwar years, rapidly reopened. Extraordinary changes were made – in 1958 all of Northallerton's 98 long term prisoners were moved by train to Eastchurch on the Isle of Sheppey in a single day.

But it was not enough.

The Government White Paper "Penal Practice in a Changing Society" published in February 1959 recorded that:

"The great majority of men…. serve their sentences in …grossly overcrowded conditions and without adequate facilities for work or training" (para 52). The report notes that there were "6000 men sleeping three in a single cell".

One of the principal recommendations of the White Paper was to press ahead with new remand centres – which unfortunately would prove highly unsatisfactory and become heavily overcrowded. The opportunity to review why overcrowding had come about and to seek a lasting solution was lost.

During the nineteen sixties, Roy Jenkins was Home Secretary and expressed the view that if the prison population was to exceed 42,000 prisoners that would be "intolerable".

The impact of overcrowding dominated the Prison Service for decades – Chris Train, Director General, had this to say to the Woolf Inquiry in 1990:

"The life and work of the Prison Service have for the last 20 years been distorted by the problems of overcrowding. That single factor has dominated prisoners' lives; it has produced often intolerable pressure on the staff and as a consequence it has soured industrial relations".

A summary of the impact of the first thirty years of overcrowding was published in evidence to the May Inquiry in February 1979 by the Governors Branch:

"Overcrowding of prisons did not exist this century until 1945. From 1945 to 1978, the prison population rose from about 12,000 to 42,000. This increase of over 300% has been contained by good management and skilful improvisation. The majority of prisoners are held in the 42 establishments built before 1900 and the 4 built between 1900 and 1939. Much of the remainder are held in "temporary" establishments improvised out of army camps, country houses and similar buildings. A small proportion of the population is housed in the 20 odd new establishments built since 1956. Less than a quarter of our accommodation is twentieth century purpose built."

Overcrowding was heavily concentrated in the Victorian local prisons. The training prisons and the borstals were largely exempted – as those at the top of the Service tried to preserve and protect positive regimes. As a result, the local prisons suffered excessive deprivation and the living conditions for prisoners, and the working conditions for staff, such as I experienced at Winson Green from 1977 to 1980, were all too typical of Victorian local prisons all round the country.

When leading staff inspection teams, described in Chapter 18, I also studied the accommodation available in a cross section of older prisons. I discovered that cells were often of different sizes; a few had quite large windows and a number had been taken over for purposes other than housing prisoners, for example stores or offices. Most smaller cells could not be used for triple occupation; the ones with big windows had originally been used for sick prisoners – for example some were originally designated as "TB Cells". The loss of cells for stores and offices had occurred with little planning – and sometimes these were cells that had practically no natural light or some other deficiency. From Du Cane's time, the warders, renamed "officers" from 1920, were not expected to have offices although "landing officers" were allowed very small "desks" out on the landing to conduct any business. Pressure on cell places from 1945 onwards resulted in efforts to recover lost cell accommodation.

Overcrowding and cell sanitation

What was the impact of overcrowding? Perhaps the worst problem was the combination of overcrowding with the lack of in-cell sanitation. Prisoners had no access to toilets within cells but had to defecate and urinate into either chamber pots or buckets. Overcrowding of cells substantially worsened what was already a deplorable situation – it meant that prisoners were compelled to relieve themselves in front of their cell mates. This was unpleasant and degrading for all three prisoners in an overcrowded cell.

When cells were opened the following morning, the contents of buckets

Above: Recess (toilet area) on prison landing.

and chamber pots then had to be emptied out in the nearby "recesses" – the infamous "slopping out" procedure. The 1981 Inspection Report on Manchester noted that the recesses were so inadequate that 40 prisoners had to share one toilet between them. Cleaning of used chamber pots and buckets was very difficult and hygiene standards were at the best variable and often very poor.

The complete lack of in-cell sanitation was not addressed as overcrowding took hold in the late 1940s. It was not until the 1990s that a substantial effort to provide integral sanitation in cells started to make a real difference to prisoners' living conditions and to staff working conditions.

In the early 1980s, HQ began work as to how the sanitation problem might be resolved. A number of new prisons – Featherstone was one as described in Chapter 20 – had been built in the 1970s with toilets in each small cell. But the real challenge was what to do about the large Victorian prison cells. One proposal was to take the middle cell of three in each Victorian prison and turn it into two "sanitary annexes", one being accessed from each cell. The two cells would be treated as either double or triple cells so a maximum of 6 prisoners could be accommodated between the three cells. Each sanitary annexe had a door so this proposal had the benefit of giving each prisoner some privacy. Experiments of this "three into two" solution were conducted at Stafford Prison – one of the few highly overcrowded training prisons – and the results looked promising. But a major programme of the "three into two" solution would result in a considerable loss of capacity – three Victorian cells could accommodate up to 9 prisoners: the "three into two" would reduce that capacity to a maximum of 6. With prisoner numbers still rising, both the politicians and HQ were reluctant to implement this solution.

Publication of increasingly critical Inspection Reports – highlighting the need to tackle "slopping out" – gradually built up pressure for improvements. It was not until the Woolf Report in 1991 that ending "slopping out" became a very high priority.

Eating meals in cells

The solutions proposed by the Stafford experiment expose a further issue around the use of cells. If a lavatory is installed in a cell, can the cell be used for eating meals? The practice of eating meals in cells – often because there was no alternative – had gone on for centuries. Given that modern hygiene rules require lavatories to be enclosed and separated from areas where food is prepared or eaten, current practice in prisons is very difficult to justify. The "three into two" solution – providing a discreet sanitary annexe to each cell – excepted, much of the rest of the in-cell sanitation may be in breach of modern hygiene rules. Many cell toilets are not fitted with lids which would at least reduce the danger of food contamination. Flushing lavatories projects aerosol particles into the cell, potentially spreading infection. In cells housing more than one prisoner this danger is increased.

Cleaning toilets to an acceptable standard, including when prisoners move from one cell to another, is a further complication.

Eating meals in cells with chamber pots and contents, before the introduction of in-cell sanitation, was at least as great a breach of modern hygiene rules.

Much more research is needed – especially whether such apparent breaches of modern hygiene rules cause ill effects to prisoners.

Unless there is a derogation from modern hygiene rules that apply across the UK and beyond, it is difficult to see how prison authorities can justify placing more than one prisoner in a cell with a toilet and without a full review of the dangers of eating meals, indeed any food, in cells with toilets. Avoiding such a breach of modern hygiene rules would require many penal establishments to provide facilities for prisoners to dine out of cell. This could only be achieved with a much reduced population together with considerable building work and reorganisation. I shall return to this question in Chapter 42.

The legality of eating meals in the same room as a toilet will have implications for the use of cells in court complexes and in police stations.

Overcrowded cells – other consequences

To accommodate the additional prisoners, bunk beds were installed in prison cells, hugely reducing the limited space within the cell. The use of upper bunks also increased the danger of prisoners being injured through falling off the top bunks, a danger said to have increased significantly with the greater availability and use of more dangerous illegal drugs in recent years.

Vandalism, equipment damage and loss of kit increased considerably with overcrowding and staff found it very difficult to assert control – all three occupants would deny knowledge and the turnover of cell occupants would often allow the blame to be placed on those just transferred to another establishment or discharged. All this added to the poor conditions for prisoners and increased the frustrations of staff. My experience of the initial impact of overcrowding at Manchester Borstal Allocation Centre in 1966 is described in Chapter 8.

One immediate and practical issue for staff from the start of overcrowding was selecting which prisoners were placed in overcrowded cells and which combinations of prisoners were placed in cells together. Given the time prisoners were locked up together in cells, the scope for bullying, abuse, and contamination was considerable. Once prisoners were placed in overcrowded cells, incidents increased involving injuries to prisoners, often reported to be accidental. I have referred to one incident at Manchester in Chapter 8 when two borstal trainees attacked a third.

Prisoners moved around the country

Another consequence of overcrowding was the pressure to move prisoners from one prison to another to make room for the next expected intake from the courts. Local prisons were expected to quickly interview and allocate prisoners to training prisons. Closed training prisons were required to review their prisoners to see if anyone was suitable for moving to open prison. Open prisons were not easy to keep full and HQ and Regional Offices were constantly exhorting Governors of secure prisons to downgrade the security category of some of their prisoners and move them to fill vacancies.

This "churn" of prisoners was often not in their best interests. Open prisons generally had better facilities and were less regimented and gave more freedom. But they were often converted from other uses – for example old military camps – and the accommodation could be very basic. Less staff meant less supervision so misbehaviour such as bullying and smuggling contraband was often a problem.

The damage caused by the "churn" included that prisoners who had commenced a course in one prison were suddenly uprooted and compulsorily transferred to another prison losing the chance to complete the course. Some of the "churn" of prisoners moved them hundreds of miles from their home areas making it much more difficult for relatives to visit. Given the importance of family support to successful rehabilitation, the impact of "churn" on prisoners was and is highly regrettable.

If prisons were to work well, the relationship between staff and prisoners was crucial. To achieve this, continuity of both staff and prisoners was required. Moving prisoners about, in response to the pressure of numbers, often had a very damaging impact on relationships as it took time for staff and prisoners to learn how to work together. So developing effective prisons with positive regimes required two crucial elements – continuity of staff and continuity of prisoners. The pressure to move prisoners around, caused by overcrowding, damaged relationships and made it difficult to run positive prisons.

Overcrowding damages regimes

As numbers grew, Governors found that other facilities – exercise yards, workshops and visits rooms – all came under pressure leading to some prisoners spending considerably more time in their cells because of the lack of alternative activity. I describe the impact of overcrowding on exercise in Chapter 19.

Contamination dangers

Overcrowding potentially increased the likelihood of contamination. Prisons have considerable potential to be the breeding ground for future crimes. "Half the robberies in and about London are planned in the prisons" wrote John Howard in 1777. Experienced prison staff recognised the dangers. Security Principal Officers – a post Mountbatten initiative – rapidly became involved in liaising with their local police contacts to try and counter future crime being planned in prison – among many other priorities.

Not all prisoners regarded cell sharing as worse than being on their own. If sharing with prisoners they got on with, cell sharing was preferred by some. But little research has been carried out on the impact of overcrowding on prisoners and especially on re-offending rates. In particular, the extent that overcrowding encouraged contamination between prisoners is largely unknown. Before overcrowding began around 1947, strenuous efforts were made to keep prisoners in "single cells" i.e. on their own. This was because of concerns for the "moral welfare" of prisoners if they were allowed to associate together unsupervised. The Annual Report of the Commissioners for 1947 comments:

"When there are three times the normal number of prisoners on a landing to be locked up and unlocked, 'slopped out', searched, served with meals, speed must tend to take the place of care. It is a situation in which an officer can rarely feel satisfaction in his work and is particularly bad for the training of so many young officers."

the UK was achieving. The May Report concluded:

"It is difficult to be confident that our more grossly overcrowded accommodation can be defended."

A helpful foundation for improvements to the Prison Service from 1980 onwards was provided by the May Report. But the question of abolishing overcrowding remained unanswered – bringing the tasks and resources of the Service into balance was a very long way off.

The Governors' Branch met Home Secretary Willie Whitelaw on 1st December 1981 to discuss overcrowding. Our accompanying media release said:

"Enough is enough. The prison system has places for only 37,000 prisoners – the present population of 44,000 is quite intolerable. Conditions for staff and prisoners alike are an affront to a civilized society."

In a debate on prisons on 2nd December 1981, Home Secretary Willie Whitelaw spelt out the realities of overcrowding thus:

"The latest total is about 44,000 prisoners against a Certified Normal Accommodation of less than 39,000. In practice more than 37,000 means a degree of overcrowding. The global figures mask considerably greater overcrowding in local prisons. For example on 31st October Birmingham Prison, with room for 537 prisoners, held 927 of whom 576 were 3 to a cell. The sharing of cells is not necessarily wrong in itself but when it is enforced and 3 to a cell, it is intolerable."

Overcrowding was the result of a rising prisoner population and insufficient resources to house prisoners. But why did the population keep rising? It was not always so as the fall in the numbers between World War One and World War Two demonstrates. But from about 1945 the prisoner population has risen more or less continuously from 15,000 to 85,000 or more today.

Causes of rising prison population

Why was the population rising? The total number of receptions into prison in 1904/05 was marginally under 200,000. In 1967 it was 98,118. Yet the overall prison population was 20,000 in 1904; it was 32,000 in 1968. Far more people were being committed to prison in 1904, but they were serving very short sentences. A major factor in the rise of the prison population was the increase in the length of sentences being imposed. There has been a marked increase in prisoners serving very long sentences, including life sentences, compared with the situation fifty years ago. Looking back at the prison population in the early twentieth century, it is striking how many prisoners were serving very short sentences indeed – many of less than 3 months.

Part of the problem is inappropriate use of prison sentences. It is not defensible to send sick people to prison yet the prisons have been and are overwhelmed by people with mental health problems. The figures for the number of mentally ill people in prison produced by the regular "Bromley Briefing Reports" from the Prison Reform Trust are highly alarming. Why are we not doing more as a community to treat mentally ill people instead of locking them up in prison?

The growth in the number of people in prison with mental health problems may be related to reduction in the capacity of the former asylum system. Reformers pressed for a different way of managing and treating those confined within asylums. The huge Victorian institutions were gradually closed and demolished but the alternatives for the former patients were often inadequate, so many were committed to prison. This is a failure of "joined up" Government as the Department of Health's inability to cope with some mentally ill offenders has put further pressure on very overstretched prisons which have few resources for containing, let alone treating, those with mental illnesses. Research is needed to establish what part the reduction in capacity of the asylum system, together with insufficient community alternatives, played in the growth of the prison population.

Most new laws passed by Parliament rely on fines or imprisonment as the ultimate sanction. More laws – more potential prisoners. Reducing crime, protecting society and reducing re-offending are complex and difficult tasks. But that is no excuse for inaction. Gross and prolonged overcrowding leaves the Prison Service with a near impossible task. This is especially true in the light of the research evidence of what reduces re-offending, as discussed in Chapter 40.

Overcrowding after 1980 is considered in Chapter 35.

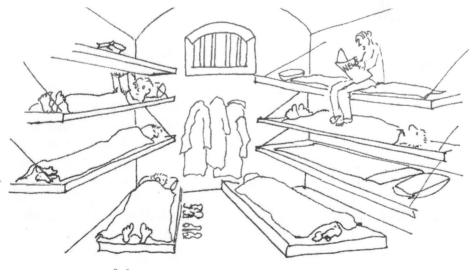

" GOOD NEWS — THE PRISON POPULATION IS
NOT AS HIGH AS PREDICTED."

15. PRISON STAFFING

Background

The underlying cause of the many crises experienced by the Prison Service since World War Two is the toxic combination of two factors: cell overcrowding and staffing difficulties.

What is so important about prison staffing? It is this. The key to delivering an effective regime for prisoners is through managing and motivating staff.

The Prison Service is required to provide staff 24 hours a day, 7 days a week and 365 days a year. What are their duties? To supervise and influence prisoners. Many prisoners have had extremely poor experiences of authority figures, including parents, teachers and employers, so starting to repair the damage of earlier years by exerting consistent, balanced and interested supervision is vital. To be effective, staff require adequate training and support and leadership from supervisory and senior staff.

The name of basic grade uniformed staff had been changed from "prison warder" to "prison officer" in 1921, but the media continue to use the older inappropriate term. Showing leadership and influencing prisoners was a different and more demanding undertaking than merely "guarding" prisoners. But for many years after 1921, the involvement of basic grade staff with prisoners was patchy. Borstals and training prisons encouraged staff involvement with prisoners and young offenders. But other more traditional prisons discouraged staff involvement.

Much of the work of prison staff was and is about following routines which are similar day after day. Supervising and

Above: Prison Warders at Castle Rushen Prison, Isle of Man. © *Manx National Heritage (PG/9395).*

influencing of prisoners occurs within that framework. Achieving consistent high performance by staff is challenging – the bedrock of working in a penal establishment is about "doing the basics well".

How were staff paid? In 1947 staff received relatively low rates of pay, calculated by the number of hours worked each week with some opportunities to work overtime. Staff worked for 12 duty days in every 14 day period. Meal breaks were unpaid.

Challenges Prison Officers faced

The challenges faced by prison officers should not be underestimated. Their work of supervising and inter-reacting with a wide cross section of prisoners exposes staff – especially officers – to inmate subcultures and pressures that can easily impact on their own attitudes. The possibility of violence, either between prisoners or towards staff, while rare in some establishments, could be all too common in others. Staff spend much of their duty time, when supervising prisoners, with a demanding mix of people, mostly convicted offenders. Unlike the police working among the public, prison staff are dealing solely with either offenders or those charged with offences. Part of the importance of regular staff training is to counteract the impact of criminal subcultures.

Importance of staff selection and training

Paterson, the great prison reformer of the interwar years, emphasised the importance of staff:

"The choice of a staff suited to the needs of the establishment is the foremost task of a prison administration...... If you want to exert an influence on human beings, you must call upon men capable of exerting that influence. It follows that it is necessary to exercise extreme care in the selection of such men, to submit them to a rigorous course of training and to pay them properly."

After 1946, there was insufficient training and support for staff and staffing ratios were often very low. I was told how one newly appointed officer – around 1950 – having completed initial training at the Prison Officers Training School arrived for his first morning at Bristol Prison. At the staff parade he was detailed to work on A Wing – on his own – and as he marched off in that direction was fortunate to be told by another officer – "First job – Unlock Cell 23". He did so – out came the Red Band – a trustee prisoner – who said "You are obviously new – just follow me" – and that was how he learned his duties – from a prisoner – on his first day.

Similar examples of the misuse of inexperienced staff were reported to me in the early 1970s at Birmingham's Winson Green Prison when staff undertaking initial training, who should not have been used operationally, were required to unlock prisoners at times when there was a shortage of staff. This misuse of staff was the result of a lack of understanding of staff working systems by management. Misuse of staff contributed to the rise in militancy by the POA.

Organising staff – local and central control

Organising staffing to cover duties over 24 hours, 7 days a week and 365 days a year was a key management task in running prisons. There was a history of conflict between staff and management over duty days and shift patterns, equalising unpopular duties and arrangements for covering unexpected events.

Staffing difficulties may have their origins a century ago or earlier. The setting up of a national service for the convict prisons and the nationalisation of the local prisons meant that prison staffing was controlled from the centre without any significant contribution from Governors. A recent article in the Prison Service Journal about the Governor of Dartmoor Prison from 1870 to 1872 emphasises his lack of control over the appointment of staff. This lack of local control continued for many decades – something that might have worked adequately in a small service and before the arrival of trade unions. Unfortunately, necessary changes were not developed after 1946 – probably in part because the Prison Commission was so absorbed with the overcrowding crisis.

In 1964, following the abolition of the Prison Commission, work on prison staffing at HQ was moved into the "Establishment" part of the Home Office and was dealt with by a separate Division known as "ED3". Prison staffing issues failed to be "joined up" with prison policy and operations. There was no proper co-ordination – the Prisons Board had no authority over those organising prison staffing. This was disastrous.

Regular overtime introduced

Regular overtime working for prison officers, the "Morrison Hour", was introduced during World War Two. This authorised staff to work for an additional hour each weekday to provide longer working hours for prisoners. Unfortunately, this led to regular overtime becoming an expectation as staff saw it as part of their guaranteed conditions of service.

Five day week working

In the 1960s, as 5 day week working had to be introduced, a small team of Home Office "ED3" staff devised, in negotiation with the POA, a new staff shift attendance system called "Vee Scheme" to bring 5 day week working into local prisons.

The POA sought to keep earnings high. The new "Vee Scheme" built in overtime, especially at weekends, when the rates of overtime pay were higher. Consequently management became dependent on the willingness of staff to work overtime to deliver the regime. Vee Scheme was an odd complex system with a matching set of odd complex operating rules. The management side of the negotiating team did not appear to understand the importance of continuity. No adequate provision was made for ensuring that staff worked in groups with the same prisoners. Consequently, staff lost the job satisfaction that derived from working consistently with the same group of prisoners.

A few years later – at the beginning of the 1970s – a simpler attendance system called Functional Group Working (FGW) was introduced for training prisons and borstals. Unfortunately, some training prisons were already working the Vee Scheme and it was impossible to obtain staff agreement for any change to a more appropriate system of attendance. This was because of the growing staff dependence on overtime – as they would put it "to protect their standard of living".

The introduction of these new more complex shift systems did not receive the management attention that it should have done. The potential damage to staff continuity was not properly understood. Consequently relationships between staff and prisoner deteriorated; Governors became very frustrated with their inability to prevent this happening. HQ – whether Policy, Operations or ED3 – largely did not understand the problem. However other consequences alerted HQ to difficulties ahead.

Overtime earnings increase

Following the introduction of Vee Scheme, overtime earnings started to rise sharply. Prison budgets were under pressure and HQ grew increasingly anxious. The rise in overtime was partly caused by the implementation of the Mountbatten Report recommendations which required either more staff or more overtime. The continuing rise in prisoner numbers made matters worse. None of these additional costs had been adequately assessed or costed.

Towards the end of 1970, in an attempt to control the growth of overtime, HQ decided to try and prevent any further growth of prison officer work. Circular 80/1970 instructed Governors not to introduce any new officer task without HQ authority. To support this change, HQ introduced new staff inspection called "Manpower Control". Teams of experienced operational staff were formed and a programme of inspection visits began. Manpower Control came directly under the Prisons Board – not ED3.

Early inspection visits revealed: the extent of the misuse of staff. Perhaps the most startling was the continued existence of the "Pony Patrols" at Dartmoor – a throwback to a much earlier era. More examples of staff misuse will be found in Chapter 18. However, effecting change in establishments, given the opposition of the POA, was a difficult task, further complicated by weaknesses within management structures at establishment level which I will examine in Chapter 16.

Across the Service, there were many inefficiencies and "Spanish customs", traditional practices carried out without regard to effectiveness. Driving much of this bad practice was the desire to preserve overtime earnings.

Court and escort work

Local prisons and remand centres had to provide staff for courts and escort work. Prisoners had to be produced at court. While the duties were shared with the police, much of the work fell to the Prison Service. Exact staffing requirement for court sittings for the next day could only be finalised in the early evening. Court work was unpredictable – planned trials could collapse without warning so that staff were not required. Other trials ran for longer than predicted meaning extra resources had to be quickly found.

Transferring prisoners between prisons required escorting staff. While these duties were more predictable than court work, very short notice escorts would sometimes arise. For example ill or injured prisoners had to be escorted to hospital and required continuous guarding.

Some staff saw court and escort duties as attractive options as additional allowances might be claimed, opportunities for overtime might be greater and the work was a change from the grind of working within an overcrowded local prison or remand centre. As a consequence, local POA committees sought to ensure that such duties were shared around fairly.

Another complication was escorting contractors working within the prison. Too often, contractors would fail to appear when scheduled or arrive without notice. If the work was critical – repairing malfunctioning machinery in the kitchens – escorting had to be given priority even if that meant cancelling inmate activities.

Unsocial hours payments

During the 1970s, there were increases in "unsocial hours" payments. Prison officers benefitted through "premium payments" for unsocial hours. Weekend working became more attractive: local POA committees sought to equalise opportunities for staff to earn premiums and overtime at weekends.

Other allowances were also payable – for example "inconvenience of locality" for working at the more distant establishments, such as Dartmoor or on the Isle of Wight.

Recruitment and staff shortages

During and before the 1970s, prison officer recruitment was difficult. Despite the uplift from the 1958 Wynne Parry Report, the pay scales for prison officers did not attract the number and calibre of recruits required. Yet the Service continued to need more staff as new prisons were built. More courts were in use and sat for longer. The recommendations from the Mountbatten Report required additional staff. So many prisons were short of staff against their authorised complement. Those suffering the greatest staffing pressures were allowed to supplement their staff by requesting additional staff on "Detached Duty", that is, borrowing staff from other establishments for a period to help

Above: Prison staff in the 1960s.

meet acute staff deficiencies. There were allowances for staff on detached duty which made this opportunity financially attractive. But allowing staff to go on detached duty reduced staffing resources at the officer's home station adding to the pressures on the remaining staff.

The staffing shortages became worse as the Northern Ireland situation deteriorated. The Service in England and Wales sent staff on detached duty to Northern Ireland. This continued for years and had an adverse effect on establishments. Then an acute shortage of staff at Brixton Prison – caused by opening additional courts in London – led to other establishments having to provide detached duty staff to Brixton – causing even greater staff shortages everywhere.

Staff continuity collapses: regimes suffer

A serious consequence of these pressures was that internal duties in prisons suffered greatly from a loss of staff continuity. Prisoners felt they were dealing with different staff every day. Requests made to one member of staff were either not dealt with or that staff member was absent the next day and unable to explain to the prisoner what was happening. Internal continuity was not easy at the best of times because staff worked five duty days a week, with two rest days, so there would be a change in staff personnel on any wing from day to day. Absences through sickness, annual leave and diversion to night duties added to the discontinuity.

This lack of continuity affected both staff and prisoners. While prisoners became frustrated with not having requests followed through, staff lost job satisfaction and their frustrations grew. Far from being empowered to work with prisoners and to deliver results, staff felt they had no clear role. Interesting work with prisoners was increasingly falling to specialists – chaplains, probation officers, education staff, instructors and others, as these specialist staff were regularly in touch with prisoners. Many staff felt undervalued and bored: they lacked ownership of their work.

Good staff performance in the Prison Service, in my experience, usually came about when staff felt ownership of their work, became involved with the issues and were committed to achieving positive results. This was not understood by many at senior levels in the Service. Hardly surprising – as many people at HQ had never worked with prisoners or in establishments operating for 24 hours a day, 7 days a week. The degree of ignorance of the realities of prisons and prisoners was astonishing among some senior people.

To achieve ownership, continuity of staff work, coupled with staff working together in teams, were two important building blocks to achieving better results. Managing and organising staff so that continuity of work was the norm required considerable organisational effort and the manpower management project was one of the ways of achieving some progress. But it would not be until the Fresh Start project in 1987 that we properly addressed these issues.

A further consequence of staff shortages was severe disruption to the prison regime. Workshops that required any prison officer supervision were regularly closed – often at short notice. Not only was this bad for prisoners, but workshop staff also became very frustrated and prison industries increasingly could not deliver the output expected. Other regime activities became spasmodic. Prisoners spent more and more time in their overcrowded cells with nothing to do. An example of how inefficient prisons were becoming can be found in the Inspection Report of 1980 into Manchester Prison which reported only 40 prisoners on average in the prison's workshops – 10% of the capacity of 400.

The Meal Break disputes

During the 1970s, the situation deteriorated even further as the staff discovered opportunities to claim that they should be paid for some of their meal breaks. This turned out to be a particularly serious example of the lack of management focus and attention to staffing matters. The detail of the meal break claims lay in the complex set of rules around the working systems and various instructions issued by HQ to try and clarify issues. The "Meal Break" or "Continuous Duty Credit" disputes rumbled on through the 1970s absorbing an increasingly high proportion of management time, punctuated with many threats of industrial action and occasionally industrial action. The Meal Break disputes was the key factor leading to the May Inquiry of 1978, as described in Chapter 17.

Addressing the many developing staffing issues required a management structure that could handle difficulties and deliver change. So how did the prison management structures cope with the growing staffing challenges?

16. MANAGEMENT WEAKNESS

Background

When I joined the Service, the management and command structure was regarded as long-established and clear. The Governor was in charge: in his absence the Deputy Governor took over. The Wynn Parry Report of 1958 included the following definition of the responsibilities of the in-charge Governor:

"The Governor is responsible to the Commissioners for everything that goes on in his establishment."

The Chief Officer was in charge of the uniformed prison officers, although some of them were specialists such as Hospital Officers, Cook & Bakers (later renamed Caterers) and PEIs.

The Steward (later renamed the Administration Officer) dealt with finance, the Clerical Staff, Storemen and Civilian Instructors.

Building and maintenance was the responsibility of the Senior Works Officer, the equivalent of the Chief Officer, known as the Foreman of Works. His staff included a number of uniformed officers, known as Trades Officers, and also civilian (i.e. non-uniformed) tradesmen including boiler room staff.

Difficulties and complexities

But experience of the traditional command and management structure revealed difficulties. An example was the staffing of the industrial and trade workshops. The task – the main provider of occupation for prisoners through productive work – and achieving output targets – was important. But control of the staff was split – uniformed officer instructors came under the Chief Officer; the civilian instructors under the Steward. Consequently unresolved difficulties over staffing had to be referred to the Governor.

The Chaplain and the Medical Officer had their own professional external regulatory bodies – but still answered directly to the Governor. Exactly how this worked in practice as regards accountability and reporting on performance was often unclear – and difficulties with performance occurred.

The position of Assistant Governors – or Housemasters as they were known in borstals – was more confusing. Were they responsible for staff? It varied greatly from one establishment to another. The interface between Chief Officers and Assistant Governors was sometimes difficult. HQ – who had first introduced Housemasters decades earlier – had never laid down how the management structure was to work.

In the 1960s, trained probation officers were introduced into prisons to provide an improved "welfare" service to prisoners. The previous arrangements were often haphazard; some of the "welfare" staff had little training or qualifications. But Governors were unclear how new lines of accountability would work. To what extent were Probation Officers responsible to their external professional supervisors – how far to the Governor?

Probation Officers were not the only new arrivals. Increasing numbers of specialists further complicated management structures. Psychologists, Tutor Organisers (later renamed Education Officers), Industrial Managers and Farm Managers all became increasingly common. Who reported directly to the Governor? If not the Governor, who did they report to? How were activities to be co-ordinated? How were conflicts to be resolved?

The recommendations of the Mountbatten Report created further groups of uniformed specialists – the dog sections, the staff who manned the emergency control rooms and the Security Principal Officer. Who – if any – reported directly to the Governor? Additional Governor and Chief Officer posts complicated local organisation further unless there was clarity about their responsibilities and to whom they reported.

By the mid-1970s, without adequate local management structures, Governors could find themselves with 15 or more people claiming to report directly to them – making it impossible for the Governor to properly supervise and support that number of subordinate managers.

Governors also had to deal with the Visiting Committee or Board of Visitors, whose powers of access to the establishment and duty of inspecting, required direct access to the Governor. From the late 1960s, some Governors were involved with the new "Local Review Committee" charged with assessing and recommending prisoners for release under the parole schemes.

Traditionally Governors had taken applications (requests to see them) from prisoners; had conducted adjudications on prisoners and were required to visit all parts of their prisons – including periodic Night Visits – to ensure that staff were performing their duties satisfactorily.

Staff management

The complexity of the staff working systems, together with the many rules associated with the systems, made it difficult for Governors, Chief Officers and other managers to understand. Consequently arranging duties for uniformed staff, especially compiling the daily "detail" of duties for the staff, became something of a "black art". Some Chief Officers were well informed, but too often they were unfamiliar with the intricacies of the staff detail and unable to exert control. As we have already seen in Chapter 15, controlling staff was the key to regime delivery so management's inability to adequately control staff was a fundamental flaw in the prison management system. This became even more critical as the challenges from the POA became more prevalent.

Management control over the appointment, promotion and transfer of staff was highly centralised. While Governors had discretion over the use of staff locally, in the 1970s, most appointments promotions and transfers were decided by HQ. Only a few staff – night patrol officers and storemen for example – were locally appointed.

Assessing the work of staff was very confused. The system of annual reporting followed a variety of management lines, often not the person who actually supervised the work of the staff member being reported upon. All uniformed staff reports were scheduled to be under control of the Chief Officer, even if in practice they spent much of their time working for an Assistant Governor. Worse, because of the lack of continuity within the attendance systems it was sometimes difficult to find a manager who regularly saw the work of an individual officer and was able to provide an informed assessment.

A historical legacy was that all prison officers were seen every 5 years by a visiting Director for a written assessment – this was standard procedure in the 1960s and reflected an early era of a much smaller service where such a requirement may have been of value.

Weaknesses in the management structure were mirrored by weaknesses in meetings structures. Terms of reference of meetings, the relationship between meetings and the machinery for adequately minuting meetings, were often seriously flawed. Decisions taken by the Security Committee could contradict other establishment priorities such as providing work for prisoners: meetings lacked a hierarchy for decision making.

These organisational difficulties hindered tackling the key issue of continuity of work for staff. Continuity would have increased job satisfaction, given staff experience of working in regular teams, providing opportunities for staff to be consulted over decisions, thus developing staff ownership over the issues and challenges they faced.

Position of Governing Governors

A fundamental issue was the discretion Governors should exercise. The principle of subsidiarity – decisions taken at the lowest possible level – was not practised. Prisons were caught between a culture of HQ knows best and the fact that good delivery and improvements depend crucially on the performance of local management, the Governor and his senior team.

How then did Governors relate to HQ? Who supervised Governors and what did supervision amount to? The answers to these critical questions were far from clear. Broadly Governors reported to Assistant Directors at HQ. Assistant Directors were selected from senior Governors and supervised a group of establishments. But Assistant Directors were not an integral part of HQ decision making structures. Thus parts of HQ responsible for aspects of policy or resource management would issue instructions direct to Governors – often without the agreement or the knowledge of Assistant Directors.

"Doing the Basics well" – this fundamental principle of prison work was rarely adequately understood by those at HQ who had not worked in prisons.

Consequently the vital task of leading, encouraging, supporting, supervising and correcting staff was rarely seen at HQ as important management work and certainly not as a priority.

HQ was largely – sometimes exclusively – interested in the latest initiative – especially if it was what politicians sought to implement. Consequently, it was difficult for Governors to give sufficient time to the basics because of the increasing deluge of initiatives and instructions pouring out of HQ. If Governors raised issues around the basics of prison work, HQ often ignored or failed to understand what Governors were concerned about. A good example is the issue of finding time for staff training which I raised with HQ when I was Governor of Strangeways – see Chapter 26. Another example is the analysis conducted by General Learmont in his 1995 report into the number of political initiatives and issues that subverted and superseded normal management work at HQ – see Chapters 32 and 37.

HQ was responsible for the posting and promoting of Governors. For much of my time in the Service, there was a lack of stability in establishments by not giving Governors long enough to implement improvements. Too many changes of Governors often led to a leadership vacuum at establishment level, something that some local branches of the POA could be quick to exploit. This is a continuing problem as improving continuity of management was a theme of Lord Laming's Review of Prison Management in 2000, an example of how difficult it appears to be to bring positive change to the Prison Service.

Underlying structural management issues was another fundamental question. Was the governing or "Number 1" Governor merely a cog in a command line from HQ; or was the Governor "independent" from HQ management control? One key test was when an operational issue – handling a violent incident for example – arose. HQ was generally quick to emphasise that the responsibility for resolving the issue was with the governing Governor and generally showed a marked reluctance to interfere in operational issues. The question of who might be to blame would hang heavy in the air. HQ always looked to protect their political head – the Minister – and good civil servants knew that their priority was never to embarrass the Minister.

So where does the position of "Prison Governor" originate? Section 7 of the Prison Act 1952 states:

"Every prison shall have a Governor, a Chaplain and a Medical Officer and such other officers as may be necessary."

It is this statutory position that places Governors in an interesting and sometimes uncomfortable position in any management line. Lord Bridge – (Leech 1988) identified that when adjudicating, the Governor "is exercising the independent power conferred on him by the rules." There are a number of other examples where a Governor has autonomous use of statutory powers. This is why it is appropriate to apply the term "sui generis" to the Governor of a penal establishment to distinguish the office from the majority of civil servants. It means that the leadership role of the Governor is distinct from many others in the public service – the Governor has a considerable degree of personal discretion over some important decisions.

During the 1970s and 1980s, new operational issues started to affect the relationship between Governors and HQ. In Chapter 11, I describe the first Gartree riot, which underlined the need for more effective precautions against riots. Good contingency plans were required, along with the capacity to practise such plans, so that an effective response could be delivered if a disturbance broke out.

Industrial Relations

From the 1970s, Industrial disputes became more of a problem for Governors. Frequent meetings with their local POA committees; internal management discussions about options; meetings with Regional Office and HQ staff about disputes: a much greater proportion of Governors' time was being taken up by Industrial Relations issues.

Before and during the early seventies, Governors had received little – if any – Industrial Relations training. HQ had not appreciated how serious the problems of staffing and Industrial Relations were becoming. When I requested taking an Industrial Relations course at Warwick University in 1971, HQ showed no interest. At the time some of my colleagues were being seconded to study social work. The priorities were wrong.

Developing improved structures

Between 1974 and 1984, some spasmodic development work went on at local and at national level to develop sensible management structures for penal establishments. It was generally regarded in management circles – at that time – that having 6 to 8 people reporting to a manager was about the maximum – so ways had to be found of making better use of the senior and middle management to develop effective institutional management.

One priority was developing a clear role for the Deputy Governor. I have explained that many Deputy Governors took charge of allocating prisoners to work and chaired the Staff Training and Security Committees, but the extent of their responsibilities was rarely well defined. Early developments gave Deputy Governors a clearer role in Industrial Relations, in co-ordinating operational matters and in some cases making them responsible for co-ordinating staffing matters.

In the 1970s, management development was hindered by a lack of information. Financial information was difficult to access and even more difficult to interpret; other management information such as about the regime – how many hours were prisoners engaged in any activity in a week – was not collected and reviewed systematically. Workshop hours, the number of hours worked by prisoners per day and per week in each workshop, were recorded but little else about regime activities.

So the crucial link between staff performance and the regime provided to prisoners was difficult to monitor. There was insufficient delegation to establishments coupled with poor – or non-existent – systems for recording data.

One of the most fundamental pieces of data in a prison was the number of prisoners and their location within the prison. This was dependent on paper records such as index books and card indexes. In those establishments with a high daily turnover of prisoners – in some prisons over 100 prisoners a day – it was difficult even keeping track of where each individual was.

An outbreak of "Hostage Taking" by prisoners provided another very serious new operational challenge. New procedures had to be devised; training for commanders and negotiators provided. I shall return to this in Chapter 21.

So in the 1970s, the management of prisons at local level was too often disorganised and far from fully effective. Little was being done at HQ to address the problem largely because it was not properly recognised.

JAIL

Four high walls cold and bare
You look around there's no-one there
A hollow voice that has no face
An echoing noise about the place
Lonely hours to think of my past
The shame and sorrow I have cast
I pinch myself to no avail
And accept the fact that I'm in jail

17. INDUSTRIAL RELATIONS 1963-1980

History of poor Industrial Relations

Research into Industrial Relations published in the May Report revealed a difficult relationship between prison officers and the Prison Commission going back over many decades. Around the First World War, officers sought equal treatment with the police. This was not granted but it was a theme officers would return to. Given the issues around the right to strike, described in Chapter 36, the desired police link is an interesting one.

Significant figures like Sir Lionel Fox, Chairman of the Commission from 1942 to 1960, did not appear to sympathise with uniformed staff and failed to build the commitment needed from all staff towards the training and rehabilitation of prisoners.

Fox is reported as having opposed the implementation of the Wynne Parry Report in 1958 which raised officers' pay significantly. To many uniformed staff, HQ were more concerned with improving life for prisoners than for both staff and prisoners. The Wynne Parry Report (Paragraph 52) had this to say:

"Substantial improvements have been made for the prison population with the emphasis now on training and rehabilitation, but in our view parallel improvements had not been made for the staff."

This failure by the Fox administration to commit staff to the new objectives of the Service may be one of the underlying causes of subsequent Industrial Relations problems.

The 1959 White Paper "Penal Practice in a Changing Society" stressed the importance of staff:

"The success of the system will, finally, depend on the quality of the staff which will administer it. The Prison Service as a whole must work together as a team inspired by a common purpose which every officer understands and in the achievement of which he has a real concern." (Paras 100 & 103)

Why did these aspirations not work out in practice?

The Prison Commission was dissolved on 31st March 1963 and the Home Office assumed all its former functions and properties. Prisons became the responsibility of a new department of the Home Office. Chapter 15 has already described how staffing matters were given to a different division (ED3) of the Home Office's Establishment Department, with disastrous results.

Compounding this legacy of failures was the way 5 day week working was handled. The loss of staff continuity, described in Chapter 15, deepened the distrust of HQ by many uniformed staff as their job satisfaction worsened.

Position of uniformed staff in the 1970s

During the 1970s prisoners seemed to have increased freedom to do what they wanted. They could change their appearance; they became involved in demonstrations without suffering great penalties. Even charging prisoners with offences became more difficult as the internal prison disciplinary process became more legalistic.

Officers started to question whether they were really part of a disciplined service and became inclined to question instructions rather than automatically obey orders. Prison officers were a uniformed service. But attitudes to uniform were quite mixed; some staff were pleased to be able to wear civilian clothes – and be paid a "clothing allowance" – as was the case in borstals. Enforcing a reasonable standard of uniform was another issue. Should the staff wear their caps at all times? This was sometimes not welcomed when a new Governor sought to raise standards and insist that caps be worn. HQ showed little interest in uniform other than in the cost of any changes requested by the POA. Some staff, who liked wearing their caps, "slashed" the peaks of their caps. This made it more difficult to see their faces, an obstacle in building relationships with prisoners.

Uniformed staff were expected to "parade" at the beginning of their shift so that the officer in charge knew how many staff were available and could allocate them to their duties. Staff also paraded for formal occasions such as presentations of awards and at staff funerals. But parades were increasingly a token gesture, difficult to equate with industrial action.

Industrial action

Staff began to pursue their own objectives such as protecting "take home" earnings by using industrial action. Governors were faced with staff refusing to undertake some duties, leaving the prison during their duty time or refusing to leave the gate area to perform normal duties.

In some prisons, local POA officials started to wield a disproportionate degree of power. At Dartmoor and at Ashford Remand Centre, Governors found more and more of their time being taken up in arcane negotiations with local POA officials around the rules of the staff working systems, especially where careful manipulation of the rules could result in more overtime earnings. This led eventually into the meal break rules disputes – known as "Continuous Duty Credits" or CDCs – which provided considerable scope for additional earnings by ensuring some meal breaks became paid.

Governors' Branch Action

Throughout the 1970s the industrial relations problems – together with overcrowding – greatly concerned most Governors. The tension in the prisons became so bad and the pressure upon Governors so intense that on the 27th October 1978, the Governors' Branch took the drastic step of publishing an open letter to the Home Secretary exposing the extremely serious state of the prison system and calling for a wide ranging Inquiry to try and resolve an increasingly impossible situation. We said:

"There is a more serious danger. We have yet to experience a serious prisoner reaction to restrictions caused by staff industrial action but the signs are there. The recent disturbance at Gartree is a salutary reminder of how quickly prisoners can wreck an establishment. So far we have successfully avoided loss of life during serious disturbances but if the present trend continues there will be a serious loss of control which has to be quelled by armed intervention by another service. In such circumstances, there is a probability of both staff and prisoners being killed. There are precedents in other prison systems."

The letter was signed jointly by David Heywood, Assistant Secretary of the SCPS, and me as Branch Chairman of the Governors' Branch.

Our letter was circulated to the media and there was considerable publicity. The pressure on the Government to take action increased and finally produced results.

The May Inquiry

The Government announced on 17th November 1978 that it was to set up a major inquiry into the UK prison services; this was primarily triggered by the worsening Industrial Relations that the Governors had complained about. This Inquiry was headed up by Mr Justice May, supported by nine members, and reported in October 1979.

The Governors' Branch prepared written and oral evidence to the May Inquiry. In written evidence, we raised the fundamental question of whether prison staff should have the right to strike. We referred to the 1978 Edmund – Davies Report which had reviewed the right of the police to strike and concluded:

"On such a fundamental issue as the preservation of law and order, the withdrawal of labour would be incompatible with the responsibilities of the police services and contrary to the interest's of the nation." (Para 87)

We drew a parallel in our evidence:

"Governors consider that the recent events have demonstrated that the withdrawal of labour by prison staff constitute a comparable threat to law and order."

We also highlighted other dangers:

"The Chief Inspector of Prisons in paragraph 377 of his Report on the Hull Prison Riot drew attention to the hesitancy of some staff to comply immediately with orders. Governors are well aware of the problem particularly in the light of the evidence emerging from the trial of Hull prison staff. Industrial action almost always involves disobeying orders."

Our evidence to the May Inquiry suggested that the problem might be resolved by an agreement to limit industrial action or by "buying out" the right to strike. However, the May Inquiry – which looked at the many options for improving Industrial Relations including a statutory ban on industrial action – concluded that:

"There was no scope for a change in the status quo – even if such a change were desirable."

This is an interesting conclusion given what happened in the crises of 1994 and the revelation that the ban on industrial action applied to both police and prison officers – this is described in more detail in Chapter 36.

The May Report also usefully set out the history of Industrial Relations in the Prison Service and debunked the myth that this was a new problem. It also chronicled more recent history, including the walkout of staff at Cardiff Prison, the first example of this behaviour since 1919.

The Secretary to the May Committee was Mr RM (Bob) Morris, a talented civil servant with a splendid sense of proportion. In reply to a question about conspiracies – Governors often felt they were the victims of conspiracies – Bob Morris replied "When things go wrong that has probably more to do with muddle rather than Machiavelli." I always felt there was much sense in this opinion.

Much of the work of dealing with the recommendations of the May Report fell to the incoming Conservative Government led by Margaret Thatcher. She appointed Willie Whitelaw as Home Secretary and he gave much time and energy to the Prison Service with positive results. Some of the underlying problems of the Service started to be recognised and addressed. Chapter 24 will describe Industrial Relations after the May Report.

Above: The May Report.

18. STAFF INSPECTION 1974-1977

Working at HQ

In 1974, following promotion to Governor Class Three, I was asked to lead the Manpower Management project, a form of staff inspection. This enabled me to acquire vital knowledge and experience of prison staffing. During the next three years, I led staff inspections in fifteen establishments which were generally the larger, complex and more challenging ones. Highlights included Dartmoor in January 1975 and Wormwood Scrubs later that year.

Based in P6 Division at Headquarters in London, half my time was spent inspecting establishments. We moved from Preston to Rugby – not far from Onley. We bought our second house, giving us more room for our family of 5 children. I commuted by train to London when working in the office. Prison Headquarters, known as Eccleston Square, was located by Victoria Station.

I learned the technical aspects from my predecessor, Gordon Lakes. After service in the army in Korea, the Prison Service was Gordon's second career. He became Deputy Director General from 1985 to 1988. He and I were to work together after retirement, some 25 years later, applying our knowledge and experience to the staffing problems of the Irish Prison Service as described in Appendix A.

I headed up a small team comprising Governors, Chief and Principal Officer grades responsible for undertaking the inspection of the more difficult establishments. Tom Rielly, who subsequently in 1977 was appointed to take charge of the Isle of Man Prison (see Chapter 2), was one of my team. During the next 3 years the team uncovered evidence of inadequate management of staff and substantial overtime abuse.

Dartmoor and other inspections

Perhaps the most striking example of overtime abuse was at Dartmoor, which had required greater staffing in the past to manage high security prisoners. A reduction in the number of high security and difficult prisoners had not been accompanied by any reduction in staffing. Dartmoor was a training prison and should have been working to FGW: but it had adopted Vee Scheme some years earlier and was not going to change. Dartmoor's branch of the Prison Officers Association had a militant reputation. Examples of overstaffing were to be found across the prison – especially staff manning the "staff tea room". Their prime function was – allegedly – to answer alarm bells – but actually to provide tea reliefs for staff around the prison. This was an expensive and indefensible misuse of staff. Further investigations revealed that there were unofficial "tea funds" being run with the proceeds used to support POA funds. I was to find further examples of this practice years later at Strangeways.

Princetown, the village next to the prison high up on Dartmoor, was virtually a "prison" village as many of the houses were prison quarters. In the seventies

Above: Dartmoor Prison.

with the growth of car ownership some staff started to live away from the prison in Plymouth, a group the staff promptly nicknamed the "Plymouth Brethren". Some of the villagers could behave quite irrationally. Members of my team were refused service in the village shop one morning – by relations of serving members of staff – when it became apparent that we were advocating staffing reductions. However, by consulting with everyone, we avoided the industrial action that had occurred when an earlier staff inspection team had visited. Some staffing efficiencies eventually resulted from our visit.

The task of my inspection team was to examine records of how staff were utilised and to also observe the staffing arrangements in action around an establishment. We prepared a report itemising what we found and made recommendations for better – especially efficient – use of staff. This involved demonstrating how many staff were needed to cover the work of the establishment. We discussed our findings with the Governor and his management team and with the POA. That could be challenging when we were recommending staff reductions or less overtime.

On one training exercise – for new staff inspectors – to a small local prison, my team uncovered a complete imbalance in numbers between the two divisions into which the staff were split. This was causing considerable additional overtime. On our final meeting with the Governor, we suggested this should be rectified. "But that is the golfing division" came the reply, "we cannot possibly change that"!

At another prison, a member of my team interviewed a middle manager and had difficulty establishing what he was responsible for and what he actually did. Eventually the manager in frustration burst out "I am not the only one in this prison without a proper job."

Implementing our recommendations fell to regional and local management. In the face of POA opposition, progress could be extremely slow. Some of our recommendations were to supply additional staff – if these could not be provided, then the recommendations could hardly be applied.

Three years of staff inspection was invaluable as I gained a much greater understanding of how we could deliver improved use of staff. I became increasingly interested in staff motivation and what could be achieved by empowering staff. This could lead to increased ownership by staff of problems and encouraged staff to seek solutions. But to implement such an approach effective management teams were essential – teams that consulted and took proper account of the ideas and views coming from staff working closely with prisoners.

If staff were empowered and felt ownership for their work, so could prisoners. While many prisoners professed indifference or were negative, others were genuinely interested in improving their own skills and abilities and could feel ownership of programmes in which they were involved. Achieving such ownership was challenging.

My experience of staff inspections helped me develop a much broader perspective across the Service from seeing some 15 different establishments in detail and the results being achieved by different Governors and their management teams. I was sure that much could be done by encouraging greater involvement of staff with prisoners; by integrating the efforts of different departments and by being ready to tackle bad practice. To achieve progress required an understanding of the way staff and management systems worked. It also needed clear leadership setting out to staff what Governors expected.

I was sure we needed much more staff training so that staff at all levels acquired the skills to interact better with prisoners and to address the difficult issue of handling verbal and physical violence from disturbed or angry prisoners. This was a service-wide problem – developing policies for dealing with difficult issues and finding resources to provide training to develop staff skills. I shall return to the issue of dealing with violence in Chapter 21.

Other activities

Once promoted to Governor Class Three, I was expected to attend the annual Governors Conference. At my first conference in 1974, one of my more experienced colleagues – with a twinkle in his eye – greeted me "Now that you are a Governor Three, Brendan, you need to be aware that there are senior

Governor Threes and junior Governor Threes!" There was little danger at that time in the Prison Service of getting ideas above your station!

One interesting and memorable diversion during 1976 was to accompany my parents to Buckingham Palace when my father, Dr AJ O'Friel, was presented with the MBE. This was awarded for his work in Ellesmere Port over many years, especially assessing those seeking compensation for industrial injuries. My father had a strong sense of social justice which sometimes conflicted with his conservative views: in respect of industrial injuries, he regarded social justice as a priority. This trip to Buckingham Palace was the first of several visits. Thanks to the Princess Royal's patronage of the Butler Trust, Barbara and I would accompany award winners from HMP Risley to Buckingham Palace and Holyrood.

By the end of three years of staff inspection, I was ready to return to working in a prison to see what improvements it was possible to deliver. All of the major prisons had Deputy Governors who were graded as Governors Class Three so a move to either a top security prison or a big local prison seemed likely.

19. BIRMINGHAM PRISON 1977-1980

Background

Early in 1977, I was posted as Deputy Governor to Birmingham's Winson Green Prison, the major local prison for the Midlands. We found a house in Sutton Coldfield handy for good schools and moved during the summer holidays. Barbara had been brought up in Birmingham so she had a familiarity with the city that I could never match. We were to live in Sutton for nine years which provided some stability for the family, especially schooling, while I took on several different posts.

Winson Green had become notorious through the escape of Charlie Wilson, Train Robber, in 1965 with suggestions of staff collusion in the escape. More recently, the mistreatment of the men accused of being the Birmingham pub bombers cast a shadow over the prison. These men were beaten up following their arrest. It appears that part of the responsibility lay with the police who then quickly, with very little notice, moved the accused to the prison; unfortunately this was badly handled by the prison authorities and the men were further beaten up in Winson Green. Subsequent police investigations resulted in some staff being charged with these offences. A jury acquitted the staff – what apparently happened was that the staff charged were those officially listed as being on duty in the prison reception – the misbehaviour came from others who were on duty elsewhere in the prison. There had been huge provocation because of the casualties that had occurred in the pub bombings but this was no excuse for totally unacceptable and unprofessional behaviour. I was puzzled at first by some of the tensions between staff at Winson Green: it was only after staff got to know me well enough to tell me some of the story that I appreciated why the feelings existed between the staff who had misbehaved and not admitted it, and the innocent staff who had had to face serious charges in court.

I also heard accounts that there had been a failure at the highest level by management to intervene at the time that the alleged bombers were received into Winson Green. This legacy of staff failure at Winson Green was part of the reason I was to take strenuous precautions to prevent ill-treatment of surrendering prisoners years later during the Strangeways riot.

Because of the experience of the ill-treatment of the Birmingham Bombers and the staff trial, considerable efforts were made to try and avoid any unauthorised use of force by staff when dealing with violent prisoners. The results were very mixed as staff were not properly trained to deal with violent prisoners. There were no proper procedures for recording what took place after the staff had had to use force against prisoners nor was there an agreed procedure for dealing with violent prisoners.

During my time at Birmingham, action began to advise and train staff to deal with violent prisoners. These developments are discussed in Chapter 21.

Governor Bill Perrie

I was fortunate to serve under Governing Governor, Bill Perrie, a charismatic and individualistic Scot, who prided himself on keeping fit. At lunchtime, a group of people used to emerge from the main gate and run around the neighbourhood – at one meeting with locals I was asked why we allowed prisoners to run around the neighbourhood – they were sceptical about my explanation that these were staff, especially so about the "old bald headed fellow – he looks like a convict" – that was actually Governor Bill Perrie! Bill allowed me scope to start to change the management structure and try out ideas that I had seen work elsewhere from my days in staff inspection.

Bill Perrie proved to be a very strong character. Had he been in charge at the time the Birmingham Bombers were brought into Winson Green, I doubt the assaults on prisoners would have happened. He made it clear that Winson Green was his prison and he would run it his own way. So when Prison Inspectors arrived he had a brief preliminary meeting with them but then told them quite clearly that they would deal with the Deputy Governor on all matters of detail. The lead Inspector – himself a senior Governor Class One – was not happy but would not argue with Bill Perrie. It demonstrated to me the authority of a Governor Class One in his own prison!

Bill Perrie's legacy continues. Since 1995 there have been annual "Perrie Lectures" organised by an independent committee. The lectures aim to stimulate dialogue between criminal justice organisations, the voluntary sector and those with an academic, legal or practical interest in offenders and their families. The committee also makes an annual Perrie Award to the person who has done most to promote an understanding of the work of the Prison Service and who has taken forward the development of penal policy.

Staff management

There was ample scope for improving staff performance. In the year before I was posted to Birmingham, I had led a staff inspection of the prison and had learned much about the strengths and weaknesses of the use of staff. The visit – over some four weeks – took place during the winter. One memorable moment was when I joined the team one morning to be briefed on what they were finding. One of my experienced and sceptical Chief Officers explained that at Winson Green they had a dogs section with "flying dogs" – when he had come in early to see for himself what was happening he had found the snow lying around the inside of the prison walls without a paw mark in sight..... staff had obviously preferred the warmth of the dog section office to the cold of doing their duty!

I had an unusual experience while paying a night visit. In addition to visiting all the officers on duty I called in the boiler house accompanied by the Night Orderly Officer. The boiler man seemed especially surly and failed to answer simple questions about procedures. I went into the office and discovered a mattress on the floor – we had woken him from his sleep. He blustered when asked about the mattress and then walked out of the prison. I later discovered from the Senior Works Officer, who was the line manager of the boiler men, that he had been concerned about this individual for a while – so his departure from the service was no great loss. But it illustrated the need for senior staff to be prepared to look in detail at what was happening. Otherwise that fringe of poor performers that is to be found in most groups of staff will take advantage of inadequate supervision and continue to under-perform.

Among colleagues at Winson Green was a young and very able Assistant Governor, John Marriott, who was to develop his career in the Service until the escapes from Parkhurst in 1995 placed him at the centre of a political and media storm. I shall describe that disaster in Chapter 37.

After 3 years leading a Staff Inspection team, I was much more able to tackle staffing issues because of the knowledge I had acquired about staff working systems and the rules around them. I understood the problems of the Principal Officer in charge of the "Staff Detail". The staff detail was the daily instruction, in those days set out on a big board completed in chino graph, to staff by allocating staff to their duties and authorising overtime. I was soon able to gain the confidence of the Detail Staff and to discover how they made the staffing situation work on the ground. I was able to exert increasing influence on the use of staff but it was slow work. Once again, there was the problem of the responsibilities of the Chief Officers, none of whom sufficiently understood all the rules of the working systems. However, I was able to develop discrete responsibilities for the three Chief Officers – one of whom took on inspecting the use of staff at courts.

I have already explained in Chapter 15 how court work increased overtime demands, contributed to poor continuity in the prison and disrupted the internal regime. So trying to get some sense into the "External Commitment" was a priority. I visited the courts to find out what the staff were doing and what conditions were like for both staff and prisoners. It was a salutary experience. The cells below most courts were old and dirty; there was no proper system for certifying accommodation for prisoners and the facilities for staff were generally poor. Courts were often unable to predict their work for the next day until quite late in the afternoon so the Detail Officer usually had no definite news of the staffing requirements for the coming day until 16.00 or later.

The solution to this problem, which we introduced under Fresh Start in 1987, was to have a separate "External Group" of staff deployed to the courts for a substantial period – perhaps 10 or 20 weeks. Progressing this suggestion in 1978 was like pushing water up a hill – virtually impossible. We made some ground, but real change had to wait for the revolution in staff conditions of service under Fresh Start.

Industrial Relations

I spent much time talking to the local POA committee. We had our share of staff who were "overtime bandits", working long hours at every opportunity. We exerted a little more control, but the growing claims for paid meal breaks caused endless work and were very difficult to deal with.

Most local establishments had local agreements with the POA committees about procedures and meetings. Meetings were chaired by the Governing Governor, although in the big prisons, the Deputy Governor often chaired. Meetings took place at least monthly and many extra meetings were required when a crisis emerged. Much discussion also took place informally outside the formal meetings structure. The POA had periodic meetings with their members, often in the evening in the officers' club, which rarely encouraged balanced and rational debate of an issue. Many meetings with management were productive, but a minority were very difficult with the POA threatening to ballot their members for some form of industrial action. Even the suggestion of unwillingness to work overtime could be a potent threat because we were so short of staff and therefore so dependent on overtime working to keep the establishment running.

A change of Governor

Bill Perrie retired in 1978 and Roland Attrill moved from Deputy Director in the Midland Regional Office to take charge. Roland was a native of the Isle of Wight, so he and I, from two islands, found ourselves running the most inland major prison in the UK. A nautical problem arose one weekend when sharp eyed staff noticed a maintenance barge moored on the canal running close to our boundary wall. The barge had a great beam for lifting materials and it could have provided a method of breaching our perimeter wall. There followed a good example of co-operation between prison and police security; the barge was visited by the police and persuaded to move to another more distant location.

Ethnic minority issues

Situated in a deprived part of Birmingham, the local area around Winson Green had attracted large immigrant populations. There was conflict between the West Indian youngsters and some of the Asian shopkeeper community who were often the victims of theft or worse. A review of the area resulted in a report called "Shades of Grey" which highlighted the breakdown of family relationships within the West Indian community as fathers tried to impose discipline on rebellious teenagers. Many left home, became even more out of control and some found themselves in custody.

I quickly realised that we had much to do to learn about managing the mixture of prisoners coming into Winson Green. Priority needed to be given to developing a better way to manage ethnic minority prisoners. Attracting and retaining staff from ethnic minority backgrounds was essential but this required a change of attitude at many levels within the Service. HQ were fond of producing policies about race relations but had little idea how to put them into practice. We lacked a workable method of organising staff training – vital if we were to help staff adjust to dealing adequately with the changing ethnic mix of prisoners. I shall return to these difficulties about training in Chapter 26.

Above: Victorian cell block exterior.

Conditions and activities for prisoners

Winson Green was a particularly deprived prison, heavily overcrowded with very limited facilities and far too many prisoners. The accompanying problems of damage and vandalism, to which I have previously referred in Chapter 8 at Strangeways, were rife at Winson Green adding to the miserable conditions for both prisoners and staff. For example, one problem I discovered was a lack of proper accountability for the emptying and cleaning of rubbish bins – resulting in the loss of capacity as existing bins were jammed full of decaying rubbish and were not properly emptied. I ensured this was improved but this illustrates the lack of systems and accountability.

Far too many prisoners had no activities other than exercise – weather permitting. Consequently they spent many hours locked up in cramped insanitary cells. We had not yet developed a Governor Grade post with responsibility for "activities" – that was to be introduced during the next few years and become an integral part of the "Fresh Start" changes. So there was a serious lack of co-ordination over what activities we had. Consequently it was not uncommon to find that while many prisoners were locked up there was competition between Departments for the same prisoners. This was a serious waste of resources and a missed opportunity to offer positive activity to as many as possible. This emphasises the need for a clear link between management structures and the objectives of any prison: in the seventies the question was hardly being asked except by a minority of very frustrated Governors.

Exercise

I was also starting to appreciate the thinking of our Victorian predecessors when they drew up the "timetable" for the way prisons worked. The whole arrangement was dependent on prisoners having no choice over activities. So exercise was usually after the staff returned from their lunch break – all prisoners were sent out onto exercise yards for an hour. This gave them access to toilets as well as being in the open air and being able to walk around. Part of the routine was to open all cell windows before prisoners went out on exercise – known as "the airing hour". This part of the routine was destroyed by a combination of factors. First overcrowding – there were too many prisoners to put them all out on the yards together. Second, prisoners were no longer compelled to go on exercise – it was an option for them. So cells were no longer aired; prisoners often had no time in the open air, reducing the regime still further. As a result, cells could become very unpleasant, smelly, stuffy and probably unhealthy. The loss of the old "timetable", with the guarantee of time out of cell, was never properly understood and reviewed at HQ; consequently prisoners suffered.

Exercise had always been weather dependent. In the past, despite it being compulsory, exercise in the open air often had to be curtailed because of the weather. But in the days before overcrowding, in inclement weather, efforts were made to have "internal exercise" allowing prisoners to walk around the landings on their wings. This at least got them out of their cells and provided a break in the monotony of their lives. The option of "inside exercise" was also lost to overcrowding and any attempt at reviving such activities tended to be met by substantial opposition from the POA. However, there were alternatives and the development of "association" – time spent on prison wings – especially after Fresh Start – was another way of reducing time locked up in cells.

External work

Winson Green had another side to its work. A prison farm some miles away gave the opportunity for a few prisoners to spend their sentence working outside. Some years later we transferred the responsibility for the farm to Featherstone Prison which was able to provide a better workforce and more reliable staffing.

Years earlier there had been another unusual external project. Prisoners from Winson Green were employed to help restore the Stratford-upon-Avon Canal which had been derelict for many years. This project which ran from 1960 had made a considerable contribution to the reopening of the canal in 1964, an example of prison labour providing the means to revive a public good.

Incidents

Unusual and difficult incidents occurred. One potentially very damaging allegation arose that a prisoner who had committed suicide had been assaulted. It turned out that the bruising to the body which triggered the allegation had been caused while removing the body from the prison. The suicide had occurred in a cell on the top landing of the wing only accessible by a narrow staircase. The individual was large and heavy and the task of removing the body had been difficult. But those who did so – the Coroner's Officers – had not appreciated sufficiently the importance of not further damaging the body. We revised procedures to avoid any repetition.

Another difficult incident arose when a very disturbed prisoner was brought into the prison hospital by the police. He had been walking around a crowded city area naked and the police had arrested him. In prison he proceeded to launch himself head first at the door or wall of the cell in which he was confined, badly injuring his head. In the end the medical officer decided to place him under restraint for his own safety.

Chaplaincy and psychology

While there had been a full time RC Chaplain at Manchester, his duties were largely concerned with the adult prison so I had not seen much of his work. At Winson Green I came to appreciate the role of all the Chaplains much more as they provided a very valuable outlet for the frustrations of prisoners in a very limited regime. Sometimes advice from a Chaplain led to action being taken to avoid a prisoner attempting suicide or to defuse a situation building up between a member of staff and a prisoner. Chaplains were an invaluable, informal and independent sounding board when trying to assess the state of prisoner and staff morale. I worked closely with Fr Martin Masterson, the full time RC Chaplain, who always provided me with a different perspective on an issue and taught me more about the complexities of prisons.

On a number of occasions we welcomed one of our bishops visiting the prison at Christmas. In 1977, Archbishop Dwyer said our Christmas Day Mass. Afterwards he chatted to the congregation, giving out cigarettes. A keen eyed officer kept watch to ensure that the less adequate prisoners did not lose their share of these gifts to the "hard" men. One of the "hard" men told me that he was quite shocked at how old the Archbishop looked – and was. Prisons – especially in those days – tended to be full largely of young men.

At Birmingham I began to appreciate the value of our small Psychology Department. While the main task of the Department was working directly with very damaged prisoners, the Department provided some support for analysing management problems so that we can assess the relative value of competing solutions. Later, I had the opportunity to work closely with another psychology department at Risley and was very grateful for their contribution to analysing the effectiveness of what we were seeking to achieve.

During my years at Winson Green, my wife, a qualified teacher who had experience of teaching young offenders at Onley, returned to work to teach young offenders part time at Swinfen Hall, Lichfield, a prison for youngsters serving very long sentences.

In the spring of 1980, I was informed by Headquarters that I had been selected for promotion to Governor Class Two and was offered the post of Governor of Featherstone. I left Birmingham Prison very determined to try and deliver improvements for prisoners and staff in my new post.

I visited Birmingham Prison occasionally when I was Deputy Regional Director. Years later my eldest daughter Mary would be running the two parish schools situated close to the prison.

Above: Prison chapel.   © *Catholic Pictorial.*

20. FEATHERSTONE PRISON 1980-1982

First command

In May 1980, I took charge of Featherstone Prison just to the north of Wolverhampton. This was one of a new class of prison with considerable facilities for work and education, holding some 485 prisoners. Fitted with integral sanitation, lavatories in each cell, it provided a huge improvement on the conditions I had left at Winson Green. I was the second Governor; John Sandy having opened the establishment in 1975, had been posted to Parkhurst on promotion to Governor Class One. I was to work with John, as Deputy Director, in 1985 when he became Midland Regional Director.

I had served under ten Governing Governors, one of them twice, over a thirteen year period. One advantage of working under many different Governors was that I had learned much about how to be an effective Governor – but also I had observed what leadership techniques and styles to avoid! My experience illustrates the excessive mobility of senior staff in the Service which often prevented Governors from developing and implementing a coherent and workable plan for improving an establishment. The problem of excessive mobility of Governors continues.

Developing an effective style for Governing was a new challenge. I knew the vital role of communications; I was also sure that it was important for the Governor to be seen around the establishment when on duty – not just confined to an office or tied up in meetings; I was concerned about how to achieve all this without cutting across the authority of middle managers; I knew that specialists also needed time and attention so that they understood that I appreciated their contribution to the establishment. I was out "walking the floor" most days when on duty. I used the technique of pushing issues back to prisoners – encouraging them to take up their concerns with their wing managers or whoever was responsible for the issue they were raising. It didn't always work, but I was able to build up some knowledge of what prisoners were concerned about and at the same time trying to ensure that issues were dealt with at the lowest possible level.

For managers, there were often difficult issues about which a second opinion could be useful. I encouraged discussion about more difficult decisions between colleagues or line managers. This improved decision making, and encouraged as much discretion as possible to be given to the less experienced and junior managers.

Another important judgement was how to balance time between the many competing issues requiring attention. Sensitive issues were always a priority – especially those involving prisoners. Use of force, standards of catering, managing conflict between staff and prisoners all needed to be carefully monitored to ensure minor conflict did not become something much worse.

As at Winson Green, I used my experience of staffing issues to assess how staffing arrangements were regulated. The prison was quite well organised but there was room for improvement.

I introduced occasional general staff meetings at which I briefed the staff on developments. This gave me confidence to use such meetings at Strangeways and Risley where I had many more staff. General meetings provided a valuable opportunity to set out the standards that I expected from staff and to reassure staff about my approach when something went wrong. Individual mistakes were bound to occur: if we were to develop the regime by trying out new ways of achieving results, mistakes were almost inevitable. My concern was to ensure everyone – including myself – learned from mistakes and avoided repeating them. This approach worked well with staff.

A lesson from staff inspections was the value of seeing how similar prisons had developed different ways of operating. Good ideas had often been put into practice at one establishment – and never even been considered at another. At Featherstone I started to encourage staff to visit other establishments – a practice I was to continue throughout my service and beyond. Perhaps the most helpful outcome of such visits was that staff would realise that present practices were not the only way to run the prison and that good establishments were constantly looking to improve routine practices. This happens in many organisations but parts of the Service, in those days, were very cautious and reluctant to change.

Plans to relieve overcrowding

Top of my priorities for improving and developing the establishment was action to help relieve the overcrowding I had just left behind at Winson Green. Consequently I encouraged my senior team to find ways of accommodating a slightly higher population, of making full use of any empty accommodation and of starting a programme to add to the total number of places we had available.

The staff and prisoners at Featherstone had huge advantages. Single cells equipped with integral sanitation meant that the vandalism and damage I have described as being common in overcrowded prisons was largely absent. Prisoners felt some ownership for their cells and behaved more responsibly as a consequence. That ownership extended to other parts of the establishment as many prisoners appreciated the opportunities that existed to improve their skills and their life prospects.

Activities

Featherstone had a large workshop complex – quite properly called "the factory" – with two contracts for producing garments for the National Coal Board and manufacturing and assembling domestic heaters for a commercial undertaking. Some 300 prisoners were working in close to

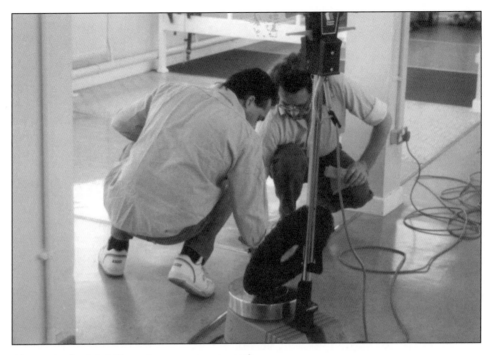

Above: Industrial Cleaning course at work.

normal factory conditions. Add in a large education centre, some good skill training courses and quite large grounds and unemployment was never a real problem. What a contrast with Winson Green! I was especially taken with the Industrial Cleaning course, a very practical job that prisoners could aspire to taking up on release. We trained and tested them to NVQ level: for many prisoners an NVQ was the first time they had achieved any qualification. And our "in house" Industrial Cleaning expertise meant that it was possible to improve and maintain good standards of cleaning within the establishment. Industrial Cleaning course members were often a classic case of demonstrating "ownership" of the establishment – something I was going to see repeated a decade later at Risley. Seeing the pride and interest taken by individuals and groups of prisoners in what they could achieve was very encouraging. Unfortunately the industrial complex was badly disrupted by the POA's national industrial action from October 1980.

We had an excellent Education Department, providing much high quality education, from teaching basic literacy and numeracy to a handful of degree students. The use of selected prisoners as tutors for adult literacy was an example of good practice but also highlighted the failure of the Service to systematically identify, promote and spread good practice. Thankfully the use of prisoners as adult literacy tutors has been taken forward by the Shannon Trust in recent years. There is a much wider issue of principle about maximising the talents of prisoners to influence other prisoners positively.

Above: "I'm afraid Sotherby's won't accept any more pieces of pottery, so we'll have to switch to knocking out a few Old Masters."

Among the range of educational classes at Featherstone was pottery. This acquired notoriety when some students developed an ability to copy the pottery style of Bernard Leach. A few of their products found their way onto the market and were sold as originals. This happened before I took charge but the fallout – including a criminal investigation – caused considerable comment and some excellent cartoons. Apparently pottery experts from one of the great auction houses fell for the deception and accepted a few of the "Featherstone pots" as genuine Bernard Leach.

We had some staff quarters on site at Featherstone and a larger quarters' estate in Cannock. Our extensive grounds provided plenty of work for an estates and grounds party. I was pleased to find proper use being made of modern gardening and grounds equipment so that prisoners were getting realistic work experience.

Management issues

The management structure I inherited needed development. The large industrial complex was managed by a General Manager recruited direct from industry. The usual arrangement was for prison industries to report to the Administration Officer (the AO). Originating as the "Steward", all establishments had an AO responsible for handling the prison accounts, the clerical, administrative and stores staff – and usually prison industries.

At Featherstone, both the General Manager and the Administration Officer reported to the Governor, an arrangement I continued. However, there was a need to co-ordinate the activities of the two posts and I took steps to try and make that arrangement work rather better by having a monthly meeting with these two senior managers to review progress with industries.

I reorganised the responsibilities of the Governor Grades and sharpened up the lines of accountability. I gave the Governor in charge of the residential area responsibility for some activities including education. This seemed to work well – the post was an early experimental example of the new post of "Head of Inmate Activities" brought in under Fresh Start in 1987.

The Service was moving towards equal opportunities for staff and as part of that development, I was asked to take the first woman Deputy Governor in an adult male prison. I was delighted to welcome Ann Hair, a Scot, to join the team. The change worked well as people adjusted to a different style and approach, but one that added to the overall effectiveness of our management team.

Adjudications

Among the important duties of the Governing Governor was to conduct adjudications on prisoners charged with disciplinary offences. Adjudications were governed by the Prison or Borstal Rules which specified the range of offences and the powers of Governors to award punishments. The procedures for adjudications were set out in further detailed instructions from HQ. There was a formality about adjudications which served an important purpose for both staff and prisoners. It emphasised that within the prison, the rule of law had priority and there had to be fairness in the way both staff and prisoners were treated.

In 1963, the adjudication procedures were often basic – one old Governor of Wandsworth was reputed to have said that if one of his officers reported a prisoner for riding a motorbike around the prison landings, he would expect that the prisoner was also charged with stealing the fuel for the bike. It sounded as if findings of "not guilty" were as rare as hens' teeth! At Dartmoor in 1974, the physical arrangements for adjudications separated the Governor from the prisoner by a grill. Prisoners were required to stand to attention during the procedures and only to speak when told to do so by the Governor.

All this – quite properly – gradually changed. There was much greater emphasis on ensuring the prisoner's side of what happened regarding any alleged offence was heard; witnesses were called if relevant; prisoners were allowed to sit on the far side of the adjudications table. A fuller record of what took place was kept and the scrutiny of the completed records became sharper. This compared with my experience at Manchester in 1966 when

Governor Maxwell often used to "write up" the adjudication sheets at the end of the week, not at the time!

Adjudications at Featherstone were reasonably civilised – reflecting the positive relationships between staff and prisoners. One of my more unusual experiences of adjudications had been at Winson Green a year earlier when one Asian prisoner insisted on calling me "Excellency" at every opportunity!

Although most prisoners at Featherstone behaved well, I was faced with one very difficult situation with a prisoner from Iran. There were concerns about his mental health but the problem he presented was that he insisted on banging on the heating pipes at night disturbing many other prisoners. When placed in the segregation unit, he continued to bang on the heating pipes which carried much further around the prison at night that we had expected. Eventually he had to be transferred as we could not cope with him. Reviewing the incident, we realised that Featherstone had not been equipped with a proper "special" cell for containing a disturbed or violent prisoner – so we set to work to provide one as quickly as possible. The new cell had to be certified by the Regional Director before we could make use of it.

Boards of Visitors

A key relationship for Governors was with the Board of Visitors. This body, required for every penal establishment under the Prison and Borstal Rules, consisted of around 12 local people appointed by the Home Secretary with power to access the establishment and talk to prisoners at all times. It derived from the former Visiting Committees of Justices of the Peace, from the days when the local prisons were a local responsibility. In more recent times, the name has been changed to the "Independent Monitoring Board" but the basic principles continue of the Board members being local to the establishment, having right of access to the prison and being able to talk to prisoners.

The Governor was expected to attend the monthly meetings of the Board and facilitate the workings of the Board. It was especially important that issues raised by the Board were properly examined and not ignored. I always attempted to give the Board time and attention and to see that staff were fully aware of the role of the Board and treated Board members properly. This was important: the Board was a vital factor when things went wrong – if the Board was doing their job properly it was able to criticise or defend the establishment depending on the facts and on the Board's view of what had happened. Having an independent Board was in part a protection for the establishment but especially for prisoners who were able to take grievances to a body which was external to and independent of the Service.

Governor's routines

So what did the Governor's typical day at Featherstone consist of? I was usually in the prison before 0800. I wrote up key events from the previous day in my "Governor's Journal", a large official book provided for Governors. Many Governors only used their journals to record the numbers unlocked in the establishment and a brief note of who was in charge. I found it a valuable record of significant events and most days recorded my principal activities.

A short morning meeting took place around 0900 with Heads of Department to deal with immediate issues and to confirm arrangements for the day and beyond. Decisions were needed about how the follow-up to any incidents would be handled – for example by appointing a member of staff to conduct an inquiry so that we were able to establish the facts of what had taken place. During the morning, I walked around the prison usually with the Chief Officer, dealt with adjudications and checked the catering by tasting a sample meal. In a large modern sprawling establishment like Featherstone, getting around was quite time consuming and of course the real value of "walking the floor" was having the flexibility to spend some time with staff and prisoners gleaning feedback and assessing the mood and morale. There were many meetings to chair; including monthly meetings of the Senior Management; meetings with the Board of Visitors and with the local POA Committee.

As Governor I had occasional staff disciplinary issues to address with a formal disciplinary code to be applied; there were staff requests for example for special leave or for a transfer. In 1980 Governors had little influence over transfers but that was to change over the next decade so that local management gained more influence and control over such moves – a valuable improvement for both staff and management.

I made a point of trying to visit the prison one evening a week at varying times and paying Night Visits at least once a month. I also attended occasionally at weekends – in the absence of one of my Deputy Governors I would work a full weekend.

For many years, Governing Governors were required to prepare an annual report on the work of the establishment over the previous year. In earlier years extracts from Governors' reports were included in the Prison Commissioners' Annual Reports. Because of the pressures on establishments, this requirement was dropped in the early 1990s – in my view a backward step as we lost another source of record of what went on at establishment level. But Annual Reports were only of value if Region and HQ studied and acted on them. As I will set out in my account of Manchester (see Chapter 26), this did not always happen.

At Featherstone, I attended my first inquest as Governing Governor following the suicide of a prisoner. Inquests are a difficult experience for relatives and families – but also for prison staff who have to relive what took place and to account for their own actions. The inquest found no fault with the way we had dealt with this prisoner but we followed up the suicide by very carefully re-examining our procedures to see if there were any improvements we could make. That was the only suicide during my period as Governor – although we experienced some incidents of self-harm.

Because of the experience I had acquired with public relations through my work for the Governors' Branch, I sought opportunities to publicise developments and achievements at Featherstone. This helped to provide information to the public in the West Midlands about positive work in our prisons and went some way to balancing the negative image of the Service projected by conditions in the old overcrowded local prisons. All was not doom and gloom.

Dangers of staff manipulation

The downside of Featherstone was that the close working relationships between staff and inmates exposed staff to the danger of manipulation and being entrapped into rackets. Some prisoners could be extremely manipulative and in the open relaxed atmosphere of Featherstone, some staff were undoubtedly involved in smuggling items for prisoners and other misbehaviour. I developed a specialised searching team as part of the management response to this threat which made some progress and probably reduced the danger for that small fringe of staff that were especially vulnerable. At my general staff meetings, I spoke about the dangers of being manipulated by some prisoners – and that this threat applied to staff of all grades and specialisms who worked with prisoners. I stressed the importance of reporting when a mistake had been made so that we could recover the situation before matters became much worse.

The dangers of manipulation by prisoners were especially acute for those staff that had not had the benefit of the training and induction given to prison officers. Considerable numbers of staff had regular contact with prisoners – all of our locally employed staff including teachers and civilian instructors and tradespeople, stores and administrative staff. Local induction programmes were able to partially meet the need but we rarely were able to provide sufficient induction training or development training to upskill and update staff.

Inspection

Towards the end of 1981, the new Independent Chief Inspector of Prisons, Bill Pearce, arrived to conduct an inspection. This was another important opportunity to learn how the Service was changing. When the report was published in 1982, it was pretty satisfactory but suggested further improvements that we should consider. Two follow-up inspections took place in early 1982: the resulting reports confirmed the progress we were making. More general issues about prison inspection are reviewed in Chapter 23.

Increasing capacity

I mentioned earlier the priority I gave to improving the use that we made of our accommodation at Featherstone in order to relieve overcrowding elsewhere. This is how we approached the problem. By making sure we ran the prison at its maximum capacity, we were able to provide places for an average of 8 extra prisoners during the second half of 1980. We reached agreement with Regional Office on using spare capacity in the Health Care Centre for suitable prisoners who were "bed blocking" in local prisons, providing a few extra places. We converted the Pre Release Unit into a "Short Term Unit" providing another 38 places bringing the total capacity – without overcrowding – to 523. We also proposed converting accommodation in the House Blocks to provide 16 extra cells at a cost of £9000. I noted in my annual report for 1980 that this initiative had been delayed by Regional Office because of cash limits on the regional budget – a very odd decision as the extra places were being achieved at a bargain price. Had we had greater access to financial information, we might have been able to pursue our conversion proposal more effectively. But at that time moving money between different subheads of expenditure was difficult. So much change in the provision of information and attitudes was needed to produce more sensible decisions.

I was especially pleased that in March 1982, when I left Featherstone, the prison was unlocking 518 without overcrowding, the highest number since the prison had opened. This meant that over 30 prisoners – instead of being in overcrowded cells in local prisons with no activity – were in good conditions and able to take advantage of our positive regime.

I left Featherstone for HQ with mixed feelings. I had considerable regret that I could not have stayed longer but having learned a great deal about what could be achieved in a relatively short space of time.

21. HEADQUARTERS 1982-1984

Security policy and advice

My move to HQ early in 1982 was rather unexpected as I had been at Featherstone for less than two years. A promotion board to Governor Class One was advertised – I applied and was successful. I did not particularly welcome the move to London as our children were at a stage when moving schools could be difficult. After the family had considered various options, I spent two years commuting from Sutton Coldfield via Birmingham International. The train did provide an opportunity to catch up with the mountain of reading that was part of this experience of working at HQ. The fact that I had twice commuted to London by train also helped when I became involved with the Rail Passengers Council and Committees many years later!

My job was to be principal security adviser in P5 Division, responsible for hostage policy and practice; security and control issues including the Dog Section. I was a standing member of the Category A Committee which reviewed the categorisation and security of all Category A prisoners. This involved long monthly meetings, a great deal of reading and learning much unpleasant detail of their offences. I was struck at how many appalling crimes had been committed while the offender was under the influence of drugs or alcohol.

Following the Mountbatten recommendations, a Police Adviser had been appointed to HQ. This mirrored the appointment at each establishment of a local Police Liaison Officer to encourage the flow of information about security issues between the Police and Prison Services. The Police Adviser and I regularly conferred.

I started to review the extent to which the Service had implemented the recommendations of reports on security and control issues. I rapidly discovered that a number of our top security prisons were still not particularly secure – that the investment required had not yet materialised and that there were significant gaps in our defences to protect public safety. HQ was often over-enthusiastic about the latest project and not sufficiently concerned about how the latest project should be prioritised against the backlog of work that had accumulated over many years.

Compared with my earlier experience of P6 (Manpower) Division, I worked more closely with senior civil servants. The Head of Division was an experienced operator who advised me not to be so precise about target dates for a project. It is better to use a season like "spring" rather than a precise date, he explained – we can always say that the "spring is late this year"!

Shortly after arriving in P5 Division, we learned of the Argentinian invasion of the Falkland Islands in April 1982. There was a momentary flurry of activity including references to the "War Book" – a manual of advice and instructions if war broke out – and an anxious question as to whether the Service would have to provide facilities to intern Argentinian citizens in the UK. Fortunately internment did not happen and we returned to conventional work.

I attended many committees considering major redevelopment projects. Usually chaired by an able – if rather irascible – senior civil servant, representatives of many HQ Divisions, as well as establishment and regional people, gathered to agree a brief for the project under review. This was only the first step. I soon discovered that programmes were often changed and important issues deferred. That is probably what had happened to the Strangeways redevelopment plan and to critical security issues like the geophones at Parkhurst, which became a hot political issue in 1995. General Learmont's Report of 1995 (referred to in Chapter 37) sets out the delays in taking critical decisions on the Parkhurst geophone issue. Major spending decisions in an operational service under substantial pressures required better decision making processes.

Hostage incidents

I was quickly faced with hostage incidents. Most of these involved a prisoner taking another prisoner hostage; occasionally a member of staff was taken hostage. I dealt with around 20 incidents in 2 years. When prison hostage incidents first began to occur, HQ issued confidential instructions to Governors about how to handle these incidents; Regional Office was taken out of the line; and the Governor worked to the Deputy Director General (DDG) though the Governor 1 in P5. So when a hostage incident took place, the DDG was the ultimate commander; I was expected to refer matters of significance to him but manage as much as possible direct with the Governor. A hostage incident often exposed a weakness in contingency planning and preparation at local level; I spent much time advising, cajoling and mentoring Governors faced with very difficult operational problems with considerable potential to go seriously wrong.

I quickly learned that the first problem was communications – finding people at weekends and at nights when an incident was first reported. This was long before mobile phones – at first, I used to contact the DDG via a Fire Service radio pager. This was quite intolerable and within a year I managed to have the Service equipped with our own radio pagers which enabled us to contact key people much more quickly. It was this system that was to alert me to the outbreak of the Strangeways riot in 1990!

Some of the incidents were very concerning. Sometimes the local commander did not know what he should be doing and needed a great deal of support. This was difficult to deliver when you were working from home at midnight. The worst incident during my two years was when a woman Assistant Governor was taken hostage at Wormwood Scrubs – thankfully the incident was finally resolved without violence. It was apparent that the experience of being a hostage and of commanding and negotiating during a hostage incident took a toll on many people. We began to pay more attention to the impact of Post Traumatic Stress Disorder (PTSD) and started to develop policies to address this difficult issue.

Managing violence

Managing disturbances was another policy issue for which I had responsibility. I started rereading reports on recent disturbances to try and ensure that the Service had learned the lessons from earlier experiences. One of the issues that stood out for me was the danger

of management losing control of staff and the result being mistreatment of prisoners. This had happened at Hull after the 1976 riot and there were allegations of mistreatment after riots at Parkhurst and Wormwood Scrubs.

To understand the problem of violence between staff and prisoners it is important to recognise the role of the "cultures" within the Service. Within the Service there were a number of conflicting cultures. One complication was the impact of inmate culture within individual prisons. As described in Chapter 15, staff spent a considerable amount of time exposed to inmate culture and could be influenced by it directly and indirectly. Inmate culture itself is complex, it shifts and develops and differs from establishment to establishment. In its most extreme form, the culture projected by disciplined terrorist groups such as the IRA can be very powerful and difficult to counteract. A constant problem is the impact of inmate culture which encourages staff to co-operate with bending or breaking rules. Unware or weak staff can rapidly find themselves caught up in inmate rackets, under pressure to bring contraband into the prison or worse. It was this culture that constantly presented issues at Featherstone, as I set out in the previous chapter.

Staff culture varied considerably. The big Victorian prisons often developed a strong staff culture, influenced by the POA, to promote a distinct and macho staff image. This image had to be tackled as part of the drive to diversify the workforce by integrating women officers and introducing more staff from an ethnic background. There was then a greater prospect of improving the approach of staff towards prisoners from ethnic minorities.

Changing the culture required us to tackle the way staff dealt with violence. In the 1960s and before, the ratio of staff to prisoners was low; if a member of staff was assaulted or threatened, an alarm bell was activated and staff would speed to the aid of the staff member in difficulty. The prisoner would probably be charged with an offence and appear before the Governor under the disciplinary procedure laid down by the Prison Rules. However, there was insufficient guidance given to staff about how they should behave when subduing a prisoner and I have no doubt that in some prisons, prisoners removed forcibly to the segregation unit by a group of staff were beaten up almost as a matter of routine.

During the 1970s, Governors had growing concerns about managing violence in prisons. After the events at Birmingham's Winson Green involving the beating up of the Birmingham Bombers (detailed in Chapter 19), serious efforts were made by HQ and Governors to change the culture. Unfortunately, initial moves were limited to warning staff that they must not use excessive force and that all use of force had to be justified. There was considerable concern about the use of batons by staff – and the possibility batons would be used to strike prisoners on the head.

But we were not training staff as to what they should and should not do to control a violent prisoner. In the late 1970s at Winson Green we had staff injuries through trying to move prisoners without using excessive force. Taking prisoners down stairs – segregation units were often on the lowest levels in the prison and incidents could occur anywhere – was a particular problem. At that time, there was no protective clothing or equipment available for staff – the use of a mattress was often the way staff would try and protect themselves when tackling an aggressive or armed prisoner.

In response to the growing concerns of Governors and staff about how to deal with violence by prisoners, the Service started to develop techniques for managing violent prisoners. Many prison staff were quite good at talking to difficult and upset prisoners. Some staff were excellent at talking to violent prisoners and were able to defuse potentially very tense situations. Much of this ability to defuse difficult situations was acquired by staff through considerable experience of dealing with difficult and violent prisoners. We reinforced the need to avoid violence if possible. Staff were encouraged to develop and then refine skills in de-escalating threatening situations. These skills were to be further developed as prison officers received training to lead "Anger Management" courses as part of the range of programmes developed to help address offending behaviour.

We also started acquiring equipment to protect staff – previously we had relied on staff defending themselves with wooden battens – without any real training – so protective shields and helmets and other equipment were brought in and trialled and increasingly used.

A more disciplined approach to groups of staff confronting rioting prisoners was developed. Initially called MUFTI (minimum use of force tactical intervention), the Service PE specialists started to develop a system of wrist locks by which staff could subdue prisoners. They built up a team approach so that the dangers to both staff and prisoners would be minimised. Three-person teams started to be used; they would practise the techniques and then apply them when required around the prison. The techniques became known as "Control and Restraint" – C&R for short. More equipment was purchased and stored for use when an emergency occurred.

This was reinforced by instructions to report what had taken place. Staff using force were required to write a report on exactly what they had done and why. Previously none of the interaction with a violent prisoner had been systematically reported, leaving scope for unauthorised use of violence.

Finding the time and resource to train staff was a constant problem and one that I shall examine further in my description of resource issues around staff training at Strangeways in Chapter 26.

These effective authorised techniques and a much more disciplined approach made it easier to encourage staff to engage more with prisoners –

because they knew what to do on those relatively rare occasions where force was necessary. This was a point commented on and endorsed in the Woolf Report in 1991.

Prison dogs, security and wider issues

I visited the College regularly as I was involved in the programme of training for Hostage Negotiators. I paid visits to top security establishments to discover whether recommendations to improve their security had been implemented. As I was responsible for the Prison Dogs Section – although most of the management work was in the hands of a Governor Class 3 – known unofficially as the "Chief Barker" – I attended a number of dog training events and Dog Trials. The commitment of the dog handlers and the skills shown by their dogs was always interesting and the contribution of the Dog Sections proved on many occasions vital in preventing escapes.

During 1983, the IRA staged an audacious mass escape from the top security prison in Northern Ireland known as Long Kesh and later as the Maze. The escape was facilitated by guns, a sign that preventing lethal weapons from being smuggled into prison was going to have to become a very high priority. We heard via the Whitehall grapevine that the Home Secretary had been summoned by Mrs Thatcher immediately after the escape and lambasted – it was only when she paused for breath that he was able to explain that the Northern Ireland prisons were not his responsibility!

I also had other opportunities to influence wider policy and practice. The impact of the Government's wider housing policy of selling off Local Authority houses to tenants led to a decision to sell off the staff quarters, at a discount. Much more flexibility was being shown about the distance Governors were allowed to live from their establishments compared with the days Governors were expected to live adjacent to their prisons. However, it encouraged Governors to travel longer distances and many were no longer readily available when a serious incident took place.

Beyond my official duties, I was invited to join a Working Group to draft a report for the Catholic Bishops developing policy and practice towards offenders. The group included Mgr Dick Atherton, then Principal RC Chaplain. This was a valuable opportunity for me to further develop my thinking about the Church's approach to offenders and influenced the articles and talks that I gave in years to come. The Report "A Time for Justice" was published in 1982 and updated and republished some 10 years later.

Earlier in May 1980, I had attended the National Pastoral Congress (NPC) – organised by the Catholic Bishops in England and Wales, which met in Liverpool. I contributed a talk to the group examining issues around prisoners and others. Unfortunately the work of the NPC was not followed up by the action many of us had hoped for. The feedback we heard was that there was little or no enthusiasm in Rome for the changes the NPC had advocated.

22. REGIONAL OFFICE 1984-1986

After two years of commuting from Sutton Coldfield to London I asked for a transfer as Deputy Regional Director (DRD) at Midland Region HQ. So in 1984, I began working at Calthorpe House, situated just south of Birmingham city centre. Setting up a new structure of four regions in 1969 had been an attempt to devolve powers and decision making from London. The Regions were reinforced after the May Report of 1979 when the four Regional Directors joined the Prisons Board. North and South East Regions were each almost twice the size – prisons, prisoner population and staff – compared with the smaller South West and Midland Regions, both of which had some 25 establishments.

Above: Geoff Lister (centre seated) Midland Regional Conference 1985.

From 1969, line management of Governors was the responsibility of the Regional Directors and their staff. This included supervision and assessment of establishment performance and the annual assessments of Governors and other senior staff.

I worked for a year with Geoff Lister, Regional Director in the Midlands. Geoff had a distinguished career having been Governor of several difficult prisons and also having worked at senior level at HQ. After he retired in 1985, John Sandy became Regional Director: he had preceded me as Governor of Featherstone.

Staff overtime abuse

I was immediately confronted with priority problems of Industrial Relations and staff overtime control. Problems of overcrowding, security and control also featured high on our "to do" list. I was soon heavily involved in a project to improve the management of staff resources across the region, a difficult undertaking particularly for those Governors and Chief Officers who did not understand the complexities of staff duty systems. My previous experience on staff inspection, coupled with practical experience of running prisons in the region, enabled me to encourage the development of some practical solutions. Overtime abuse, which was rife in a few establishments and present to a lesser degree in all of them, came under improved management control but there was a very long way to go. It would not be until the introduction of "Fresh Start" that we were able to use staff much more effectively.

Management developments

Work on overtime control included the development of better management information so that staff hours – and especially overtime – could be monitored effectively. Previous attempts to improve management information about staff usage were not successful but in the mid-eighties – partly due to the arrival of more technology – monitoring started to become accurate and reliable. Similar developments were taking place over financial accounting and monitoring the hours of inmate activities – all management information that we had previously not been able to accurately record.

Among wider developments within the Prison Service were significant new ideas from Ian Dunbar, an experienced Governor who became a Regional Director. Perhaps his most telling contribution was the report "A Sense of Direction" published in 1985. In it, he proposed clarifying the Service's aims and tasks.

Dunbar also developed the concept of "Dynamic Security" – that the close involvement of staff with prisoners in a high security regime reduced the risks of escape. Activity and Security were to be viewed as interdependent rather than opposing functions.

Much of what Dunbar advocated began to be implemented over the following years. The Prisons Board adopted a new statement of Aims and Tasks. Positive regimes became part of the "Fresh Start" initiative of 1987 which dramatically changed the way staff worked. Regime monitoring and improved management information systems started to be developed. HQ began to set national goals. These included reducing the number of assaults recorded on prisoners and on staff as well as reducing suicides and incidents of self-harm.

Prison Industries and Farms

As DRD, I was asked – together with my colleagues from the other Regions – to be part of the Board overseeing Prison Service Industries and Farms (PSIF). This involved monthly meetings in London to consider reports on current operations and to plan ahead. The four DRDs had been recruited to the Board to try and improve establishment performance in respect of Industries and Farms output – which was generally dire – as it depended on staff co-operation and availability. Both were in very short supply.

Prison Industries varied from the excellent facilities I had inherited at Featherstone to dingy workshops in Victorian local prisons doing fairly mindless work for relatively short periods whenever staff could be made available.

Farms offered better experience for prisoners but few offenders came from rural backgrounds and even fewer aimed to take up farm work on discharge. Providing occupation for prisoners was crucial to developing an active regime: traditional workshops while not popular with prisoners were often seen as better than being locked up in cells.

Making a financial return on prison industries always seemed an unlikely possibility. The workforce turned over far too frequently; the wages did little to motivate and the workshop hours during which we could provide the workforce varied and was often far too low. As management could not guarantee delivery of the workforce so Prison Industries could not guarantee delivery of finished items to their customers either within the Service or to external firms.

Financial and staff delegation

The Prison Service was also grappling with the need to devolve more control including financial control to establishments. Although each Governor was the "sub accounting officer" for the establishment, in practice there was little real financial authority at local level. This was also the case with most staff matters – and staff was by far the Service's most expensive and valuable resource. Worse, there was poor information about how much an individual prison cost to run. So Governors were frequently struggling because of a lack of information and authority. The first steps were taken to provide Governors with training so that financial delegation could be gradually introduced.

Other powers were also starting to be delegated to Governors. For staff the decision to obtain a move from one prison to another had previously been in the hands of HQ; now Governors were not only consulted but also able to recommend. Staff realised that local management were being given more influence on staffing decisions. Local recruitment was increased, meaning that the establishment could seek the sort of employee it required for a particular post rather than being sent someone from a national or regional recruitment process.

These changes were part of the background to the Fresh Start project. They provided stepping stones on the path to better prisons in the future – provided always that the issue of overcrowding did not overwhelm the Service. The other driving force for change was the continuing difficulties with Industrial Relations and the acute operational difficulties this was causing.

23. INSPECTION OF PRISONS

The need for external scrutiny of prisons had been formally recognised in prison legislation for centuries. The Prisons Act of 1835 authorised the appointment of five Inspectors of Prisons in the various parts of Great Britain and Ireland to visit and to write reports. After nationalisation, the Prison Commissioners took on the responsibilities of inspecting the prisons. So from 1870, management and inspection became part of the same organisation.

Following the Mountbatten Report of 1967, an external "Inspector General of Prisons" was appointed, Brigadier Mark Maunsell, a retired army officer with experience of working in Industry.

After Brigadier Maunsell had retired, the post of inspector was filled by ex-prison Governors. The first was Stanley Clarke, who was also appointed to the Prisons Board. Clarke's successor as Chief Inspector was Gordon Fowler who was required to investigate and report on the Hull Prison Riot of 1976 and on the escape of WT Hughes from a Leicester Prison escort in 1977. Hughes – while on the run – committed several murders. In 1979, Fowler was promoted to become the Service's first Deputy Director General (DDG) – in effect operational head of the Service. Bill Brister, an experienced Governor, was appointed Chief Inspector.

When the May Inquiry published its report in October 1979 it recommended many changes, including setting up a new independent Inspectorate, effectively abolishing the existing "internal" Chief Inspector's post.

The Home Office agonised over this recommendation – how could an independent Chief Inspector, appointed by the Home Secretary, inspect the prisons which were the responsibility of the Home Office? But Home Secretary Willie Whitelaw took the bold decision to implement. A new independent prisons inspectorate was to be created with the power to make unannounced inspections and to publish reports into the state of the prisons. The new system came into effect on 1st January 1981.

The new independent Chief Inspector was to be a complete outsider. The first appointment was Mr W "Bill" Pearce, former head of the London Probation Service.

I met Bill Pearce when he inspected Featherstone – as recorded in Chapter 20. Bill Brister was asked to take on the role of Deputy Chief Inspector and help establish the new organisation. Some might have refused an apparent demotion, but Brister undertook the task with distinction. It was complicated by the new Chief Inspector became terminally ill, leaving Brister to cover his duties until a further appointment was made. Much of the success of establishing the Independent Inspectorate was the result of Brister's work.

In recent years publishing reports about public bodies from schools to hospitals has become normal – so the decision to publish the prison inspection reports may be seen as one of the forerunners of much wider change towards greater transparency and accountability.

The second Chief Inspector (1983 – 1987) was a retired diplomat Sir James Hennessey and the third (1987 – 1995) Judge Steven Tumin. In more recent times we have had General Sir David Ramsbotham and the first woman Chief Inspector, Ann Owers. Undoubtedly Judge Steven Tumin was responsible for raising the public profile of the Inspectorate with a series of hard-hitting reports exposing the very poor conditions in many establishments – especially the Victorian local prisons.

Prison Inspection teams have grown in size and complexity over the years. Specialist inspectors have been brought in to examine education and health care giving the inspection reports greater authority.

Above: Chief Inspector Judge Steven Tumin.

The decision to publish inspection reports caused considerable concern among Governors at first – especially those from Judge Tumin – renowned for his trenchant criticism. But we gradually adjusted to this new openness and started to welcome the opportunity that it gave for exposing pressing issues within the Service.

Inspections were also conducted beyond England and Wales. The island prisons of Guernsey, Jersey and the Isle of Man were all inspected following invitations from the island governments. Reports were published.

Published inspection reports also provided considerable independent information about the state of the prisons, information previously not readily available. Inspection reports were an interesting mix of facts and opinion. As Governors were no longer required to produce their own annual reports on the state of their establishments after 1992, the inspection reports go some way to filling the information gap but with the advantage of providing an independent opinion on the state of any particular prison. These reports may prove to be a valuable resource for future researchers. Inspection reports were produced before 1980 – but none of them were published or easily accessible to the public.

24. INDUSTRIAL RELATIONS 1980-1989

Following the May Report, Industrial Relations received much more priority but continued to cause great concern. Staffing issues became the responsibility of the Director General with a Director of Personnel and Finance being appointed to the Board. But the underlying problems of overtime and conditions of service continued to fester and the Prisons Board recognised that major reform was needed. The process that led to "Fresh Start" began.

An example of the difficulties Governors could face occurred in 1983 at Preston. The Governor was away; the Deputy Governor in charge. The POA decided to test the limits of the authority of Deputy Governors – probably to try and drive a wedge between Chief Officers and Governor Grades. At Preston, two Principal Officers refused to obey the instructions of the Deputy Governor to accompany him on his rounds of the prison. The Governors' Branch had to step in to support the Deputy Governor and I had an exchange of correspondence with John Chilcott, Director of Personnel, about the way the Deputy Governor was treated. This led to the issue by Headquarters of a Notice to Staff about Industrial Action dated 29th September 1983. The notice spelt out the position clearly:

"Failure to recognise the lawful authority of the Governor or of a person to whom his duties and powers are lawfully delegated under Rule 98 of the Prison Rules constitutes a fundamental breach of an officer's conditions of employment".

But the fact that this had to be spelt out demonstrates the chaotic world in which Governors had to operate.

Police cells

One of the ways the POA applied pressure on HQ was by restricting the number of prisoners received into prisons. POA members would refuse to accept new prisoners from the police, leading to displaced prisoners being sent to police cells increasing Government expenditure. This tactic was used in October 1980 when the POA were in dispute over meal break claims. Thousands of prisoners were soon being held in police cells. Many Governor Grades were deployed to provide advice to local police forces over the practical problems that arose from holding prisoners in their cells for weeks without proper facilities.

To alleviate this, emergency legislation was rushed through Parliament – the Imprisonment (Temporary Provisions) Act 1980. This allowed the use of military personnel to assist Governors in running two temporary prisons – one a top security prison under construction at Frankland; the other Rollestone Camp on Salisbury Plain. In both cases, Governor Grades played a crucial part in making the emergency accommodation work reasonably smoothly as the military were not accustomed to dealing with prisoners.

This demonstrated the Government's determination to stand up to what it regarded as unreasonable demands. The POA learned that industrial action did not always pay dividends.

1986 disturbances

Early in 1986, there was a serious breakdown in Industrial Relations over the right of management to set manning levels in prisons. This led to a ballot by the POA for industrial action with a majority voting in favour of taking industrial action. In April 1986, many officers at Gloucester left the prison over this issue creating a crisis which was only averted by Governor Grades from across the country assisting the Governor by undertaking some prison officer duties.

At the end of April, the POA ordered an overtime ban. This was followed by a wave of prisoner disturbances at forty establishments and considerable damage to some prisons. Northeye, near Bexhill, was severely damaged by fire; serious riots occurred at Bristol and Lewes. At Lewes, the Governor was John Marriott and he came through a terrible ordeal with considerable credit. I doubt that what he had been through at Lewes was remembered when he was savaged over the Parkhurst escapes years later. Forty-five prisoners escaped; some eight hundred places were lost from the system, over two hundred of them permanently lost. The POA called off the overtime ban on May 1st.

The Chief Inspector of Prisons, who conducted an inquiry into the disturbances, described it as:

"The worse [sic] night of violence the English Prison Service has ever known".

Following these disturbances, negotiations took place to try and avoid a repetition. The POA, HQ and the politicians were shocked by the violence and damage. A new disputes procedure was agreed between HQ and the POA and was further modified in 1989.

Douglas Hurd was the Home Secretary at the time and we know from his memoirs that the Prime Minister was deeply concerned. What remains a troubling mystery is why – in the face of such extreme difficulties and dangers – the politicians did not make use of the fact that prison officers did not have the right to strike. I shall return to this question in Chapter 36.

Developing "Fresh Start"

The prisoner disturbances of 1986 increased the pressure to find a solution to the many Industrial Relations issues. Work on the new initiative, named "Fresh Start", was given greater priority. Fresh Start aimed to reform prison officer conditions of service by eliminating overtime; to restructure management and to substantially improve regime conditions for prisoners. The initiative was eventually agreed and a programme of implementation began in 1987.

A key part of the change was to allocate staff into working groups attached to either a physical location such as a prison wing or a specialist activity like security. Groups were to be deployed and managed by a Principal Officer and as far as possible the staff would work only in their allocated work area. Continuity would be hugely improved; the first step to building up much more positive relationships with prisoners.

Fresh Start did not eliminate industrial disputes. In 1988, a further serious dispute arose at Holloway Prison in August, with Governor Grades having to cover the duties of prison officers taking industrial action. A larger dispute occurred in January 1989 at Wandsworth Prison when Governor Grades were again called on for some 10 days to perform prison officer duties. The pressure on Governor Grades, being required at short notice to answer these emergency situations, caused considerable problems as the establishments from which they were drawn were left very short of management resources.

This was the Industrial Relations background during my term as Governor of Strangeways Prison.

25. PRISON GOVERNORS ASSOCIATION 1986-1990

Fresh Start was to have consequences for senior staff representation.

Difficulties in the relationships between our parent body – recently renamed the Society of Civil and Public Servants (SCPS) – and the Governors were explored in Chapter 13. These difficulties continued through the early 1980s as Industrial Relations deteriorated across the public sector. Governors felt uneasy about any form of industrial action that impacted on prisoners. One complication was that the SCPS had two branches representing members working in prisons – the "Outstations Branch" covered the administrative grades. Inevitably, the interests of the two SCPS branches were different. The Governors' Branch was especially incensed at attempts to restrict our freedom to give evidence to outside bodies without first reaching agreement with other Home Office branches.

The decision of the SCPS to consider a merger with the CPSA caused particular disquiet among Governors. The Governors' Branch committee started to consider alternative ways of representation. One option was a new "professional organisation" incorporating the Prison Governors of Northern Ireland, Scotland, England and Wales.

In 1981, a group of Immigration Officers decided to break away from the SCPS and set up their own independent union, the Immigration Service Union (ISU), with some 1500 members. Governors watched with interest what was involved in setting up a new independent union, took note and realised that with adequate planning and determination such a change – while difficult – was possible. Recent research into the formation of the ISU was published in 2020 and is listed in Appendix C.

Meanwhile the POA was having problems with its senior members, the Chief Officers, who found the union's readiness to take industrial action difficult to balance against their management responsibilities.

Informal talks began in 1985 about setting up an independent organisation to represent both Governors and Chief Officers. A discussion paper was prepared in 1986 about future representation. This considered the options of setting up a new organisation, of joining another union and of continuing with SCPS. Decisions became urgent when proposals emerged from the Fresh Start Team to amalgamate the grades of Chief Officers and Governors.

In 1987 the pressures to set up an independent organisation became overwhelming. The Service was completely absorbed in the moves towards Fresh Start. The Governor and Chief Officer grades were to be merged with common conditions of Service: the two existing unions had difficulty in handling this change. In particular, the Bridlington Agreement which regulated membership movement between TUC trade unions meant that the POA could prevent Chief Officers from joining the SCPS. Nor did many Chief Officers wish to join the SCPS. So the need for a new independent organisation was becoming critical. As the grade mergers took effect from the summer of 1987, informal discussions continued between representatives of the Chief Officers and the Governors' Branch Committee culminating in a meeting at the Prison Service College, Newbold Revel. Those attending the meeting decided the discussions had made sufficient progress for us to act.

So at the beginning of October 1987, a group of Governors and former Chief Officers resigned from the two old unions and founded the Prison Governors Association (PGA). Independence Day marked the beginning of a period of high activity. The PGA was launched by a Steering Committee of those with experience in both the Governors' Branch Committee and the former Chief Officers' Committee. A manifesto was circulated to all potential members with an invitation to join the PGA. Recruitment proceeded quickly and by the first meeting of the Steering Committee on 15th October, the PGA had 337 members. Counteraction was taken by both the POA and the SCPS but despite their efforts, the PGA's membership continued to rise steadily over the next few months. The PGA was placed on the list of Trade Unions by the Certification Officer on 6th November 1987. Departmental recognition by the Home Office followed in March 1988; Treasury recognition in May 1988. A certificate of independence was issued by the Certification Officer on 28th July 1988. By that date the PGA had over 650 members.

The intervening months were very challenging. The Prison Service would not talk to the PGA formally although some useful informal discussions took place. "Facility time" – an allowance of time to undertake union work in official time – was not available to the PGA so everything undertaken by the organising committee, of which I was a member, was in our own time and at our own expense. Our first Secretary used his home address as the official office for the new organisation; completed application forms with the necessary bankers standing orders were to be sent there. Our Secretary reported that "Many completed applications were arriving by every post".

The Secretary and Finance Officer of the organising committee came under particular pressure, including threats of legal action, from the two unions and from the official side: the rest of the organising committee did what they could to support our two exposed officers. The practical difficulties meant that our first committee meetings were held in pubs and a great deal of work was completed in the evenings and during our weekends off duty. However, we were able to organise our first Conference early in 1988 to ratify a constitution which enabled us to hold elections for the new organisation.

Above: Paddy Scriven, PGA Finance Officer.

Following the elections, Terry Bone became the first Chairman of the PGA and I became one of two Vice Chairmen. The other Vice Chairman was David Simons, a former POA member, who became PGA Conference Chairman providing valuable and balanced leadership during our early Conferences. Paddy Scriven was elected as Finance Officer, a post she was to hold for 20 years.

By April 1988 we were holding our first official meetings with the Prison Service and were able to start to function as a proper independent trade union.

An example of the difficulties we faced was when a helicopter escape took place from Gartree Prison in December 1987, between the PGA being set up and being officially recognised, when Governors were asked to comment by the media. I decided – although it was far from clear what our legal position was – that we had to say something and with the agreement of colleagues on the steering committee was interviewed on national TV – something I had done many times before when speaking for the old Governors' Branch. Fortunately the interview appeared to go down well with our members and the wider public and there were no difficulties with the Prison Service.

In 1989 PGA published our first edition of a magazine. Later in 1989, the Northern Ireland Governors decided to join the PGA. Because we were recruiting from a wider pool of potential members – the former Governor Grades, the former Chief Officer Grades, and the Governors and Chief Officers from the Northern Ireland Prison Service, the PGA was soon representing over 1000 members compared with just over 500 in the days of the old "Governors' Branch".

Annual PGA Conferences were held at the new Prison Service College at Newbold Revel, between Coventry and Rugby. Our family had long connections with Newbold Revel as my wife had studied there for her teaching qualification between 1960 and 1963. Called St Paul's College it was run by the St Paul's Order of Roman Catholic Nuns. The Service acquired the College in 1986.

After I had retired, in 2003, the Scottish Governors also joined the PGA, further swelling their potential membership.

An interesting initiative by a recently retired Governor – Arthur Williamson – was to set up a newsletter to link those retired Governors who wished to keep in touch. I took on the editorship of this small specialised magazine "The Retired Governors Newsletter" (RGN) and continued for some 25 years. It was a fascinating experience – producing a magazine twice a year to give former colleagues a chance to keep in touch. The RGN circulated to over 400 addresses, an indication that many enjoyed being able to retain some small link with the Service. It also provided a valuable record of some Service history, not available elsewhere – see Appendix D.

In 2020 the RGN celebrated 40 years of publication with a special edition.

26. MANCHESTER PRISON 1986-1990

Background

My transfer to take charge of Manchester Prison in September 1986 was at my request. My widower father – my mother had died in 1983 – lived in Ellesmere Port and as his only child I wanted to be stationed closer to him. The Governor of Manchester Prison, John Lewis, was due to retire, and I was delighted to grapple with a big challenge. The family were happy to return to the north west. We moved house to Grappenhall near Warrington in January 1987, where we were to live for the next 19 years.

I had seen the splendid series on BBC1 by Rex Bloomstein on Strangeways, one of the first "fly on the wall" documentaries. Some of the problems stood out in stark relief – the overcrowding, the lack of proper facilities, and the unusual style of Governor Norman Brown. As mentioned in Chapter 8, I had known Norman from when he was Deputy Governor during part of my first tour of duty at Strangeways in 1966. Son of a former Governor of Dartmoor, Norman had suffered grievously in the Second World War – his scarred face a permanent reminder of how many of those who fought for freedom had been affected.

There was one dramatic scene where a prisoner predicted that the roof would be taken off Strangeways. This makes an excellent introduction to any programme about the 1990 riot. But many predictions of disorder were made by both prisoners and staff over the years, and although Strangeways had endured difficult and dangerous moments from time to time, nothing very serious actually happened until 1990. Warnings of trouble were a part of the interplay between staff and prisoners in many prisons. When investigated – in so far as it is possible to investigate warnings coming from intelligence sources – they were found to have very little substance.

I discovered that there had been at least one earlier BBC programme about Strangeways – around 1960 when Gilbert Hair had been Governor. This was an interesting record of the state of the prison at that time. When I viewed the footage of this earlier film, I discovered Jack Beaumont – one of my former Governors at Preston – had a significant role – he was then the POA Secretary.

Strangeways was opened in 1868 on a site to the north of Manchester's city centre. It consisted of two separate radial prisons; a prison for men and a smaller one for women. The Manchester Assize Courts were constructed in front of the prison, partially concealing it. The courts were destroyed by enemy action during World War Two and the site more recently was used as a car park. Consequently the prison became a much more visible landmark. The Prison Commissioners acquired land to the north of the prison across Sherborne Street and built workshops and stores. This site, known as the "Croft", had separate vehicular access – the Croft Gate. A secure enclosed bridge across Sherborne Street linked the Croft to the rest of the prison site. Constructed on sloping ground there was a considerable drop between the east and west ends of the prison so that levels within the prison appeared to be constantly changing. The height of the perimeter wall varied – and was quite low at the east end of the prison.

Initial Assessment

Physically the prison was very little changed from my first tour at Strangeways. I was especially struck by the lack of improvement to the main gate area – which was totally inadequate for coping with the volume of traffic. Getting large coaches into the prison to transfer prisoners required both sets of gates to be opened together, an obvious and significant security weakness. Interestingly, when I turned up an Inspection Report from 1981, the gate had been singled out as an area requiring urgent improvement – the problem may have been discussed at HQ over the intervening years but nothing had changed. I was to find that to be the case in many parts of the prison – a failure to deliver improvements on the ground.

The 1981 Inspection Report – published in September 1982 – described the quality of life for adult prisoners as "quite barren". The lack of continuity of staff and understaffing were also identified. In parts of the main prison, the Inspectorate reported "40 or more prisoners share access to a single lavatory". Although there were 500 work places in the workshop complex, the Inspectorate found "only 40 employed, and this was fairly typical". The Inspection Report continued: "Overcrowding had imposed such poor living conditions, the opportunity to leave the cells were so limited and the demands on staff time so heavy and unpredictable that the scale and urgency of the improvements necessary were beyond local management's capacity to achieve... the Prison Department should consider with the Governor how to improve the existing regime."

Yet nothing had happened despite the Chief Inspector's recommendations – or despite the BBC TV exposure of conditions to the general public.

One of many weaknesses was in physical security. The old cell window bars were original – no match for modern hacksaw blades. Fortunately, our dogs section was well trained and well led: time and again escapes were prevented by speedy action by our dogs and their handlers.

I inherited some very good senior staff, especially Robin Halward the Deputy Governor. Robin had joined the Service straight from university and had served in a number of establishments. He suffered from cancer and occasionally had to take time off, but despite his illness he was excellent, playing a big part in moving Strangeways forward. Robin was destined to return to Strangeways as Governor when the rebuilding was complete around 1995; he was to successfully bid to keep the establishment in the public sector by winning a "market test" process. Promoted to be Director General of the Northern Irish Service, Robin was heavily involved in the changes to Northern Ireland Prisons under the Peace Process. Unfortunately, cancer returned and Robin died in 2007, a life bravely and well lived but cut short.

On arrival, I discovered that some previous Governors had not drawn security keys. When walking around the prison they had always been accompanied by a Chief Officer to open and shut security gates. I reverted to earlier practice; at least one of the Governors that I served with in 1966-68 had regularly used security keys and gone where the mood took him. When – in my first few days at Strangeways – I appeared on the top landings of the wings, the staff were very surprised – as were the prisoners. When I visited on a Sunday morning, one very experienced Principal Officer told me that I was the first Governor he had seen going to church on a Sunday morning for over 15 years.

So I started by getting about the prison, seeing for myself how bad conditions were for both prisoners and staff, talking to as many people as I could while I assessed what could be done to improve matters. The staff needed to know that it was part of their job dealing with issues raised by prisoners – if the Governor was seen to be prepared to talk to prisoners about issues they raised – then this - for most staff – was a useful lead. But Governors who dealt direct with prisoners needed to be clear about the damage they could do to the lines of delegation and accountability. Time and again I would respond to prisoners who raised an issue with me – "what have you done about it?" I always tried to send them back to the wing staff or whoever was responsible for the issue they raised. But it had the advantage of giving me a little direct knowledge of what prisoners were concerned about – and I could inquire at wing level about the issues and how they were being handled. While there were many real issues, there were also prisoners who would "try it on" and raise matters they knew perfectly well were not for the Prison Service. But for some, the fact they had spoken to the "Number One Governor" about a concern was satisfaction enough – and if that reduced their frustration, well and good.

For prisoners, life in Strangeways was very poor. Conditions were basic; no lavatories in cells; food having to be collected and consumed in cells; very little to do – so a high proportion of the day was spent locked up in cells; very short visits with families; staff who often could not help much with problems, if they wanted to, because of the lack of continuity.

Above all, there were too many prisoners. Manchester was built for less than 1000 prisoners in 1868. We regularly locked up over 1500; during one summer we had a daily average population of around 1750 and we unlocked just over 1800 one morning. Every extra prisoner meant more overcrowding of cells – more cell sharing and less opportunity for single cell occupation. We had limited, heavily worn, supporting facilities – showers and baths; exercise yards; visits rooms; activity space. So the excessive number of prisoners was key to how prisoners felt they were being treated and how far staff felt they could cope.

The staff faced considerable difficulties. The population of Strangeways fluctuated wildly – up to 200 prisoners could leave or enter the prison in a day. For staff to develop a sensible relationship with such a mobile population was very difficult as the way staff duties were organised was largely to equalise overtime opportunities rather than provide continuity on jobs. Job satisfaction was low. The management structure did not encourage clarity about accountability; specialists felt they were largely ignored and fairly powerless.

Initial changes and challenges

I quickly introduced a new management structure giving clearer lines of accountability to senior staff, trying to involve specialists more, but above all looking for ways to allow staff and prisoners to engage more positively and constructively. I inherited a situation where the accommodation units were managed by two Governor 4s. One ran the main prison; one the remand prison. But the main prison had five wings and over 1000 prisoners; the remand prison held about 500 prisoners. One of the wings of the main prison, E Wing, was physically separated from the other four wings at the centre end and was used for sentenced young offenders. I linked this wing to the remand prison resulting in the two residential Governor 4s having a more balanced work load. In particular the Governor of the main prison could focus on sentenced adult prisoners, rather the mix of young offenders and adults. The remand prison already held young remand prisoners so there was logic in linking the remand prison and E Wing as well as trying to balance responsibilities for senior staff.

Norman Brown, the Governor who featured in the BBC TV series, regularly used the Prison Officers' Club, both at lunchtime and in the evening. I inherited a damaging culture of lunchtime drinking among staff, often followed by erratic behaviour in the afternoon. Such behaviour sometimes resulted in confrontations between prisoners and staff – something hardly acceptable when it ended with a prisoner being placed on report to the Governor. The staff considered lunchtime drinking to be normal, especially as Governor Brown had set an example. Changing attitudes was going to be a challenge!

A few staff wore symbols on their ties regarded as racist. These I quickly banned and staff conformed by not having objectionable symbols on display. Some staff "slashed" the peaks of their caps and I asked our Chief Officers to put an end to this practice. There was also a large tea room which encouraged staff to be away from their place of duty and the funds from which were under the control of the POA. The "Kardomah", as it was known, needed to be changed and placed under proper management control, perhaps as part of the staff mess. There were suggestions from some middle managers of undue masonic influence within the staff structures at Strangeways. I kept a sharp eye open for evidence of this but found none despite encouraging those who alleged such influence to let me have any evidence.

Misbehaviour by staff, whether it was in the way they treated prisoners or by contributing to an escape, was an important issue. There was a fairly arcane discipline code with a limited range of sanctions. The most important thing was to set standards, to accept that mistakes would be made and to recognise that if Governors wanted some flexibility from staff in the way they dealt with prisoners, then fairness demanded some flexibility from Governors in dealing with staff. But lines also had to be drawn to prevent abuse and some staff faced disciplinary action for unacceptable behaviour.

I had to hold an inquiry into misbehaviour following a party in the Officers' Club which affected the behaviour of the night staff. We never succeeded in dragging out all the facts but the investigation into these allegations sent an important message that misbehaviour by staff was not going to be swept under the carpet but investigated and confronted.

Staff sick absences were another problem. Managing staff that reported sick or in some cases, just failing to appear, was a considerable problem. Many prisons had this difficulty; I had confronted it before especially during the work we had done to try and improve staff efficiency when I was Midlands DRD. At Strangeways I discovered that staff were averaging about 18 days sick absence a year when I arrived; by 1990 it was reduced to around 12 days a year average, an important improvement. Management of sickness was a problem in many parts of the public service and I learned that the comparable figures for the Greater Manchester Police Service were rather worse than ours.

But most staff were strongly offended by the minority who abused sick leave and who went off duty for no good reason. Most staff knew who the miscreants were and were pleased when management action was taken to encourage better performance.

Sick absence sometimes indicated a member of staff had no ownership of their work – perhaps because their job was boring and they felt undervalued. My aim was to improve the interest in staff jobs, to encourage ownership and better performance. Publishing figures about how much staff sickness was being taken had an impact; steps to acknowledge good attendance by staff also helped and formal investigations into suspected abuse of sick leave started to change the staff culture.

The problem of managing sick leave nationally resulted in increasing interest by the National Audit Office into how effectively the Prison Service was addressing the issue. In 1999 a NAO Report (HC372) was published, documenting the challenge that the Service faced, along with other public sector organisations.

Women officers

Introducing women officers was a significant development. Initially opposed strongly by the local branch of the POA, I eventually got a measure of agreement and gradually started introducing experienced women officers transferred from Styal Prison, with very positive results. When a male officer was attacked by a prisoner at the top of one of the wings, two women officers subdued the offender and marched him down to the segregation unit. This had a marked impact on both male staff and the prisoners. Staff would occasionally say to a prisoner who was threatening to be violent that two of the women officers would take him down to the segregation unit: such a loss of face usually had the desired effect and the prisoner rapidly quietened down!

"Losing face" was a significant issue for some prisoners. If the rest of the prison was locked up, some allegedly "hard" men would walk down to the punishment block with a couple of officers in attendance without any resistance but would shout and scream as if they were being beaten up. Anything to preserve their image!

Two newly recruited women officers were posted to us and allocated to E Wing, where we housed our young offenders. A Senior Officer was appointed to act as their mentor. One day, while I was walking through E Wing on the two's landing, the Senior Officer called me over and showed me what one of our new officers was doing. Looking down onto the ones, I could see her talking to a very large black West Indian youngster – who looked twice her size. She was obviously telling him off and the interesting thing was his reaction. He was very subdued and was saying "Yes Miss" as the officer spoke to him sternly. My Senior Officer mentor said that if that had been a male officer, he was sure the young man would not have reacted so positively – and how pleased he was at the reaction mixed staffing was having on the control and management of our young offenders.

On another occasion, when walking around in the evening, an older very experienced Hospital Officer came up to me and said, "Governor – you were right about the women officers." I was pleasantly surprised and asked him what had led him to that conclusion. He explained that he had been giving out medicines to prisoners from one of our surgeries and a notorious prisoner came in and swore at him. Then the prisoner realised there was a woman officer working next to the Hospital Officer and immediately said "Sorry Miss" and didn't swear again.

Fresh Start

A major opportunity to improve almost everything at Strangeways arose because the whole Service was involved in the "Fresh Start" project designed to abolish overtime, give staff higher guaranteed earnings and improve conditions for prisoners. Strangeways was the first big prison to introduce Fresh Start on 5th July 1987. The staff by and large were brilliant, working much harder but for shorter hours. One officer came to see a Governor Grade after a couple of weeks of Fresh Start. "You see these shoes," said he, pointing at his feet, "They were new last week and they have a hundred miles on the clock already!"

We used the introduction of Fresh Start to significantly change the prison routine. Perhaps the most dramatic impact was the improvement to workshop hours. Previously there had been great difficulty in getting prison officers in sufficient numbers into the workshops to provide part of the supervision of prisoners. When the protection of overtime ceased to be an issue, so did the problem of finding workshop supervision. We already had a number of officer instructors and they were quite happy to manage their workshops without discipline officers. Even better, when staff went for a meal break at 12.30 having supervised the lunch meal and locked up the prisoners, there used to be a long gap before the prisoners could be got back to work – often around 13.45 hours. But the workshop instructors, having gone for their meal break at 12 noon, were back on duty at 13.00 and they and the Trades Officers unlocked their charges and had the workshops running soon after 13.00. This was a huge improvement and it worked very well with co-operation on all sides. It showed the fundamental benefits of Fresh Start – instead of worrying about overtime, the staff were focussed on doing the job the best way.

Prison officers were organised into work groups and spent most of their working time in either a wing group or a specialised group such as security. The results were very encouraging as staff and prisoners started to build up much more positive relationships. But it was only the start of a major change and staff needed support and training to appreciate what was now being expected of them. We were still working in a very overcrowded old prison with poor conditions for everybody. What was exciting was the way many staff started to use their initiative in bringing about small improvements. Inevitably there were some staff less happy about the changes.

A fuller description of our introduction of Fresh Start was published in the Prison Service Journal 71 in 1988 under the heading "Strangeways makes a Fresh Start".

But every improvement seems to have complications. Now that the financial incentives to work at "unsocial hours" had gone – they were included as part of the improved salary package – there was a growing reluctance to cover weekends and evenings. This was not a large problem but the change in approach to evenings and weekend working was quite startling for those of us who had experienced the enthusiasm for weekend working when it attracted premium payments!

Much of my energies went into trying to improve conditions for both staff and prisoners. We gave the staff mess some priority, improving the food and the environment. Training was another important tool in developing Strangeways and we revamped the staff training centre.

Organising much needed training for staff was not easy. The problem was releasing staff from operational duties – especially when we were short of staff. The Woolf Report describes the dilemma faced by Governors. It says:

"Few of these developments will however be achieved unless a proper and adequate amount of time is set aside for training. The Fresh Start package provided some allocation of staff time to training which it unhappily refers to as 'non-effective' time. In our view it is wholly inadequate. It is undesirable also that it is lumped together with the allocation of sickness absences and staff leave.

"On 29th March 1989, Mr O'Friel Governor of Manchester Prison wrote to the Director of Personnel and Finance expressing concern about the position

Plater who organised the prison's workshops. These two were responsible for providing prisoners with much more activity, especially work and education.

As I described earlier, Strangeways had the advantage of having a second linked site, to the north of Sherborne Street, acquired decades ago to develop a workshop complex. It was the existence of the space within Croft Workshops that gave us the opportunity to vastly increase the activity for the majority of our adult convicted prisoners. So for prisoners in the main prison we planned to have every prisoner attending an activity for part of the day and exercise in the other half of the day. Of some 900 prisoners in the main prison we gradually succeeded in involving over three quarters of them into this improved regime. Our regime monitoring figures showed that we had 350/400 prisoners in the workshops each morning and afternoon, most of them working half time, so a total of up to 800 prisoners would be in the workshops half time during the week. That compares with the 40 prisoners a day the Inspectorate had found in the workshops in 1980 – an indication of the huge improvement we had brought about by implementing Fresh Start.

One of my major concerns was the awful physical conditions for visits. They were a disgrace: cramped, dingy and far too small for the volume of visitors. In those days everyone smoked and the atmosphere when I went round was thick with cigarette smoke. And many visitors brought young children with them. It was a nightmare. We made a few minor improvements but visits were very heavily used every day. So even repainting the facilities was difficult. The real answer was to re-provide but that unfortunately had to wait until the rebuilding after the riot.

We were able to improve the regime for some of the vulnerable prisoners (VPs). These were generally sex offenders but also included others who feared for their safety at the hands of other prisoners. Sentenced VPs were located on C1 landing – which was a discrete enclosed unit to prevent contact with other prisoners. The staff developed an excellent working regime for most of them throughout each day by using the space on the landing.

Remand VPs were moved onto E 4 landing where we were not making full use of the space: North Regional Office pressed us to use every cell that we had as fully as possible. Developing a regime for these prisoners was much more challenging although we managed some improvements, for example installing some portable toilets in cells as an experiment.

Education had a vital role to play and more classes were arranged. Some staff became involved in tutoring individual prisoners as we tried to unlock the potential that many staff possessed. Probation and Chaplaincy also contributed with more groups of prisoners involved in preparing for release, addressing offending behaviour or studying their religion.

We had one major building programme completed during my time. A new hospital facility was constructed – this provided much improved accommodation for sick prisoners and freed up the old hospital building for much needed activity space. The new hospital also provided important space during the riot as it did not fall into the hands of the rioters.

In February 1990, reporting on further regime progress to Regional Office, I wrote:

"I am pleased to report that following the provision of showers in the remand gym, we are now offering 90 prisoners a day an opportunity for a second shower a week. Similar improvements are now starting in the main prison with an increasing number of prisoners able to have a second shower in the week.

"We have also opened an additional workshop in the old hospital ward employing an additional 30 prisoners working on shifts – this means we have virtually eliminated unemployment in the main prison."

Two examples of the flexibility we had developed in the regime were the staging of a performance of a play about Maximilian Kolbe, and the production of Blind Bingo sets.

I had come across the Theatre of Poland on tour in the Isle of Man in 1987. I invited them to perform their play in Strangeways which they delivered in October 1987 in the prison chapel. Before an audience of prisoners and staff, the company portrayed the meeting between Rudolf Hoess, Commandant of Auschwitz awaiting execution for his crimes, and the spirit of Maximilian Kolbe, Catholic priest, who had died in Auschwitz some years before. Hoess tries to justify his action; Kolbe agonises over whether such a criminal can ever be forgiven. The performance was very powerful with the addition of the sounds of a real prison adding authenticity to the scenes.

The Broder Bingo board was designed by prison officers at Thorn Cross Young Offenders establishment and produced by prisoners at Strangeways with the support of the Prince's Trust. It enabled blind and partially sighted, those with physical disabilities and the elderly to play Bingo. The co-operation between the two establishments working with community groups made this a special project. It attracted some prisoners who would otherwise have been reluctant to work.

More challenges

A constant concern was the danger of prisoners committing suicide. We had a number of suicides in the years I was in charge and after each one we reviewed procedures and introduced improvement where it appeared sensible to do so. One of the most tragic cases was of a young offender who received a visit during the morning. The relatives who visited gave him some very bad news but said nothing to staff. When he returned to his cell at lunchtime, this young man hung himself. We were devastated when we heard the full story from the family about the bad news. Among the procedural changes we made was a handout for all visitors explaining that if they were delivering news that might upset an individual prisoner, they should inform staff so that we were aware of the possibility of a reaction and take precautions. Such action prevented any repetition of the tragedy and I took the lesson with me when I moved to Risley a year or so later.

A practical day to day problem for staff was knowing how many prisoners we had, who they were and where they were. In 1986, our records were all on paper either in books or using card indexes. Given the large turnover of prisoners – up to 200 a day – keeping track of how many, where and who, was very difficult. We were good at getting our total numbers right – we had to – it was a critical part of the security routine of the establishment to count the prisoners several times a day. But who they were and exactly where they were in the establishment was much more difficult. Paper systems, especially those run by a number of different people, are notoriously difficult to keep accurate. And in addition to the prisoner movement in and out of Strangeways, there was considerable internal movement as staff filled empty cells, moved prisoners around who were not getting on or moving prisoners to the segregation unit because they needed protection or had been charged with a disciplinary offence.

So when we were trying to find a prisoner it was rarely straightforward. What was especially difficult was when outside agencies, or families, phoned up the prison to inquire if we had a particular prisoner. In the days of card indexes and wing or landing books, this became a lottery; one that most staff found quite difficult to explain. It was especially embarrassing when a family visited and the prisoner they had come to see had just been moved to another prison. It happened too frequently as our paper based systems proved very fallible.

The beginnings of the use of computers in prison transformed this problem. LIDS – the new computer inmate data base – was our first venture into computers and it transformed our knowledge of whom and where our prisoners were. Phone calls from anxious relatives could be answered with much greater certainty; so could calls from outside agencies trying to trace an individual. Staff responded very well – by and large – to the arrival of the computers and enjoyed developing a new skill. Some quite amusing and innovative applications occurred. One prisoner was abusing a dog handler by shouting insults out of his cell window. The dog handler was able to locate the cell and radio the control room that checked the computer to discover who the occupant was. The dog handler was able to respond quietly to the prisoner next time he shouted by using his name so that the prisoner knew he had been identified. That quickly put a stop to shouting abuse!

Some prisoners would be known by a number of names to try and confuse both the police and ourselves. The computer could record all the known aliases for an individual, making it easier to identify which prisoner he was. Similarly many common names like "Smith" were in order to identify the correct person who was being sought, dates of birth, home addresses and dates of committal to the prison could be helpful pointers to finding the right person.

As I explained in Chapter 22, work had been going on to identify the costs of running prisons so that it would be possible to delegate greater financial control locally. At Manchester, we were able to identify our running costs and how we compared with other prisons. The Prison Service's annual report for 1989/90 revealed that we had a total net budget for the year of just over £28 million. Our cost per prisoner was £230 a week – £190 of that attributable to staff costs. Only Leeds was cheaper to run – all the other big prisons in the Service cost more per prisoner.

The pressure of prisoner numbers on the establishment was a constant source of concern. The pressure was particularly acute in 1988 when in the summer we ran with a daily average population of 1760 prisoners. This was several hundred more prisoners than any other prison in the UK, including Wandsworth which had a much higher number of cells than Strangeways. The failure to even out the pressure ended when the POA took industrial action and reduced the number by several hundred. But even after this dispute was settled, population pressures were always in the background and I have no doubt that the fact it rose to around 1650 prisoners in early 1990 played some part in causing the riot.

At the beginning of 1989, a serious Industrial Relations crisis developed at Wandsworth over the change to Fresh Start. During January, many Governor Grades had to be deployed to the prison because prison officers refused to work. At the time, comparisons were being made with Strangeways – we had more prisoners than Wandsworth – but less cells – and we were making Fresh Start work. However, this was a delicate time and required all my efforts talking to our local POA to keep Strangeways moving forward rather than being tempted into supporting their colleagues at Wandsworth.

Lack of investment

One of the main problems for Strangeways was that HQ had failed to provide a building programme to modernise the prison. With the exception of a new prison hospital – and the design of that was not a great success – Strangeways had received no significant investment for many years. Other big local prisons had done better, especially our near neighbour Liverpool which had extensive building work since World War Two – probably helped by the fact it had endured serious bomb damage during the blitz.

Consequently in my annual report for the year 1988/89 signed on 31st May 1989, I had written:

"As I complete my first 30 months command of Strangeways Prison I have to balance the euphoria of how much has been achieved against the sinking realisation of how much remains to be done. Again and again, I am confronted with the consequences of at least a decade of decline. Before 1986, few internal improvements took place and were heavily outweighed by the serious deterioration in the regime. Capital investment was minimal. This means that of the major Victorian prisons in the northern half of the country, Strangeways is the most deprived of capital investment. Yet officials at HQ and Region do not appear to have grasped this unpleasant reality, perhaps because of our programme of substantial local improvements. But our internal achievements cannot disguise the overwhelming requirement for a major redevelopment scheme to be agreed. I regret to have to formally record that I have seen no sign from HQ during this reporting year of either urgency or determination to launch a sensible scheme of redevelopment."

I concluded my annual report with these words:

"I am still awaiting an acknowledgement of last year's report. It would be encouraging to know that my annual reports are actually read outside the establishment. I am still looking for a suitable response from the top of the Service to what we have achieved at Strangeways. I would settle for HQ moving forward our major redevelopment plan with the determination and urgency with which we tackle work within Strangeways Prison."

Further problems

Among the problems arising during 1989 was the poor state of the central rotunda, the hub of the 5 wings of the main prison. Even routine maintenance was sadly neglected because it was difficult to access and any work would affect the running of the prison. As a result, the leaking roof deteriorated, birds accessed the central rotunda with ease and the situation looked like getting progressively worse. Pleas to Regional Office to have the population reduced while the work was done met with a total refusal; the Senior Works Officer and the Deputy Governor agreed a way of proceeding which filled me with no enthusiasm but there appeared to be no alternative. The plan involved very large amounts of scaffolding and wire mesh to prevent – so we hoped – prisoners gaining access to the scaffolding.

Another problem during the first 3 months of 1990 was a rise in prisoner numbers from some 1400 in January, to over 1650 towards the end of March. Despite representation to Regional Office, we were expected to carry on coping with higher numbers. The rise in numbers had a variety of causes including not having suitable prisoners available for low security prisons to having to absorb problem prisoners from other establishments.

The Woolf Report notes that this rise in numbers had the effect of increasing the number compelled to share cells. In January, 103 had a cell to themselves; 111 were 3 to a cell. By the end of March only 39 prisoners had a single cell while 174 were sleeping 3 to a cell.

27. EVENTS PRECEDING THE RIOT

Incidents

There were two significant incidents in the weeks before the riot. On the afternoon of Sunday 18th March, about 100 remand prisoners refused to come in from the exercise yard, disrupting the regime. On Sunday 25th March, I attended the prison to see how the afternoon routine ran. The prison was in good order and the staff reported no problems.

On Monday 26th March, two prisoners broke onto the roof of F Wing (the roof above the Chapel). On 27th March, our negotiators talked these two down. They appeared to have no support from others and we were able to repair and strengthen the breach they had made in our defences – which we thought would prevent a repetition.

Inspection Report

The week immediately preceding the riot was partly taken up with the launch of the Report of the Chief Inspector of Prisons following his 1989 Inspection. The launch was on 29th March and the conclusions of the report stated:

"There was a feeling in Manchester that in the last three years, the prison had emerged from the doldrums. This was confirmed by all that we saw. Management are to be congratulated for providing the successful impetus for this. The Governor had put in place a management structure which worked for Manchester and he had used it strongly to promote efficient use of staff and the beginnings of a reasonable regime for inmates. It was striking to see the degree of ownership exhibited by staff at all levels and much useful energy expended searching for more constructive ways to complete tasks. Specialist staff were well integrated. We sensed that whilst this approach had been welcomed by staff there was now a need to build in more opportunities for them to have their say and know they would be listened to, whatever the ultimate decision. Overall, however, the Governor and his senior colleagues had given a first class lead.

"The prison had some awful buildings, particularly the visits area and reception for remands, but were quite unsuitable for continued use. We were greatly impressed by the way we saw staff manage in them. For all the improvements in the regime there was not enough for prisoners to do (some 3-400 remained completely unemployed). Overall in spite of improvements, the treatment of prisoners at Manchester still left much to be desired and the target of 11 hours (average) per week out of cell gives some measure of how far there is to go. There should be a comprehensive study of the regime requirements for inmates at Manchester. Whatever the future may hold for the land around the prison, the existing site should be redeveloped to provide integral sanitation and replacement buildings where necessary, and new building, to house additional work, education and PE opportunities for prisoners and improved facilities for staff. At the same time all cells should be provided with integral sanitation.

"Manchester now needs to experience a management thrust consistent with that which it has enjoyed in the last 3 years to enable the changes which have already taken place to bed down and also to enable fresh initiatives to continue to burgeon. We found some unsatisfactory features; in particular the design of the new hospital and the treatment of Category A prisoners. Standards of cleanliness and kit control were not as high as they should be but on the whole there was much more to praise than to decry in an establishment clearly going in the right direction and with an optimistic momentum."

I held a news conference with the local media on March 29th – so there were TV cameras inside Strangeways only days before the riot. One member of the press left his coat in my office: remarkably it survived the riot and he collected it many weeks later. I also held a general staff meeting to brief staff about the outcome of the Chief Inspectors Report.

Saturday 31st March

To allow the redevelopment of the Strangeways site, it was essential that we acquired the former assize courts site, situated adjacent to and on the west side of the prison, to open up options for the redevelopment of the gate complex. The purchase of this land from the local authorities was completed on the 30th March 1990. On Saturday 31st, because I had agreed to be on duty to cover one of my deputies, I walked across the site with glee knowing that redevelopment was at last possible.

I performed the usual Governor duties that Saturday morning including adjudications, visited several parts of the prison including the kitchen. All appeared normal. No staff or prisoners raised any concerns with me although I spoke to quite a number of people during the morning. At lunchtime I handed over to Gordon Morrison, an experienced Governor 4, and told him to call me if he had any concerns.

Later that day media reports began of the Poll Tax riots in London. My elder son Francis was at university there, so I spent part of the evening trying to locate him as the scenes looked very traumatic. Barbara was away in York attending a training course run by the Catholic Marriage Advisory Service while I was at home with my younger son, Michael.

One of my daughters, Anne, was in Manchester on the Saturday night and later told me that there was a very strange atmosphere in the city centre. The media coverage of the Poll Tax riots on radio was reaching the prisoners and TV footage the next day showed a few banners on Strangeways' roof referring to the Poll Tax.

In my office at Strangeways, attached to a notice board, was a postcard from Alice Springs, Australia, addressed to The Governor, Strangeways Prison,

Manchester UK. It was from my second daughter Helen who spent some eight years travelling after getting her degree. Helen knew of my interest in Alice Springs from reading the Neville Shute novel "A Town like Alice". The card read "As promised a card from Alice". It had reached me safely through the mail, having been posted towards the end of 1989. It was still there when I eventually got access to my office. Over 30 years later it has pride of place in my study, a reminder of April 1990.

28. THE RIOT

Day 1: Sunday 1st April 1990

Perhaps the first indication that 1st April 1990 was to be an unusual day occurred when I went out to my car soon after 9.00 in the morning. I found a dead magpie on the driveway and cleared it into my dustbin thinking no more about it.

My first warning of the riot was when my radio pager bleeped as I drove towards the M56 on my way to my father's house in Little Sutton. He was due back from a holiday and I had promised to check that the house was in good order before his return. It was between 10.00 and 11.00 in the morning. I decided to turn round and phone the prison from home – when I reached home my fifteen year old son, Michael, greeted me with the words – "There is an April Fool call from the prison saying there is a riot." I phoned the establishment – Governor Vic Wallace told me the facts succinctly – "Full scale riot, Sir, they have got on the roof." I quickly changed into a suit, jumped in the car and headed for Manchester with Michael still protesting "I am sure it is an April Fool Dad!"

I drove fast into Manchester along the M62 and my heart dropped when I rounded a corner and had my first glimpse of the prison. The police helicopter was hovering over the establishment – conclusive proof that there was a big problem confronting me. I abandoned the car a street or two away and ran to the gate. My progress was halted because the prisoners had the high ground on the roofs overlooking the gate and were pelting anything that moved with roof slates – lethal weapons. A shield was quickly provided and I dashed into the control centre to take charge.

The control centre was a small prison wing close to the gate that years ago had been used for a few civil prisoners. Despite being only partially converted into a control centre with rudimentary equipment, it did sterling service. The briefings on arrival were all uniformly bad – causalities, buildings lost, communications in chaos, and morale pretty low. The prisoners had seized our internal office phones and started phoning everyone – especially the media. An early decision was to cut off the phone system from the prison to the outside world – it was rather late in the day but at least it stopped the prisoners from communicating direct by phone with the media. It also stopped our communications – we retained just one line to Regional Office in working order.

The first task was containment. We had to prevent prisoners breaking out into Manchester. Some 1500 prisoners were running riot and anything could happen. During the early stages of the riot, the prisoners had seized a set of security keys from staff enabling them to unlock cells and to open other security doors and gates. I had to try and get some structure and organisation to contain and manage the situation. I started by placing the available management team in charge of various tasks – the priorities were to hold the perimeter; try and re-establish control where we could and to save life. A senior officer, demonstrating initiative and great courage, had already undertaken the vital job of double locking all the exterior doors of the prison to avoid a breakout of prisoners from the main accommodation wings. This action negated the prisoners' access to a set of security keys, so we had a small measure of control in that respect.

I quickly told Assistant Regional Director Arnie Stapleton – at Regional Office – that this was worse than anything that had happened previously and asked him to throw all the resources he could at the problem.

We later worked out that there had been 4 Governor Grade and 171 uniformed staff on duty when the riot started and some of those had been injured. Principal Officer Pete Hancox – who was also POA Secretary – appeared and asked what he could do to help. I told him that Chaplain Noel Proctor and others were trapped in the Chapel vestry – could he assemble some staff and see if they could affect a rescue? Pete was very helpful and reported back later that he had rescued a number of staff and had removed some prisoners who wanted no part in the disturbance.

We became very concerned about our vulnerable prisoners (VPs) – sex offenders largely – who were in danger of being attacked. The staff on C1 landing where a large number of VPs were located did a splendid job evacuating them to the workshops in the Croft and we were able to move them out of the prison to safety some hours later.

The VPs on remand were in a much more dangerous position as the rioters had broken into E Wing where they were located and smashed their way into the VPs' cells. What followed was mob violence and lynch law. We managed to evacuate some badly injured VPs during the afternoon – this was very brave work of a small number of staff who negotiated with prisoners at ground level while under bombardment from other rioters 80 feet above them on the roofs. This evacuation enabled us to get these VPs to hospital – one was to die, but the others survived. The behaviour of the rioters towards the VPs completely undermined any shred of justification for starting the riot.

Meanwhile in the control centre, life was difficult. There was only a door between the control centre and one of the wings around which prisoners were rampaging. The door was attacked a couple of times but not breached. More spectacularly, the rioters on the roof were starting to push off quite large coping stones some of which crashed through the roof of the control centre. Fortunately for us the slate landing above our heads did not collapse and we just had to endure the noise and anticipation of further attacks. Around about this time I asked the staff if I could have a drink – a tea or a coffee, which had a great calming effect. "If the Governor has time to have a cup of tea," they told me later, "Things must be going to be all right!"

At the time that the coping stones were dislodged the rioters decided to try and dislodge the stone cross on the top of the prison chapel. In due course they succeeded and another very dangerous missile came crashing down to the ground fortunately without causing more casualties. That was captured on camera and later was shown on TV. The sight of it made me angry. It was wanton destruction.

I was far from confident of the outcome at that stage but I was so busy with difficult decisions to take that I had little time to contemplate the worst. In the middle of the afternoon I had a message from Governor Norman Holliday who had brokered, with other staff, the release of the injured VPs. Norman was talking to a Category A prisoner with a considerable reputation for violence, having attacked and injured a previous Governor of Liverpool Prison. The Category A prisoner reported that there was a fire in the segregation unit and that there were still prisoners locked up down there – in considerable danger from the fire. The prisoner was volunteering to unlock these cells if he was given a cell key. Norman sought instructions from me. I agreed promptly and the key was handed over. It was returned later and we suffered no deaths as a result of prisoners being trapped in cells – as happened later that month during the riots at Dartmoor. This demonstrated our ability to co-operate with prisoners even in the middle of a riot. Perhaps more strikingly, other staff heard the instruction and sent a cell key into the remand prison to have prisoners released from other cells where there was danger from fire. Again the key was returned.

One of my hospital staff was liaising with the NHS and the Ambulance service as we evacuated casualties to local hospitals. In discussion with the Ambulance service he agreed that a number of body bags should be provided as a contingency. This was a sensible decision although it may have played its part in press headlines later in the week as the media sensationalised the riot and declared that there were many dead bodies in Strangeways.

Trying to assess how many staff we had available was not easy. Some staff headed for the prison as soon as they heard that there was trouble; others made themselves less available. Some staff contacted by the prison thought this was an April Fool – so my son was not the only one to be deceived! Of the staff originally on duty, some were injured, others were traumatised by the experience.

As staff arrived from other prisons, keeping track on who was here and how we deployed them, was difficult. We needed staff with full riot equipment to reduce the danger of more casualties. We had only limited amounts of equipment and many staff turned up without protective clothing.

An immediate task was to evacuate surrendering prisoners. We moved these prisoners to the Croft and a major exercise began to remove prisoners to other prisons. If anyone had said to me the week before that I was required to remove in excess of 1000 prisoners from Strangeways in under 24 hours, I am sure I would have responded that this was an impossible task. Yet the Service rose to the challenge and well over 1200 prisoners were moved away without any escapes or further serious incidents.

Another urgent concern was feeding the staff, especially as additional staff started to arrive. The Staff Mess did excellent work providing short term sustenance to staff – and HQ's Catering Branch had sensible contingency plans involving aircraft meals which worked pretty well.

Throughout the afternoon and evening, prisoners set a number of fires. The Greater Manchester Fire Brigade did a first class job tackling blazes wherever possible, supported by our staff. Rioters treated the Fire Service staff no different from anyone else and threw missiles at them.

Reports from the various "fronts" indicated that prisoners were building barricades to prevent us launching attacks on their positions. A huge barricade developed in F Wing with piles of debris from cell beds, broken furniture and scaffolding poles. I was receiving a constant stream of information, requests and occasionally very urgent messages requiring immediate decisions. I have often been asked about how scared we were in the midst of the mayhem we confronted. In my case I was almost too busy to be scared – but when one of those huge coping stones crashed through the roof above us I jumped as high as anyone.

By Sunday evening, we were receiving substantial numbers of riot trained staff and I was keen to see if we could recover some of the accommodation that had been lost.

We were able to move from containment to considering a counter attack. We decided to attempt an incursion into E Wing. This was a difficult operation as we discovered that the prisoners were able to attack staff from above the security mesh at the top of the wing and could launch missiles including scaffolding poles at staff, causing some casualties. We took the decision to withdraw after a period to avoid further casualties and fighting in the dark was not a sensible option unless absolutely essential. The incursion was valuable because it gave us better knowledge of what we were up against and enabled the C&R commanders to consider options for the next day.

At around 22.00, I handed over to my colleague Ian Boon, Governor of Risley, who had been asked to cover the night time. I drove home, fell into bed exhausted and enjoyed a few hours sleep.

Earlier in the day, my family started to rush home realising the crisis I was confronting and that our fifteen year old Michael was "home alone". There were many phone calls largely from friends and relatives although one national newspaper reporter asked one of my daughters, "How many dead are there in Strangeways?" Within a day or two, my elder son Francis was doing sterling work monitoring the media for me and briefing me each night on the issues being raised. That was of great assistance when I had the time to hold press conferences.

Day 2: Monday 2nd April

I drove back to Strangeways arriving soon after 07.00. It took a while to catch up on all that had happened overnight as the evacuation of prisoners had continued through the night. By 09.00, I decided we might see if the remand prison could be retaken as it appeared almost unoccupied and the remaining rioters were congregating in the main prison. After discussion with HQ, I gave instructions for C&R teams to enter the remand prison. This was a successful operation; six prisoners were captured and the remand prison secured without difficulty. However, the extent of the damage was very disturbing – I was anxious to get hold of cells that were usable for locking up surrendering prisoners but there were only a few in the remand prison and the undamaged cells were scattered in such a way as to not be of much use even as a temporary holding centre.

Although it was some time before the Service came to appreciate what had been achieved on the first day, it was remarkable that well over one thousand prisoners had been moved out of Strangeways in under 24 hours and distributed widely around the country. Some were in police cells but many had been moved to other prisons with staff working very long hours to escort them. No prisoner escaped from escort despite the difficulties that the escort staff faced. We would not have been able to move that number of prisoners so quickly except for the "Croft Gate" which gave us an invaluable extra entrance and exit to the prison. At this stage we were unclear as to how many prisoners were left, who they were and how many were serious offenders. We had insufficient information even to identify the leaders of the disturbance.

During the morning I asked the C&R commanders working with Robin Halward to come up with a plan to retake the main prison and restore order. I also appointed a senior officer to work as my staff officer. He did a valuable job in keeping a log of what I was doing and of my decisions. He also visited staff in other locations to give me feedback on how people were coping.

By the middle of the day, a plan to retake the prison was starting to shape up. We knew that we could move large numbers of staff into the prison chapel and into E Wing. If we mounted a major assault, that would increase the prospects of any of those on the fringe of the hard core rioters quickly surrendering. There was no guarantee of success, but we expected to retake much of the main prison and to drive a small hard core either onto the roof or into a relatively confined space. Part of the plan was co-ordinating any attack with the police helicopter which provided us with direct intelligence as to the behaviour of the rioters on the roof, something we could not see from ground level. Moreover, the approach of the helicopter caused some of those on the roof to seek shelter and the helicopter had a noise-making machine, a "Distractor", which caused some prisoners to move off the roof.

Communications continued to be very difficult; this was long before the age of effective mobile phones and we were relying on one line out of the prison. I had a couple of short exchanges with Brian Emes, who as Deputy Director General (DDG) was in operational charge at HQ. However, we agreed to work via Regional Office which was the usual line of accountability and communications. I therefore briefed senior staff at Regional Office about our emerging plans to retake the prison.

There were two different command systems used in operations at this time in the Service. For hostage incidents, as described in Chapter 21, it was clearly laid down that decisions lay between HQ and the field Governor – Regional Office had a supportive role rather than a line role. There were detailed and well worked up arrangements for this which I knew well. But for other crises, the line was from the local Governor to Regional Office. We had plenty of experience of that during a number of major disturbances over the years. It was through the Regional Office that the command structure had worked during the 1976 Hull Prison riot, which although a shorter and smaller disturbance, had interesting similarities with what happened at Strangeways.

I had acquired staff from all over the Service and although I was the commander on the spot, it was quite proper for others to have a say in major decisions. What we lacked was clarity about how this should work in practice. That was a failure on all our parts to have adequate contingency plans and opportunities to practise and refine them. This was part of the damage caused by overcrowding. Insufficient time and resource was available to deal with anything other than the daily running of many establishments – especially the local prisons and remand centres.

I was entirely unaware of what had been going on at HQ. I learned later that the DDG had been continuously on duty since he was alerted on the 1st April at the start of the riot. He had been on duty for 24 hours without a break. That afternoon he was scheduled to meet and brief the Home Secretary.

So when the DDG phoned me around 1500 hours, everything was wrong. He had not been adequately briefed – and I was unaware of that. He called me from a side office next to the Home Secretary's office – he was away from the HQ control room where his aides were working and had the latest information.

For my part I was in a cell in the control centre with no privacy, many staff around and continuing noise from the prisoners. I was extremely conscious that if I was instructed not to attack I would have a major problem on my hands with staff morale. I was also concerned about staff following orders as staff were keyed up for the proposed attack. The difficulties with staff obeying orders around the Hull prison riot – see Chapter 12 – demonstrated that this was no theoretical problem. Hence I decided quickly that I would not argue with the DDG as this would expose rifts in the command structure to the staff. I concentrated instead on getting authority to seize the kitchen because I wanted to cut off the prisoners from any food supplies that could prolong the siege. Fortunately we got permission and the alternative limited attack went ahead and was reasonably successful. The DDG made it clear that no other attacks were to be launched without HQ authority.

But the impact on staff morale was horrendous. We knew that the prisoners would believe that we had backed off – and this would embolden them to continue the disturbance. The staff felt that they had been prevented from taking back the prison: the local Manchester staff felt this very much indeed. Fortunately they understood that I had been prevented from launching the planned attack on 2nd April; they remained loyal and on the whole remarkably well behaved given the provocation we were all under from the rioters.

Before the end of the day I was able to announce that emergency payments had been authorised for staff by HQ. This helped morale, especially after the anti-climax of the afternoon.

The decision taken by the DDG to cancel the planned attack was regrettable. It must have contributed as a cause of the riots that broke out in a number of other prisons. The decision was fully explored in the Woolf Inquiry. But there remains a feeling among some professionals that there was political interference for which the DDG took the blame. I have seen no evidence of that; the Woolf Report ruled it out. When the Home Secretary visited on 22nd April, I formed a very clear impression that he had not known about the planned attack when he was briefed by officials on 2nd April. Perhaps any doubts will be cleared up from a study of all the official papers by future researchers.

Recommendations flowed from the Woolf Report to try and ensure better handling of major disturbances in the future. The test of the changes to contingency plans will be when another enormous disturbance occurs. I sincerely hope that it doesn't but occasional major disturbances are an unpleasant fact of prison life across the globe.

Day 3: Tuesday 3rd April

When I returned to the prison the next morning we were confronted with a serious attack on the fabric of the building as the rioters attempted to break into the prisoners' records area. Because of the sensitivity of prisoners' records, I judged this to be a "red line" that we would defend. We sent a force of C&R staff into E wing and this incursion drew off the attempt on the prisoners' records area. The fighting in E Wing went on for some time; at one point a prisoner was paraded on the roof with a noose around his neck; but within E Wing both staff and prisoners slowed the fighting and began some dialogue. I encouraged this as every time we got into dialogue we learned more about the

Above: Staff guarding gate.

number and names of the prisoners left within the prison; we were still trying to establish which high security prisoners were left. We were also concerned about possible attempts by some prisoners to break out through the maze of Victorian tunnels built for ventilation and other purposes known as the "Undercroft" below the prison.

The question of how many prisoners we were dealing with was rapidly becoming a priority. How many prisoners were there in Strangeways at the start of the riot? How many had been rehoused elsewhere? How many were left in the prison? Media stories about deaths in the prison pressurised us to try and establish the facts; but our inability to check on all the facts – because we couldn't access many of the records in the main part of the prison – made this a very challenging task. Excellent work was done by staff in identifying individual prisoners when they showed themselves on the roof or when any opportunity arose to open dialogue, and staff were able to ask rioters questions. One very shrewd senior officer established regular contact with rioters through a barricade and occasionally sent for a prisoner we wanted to check on in order to establish if he was indeed still within the barricades. We eventually established that there were 1647 prisoners in the prison when the riot broke out – so we had to account for each and every one of them to be certain there were no dead bodies in the prison.

News reached us that one of the prisoners in hospital, Mr D White, had died.

During the day, an offer was made by the Manchester Evening News that the editor was willing to act as a go-between to see if a negotiated end could be achieved. He and a well-known local solicitor, Barry Cuttle, came into the prison but the prisoners, while showing some distant interest – probably with an eye to encouraging publicity – did not really engage.

Another development was that we set up staff support, conscious that the stress we had all been through would take its toll sooner or later. Prison Service had quite well developed plans for supporting staff involved in hostage incidents, and in incidents of suicide. We used this experience on a much broader front to try and start and address the impact that stress would be having. In times past, stress – like shell shock – was not recognised for what it was and what it did to people. We made a conscious attempt to recognise staff needs and give them opportunities to talk to trained colleagues about what they had been through.

Relationships with the media

Because the disturbance took place in an accessible place, close to the centre of Manchester, and the prisoners used their access to phones to call the media in the middle of Sunday morning, the Strangeways riot became the centre of a huge media circus. Unfortunately I was unable to contemplate talking to the media during the first 3 days because the operational pressures on me were so great. On Wednesday 4th, I held my first news conference and held another 7 before the incident was over. Fortunately I had had considerable experience of dealing with the media as Chairman of the Governors' Branch as described in Chapter 13 – which proved to be very helpful. I also benefited from the daily briefings provided each evening by my son Francis, monitoring the media stories at home as they arose. It was at the first news conference that I described the riot as "an explosion of evil". This reflected my anger at the serious assaults on vulnerable prisoners, the injuries caused to staff and the wanton destruction of facilities including those that benefited prisoners.

The Manchester Evening News ran a story on 2nd April alleging between 12 and 20 prisoners were dead in the prison. This allegation, based on rumours and speculations from a number of sources, unfortunately became a considerable distraction to managing the disturbance and bringing it to an end. There was pressure from HQ, responding in part from questions from the media and politicians, to try and establish if there were dead bodies in the prison. We had trouble enough trying to establish how many prisoners were at the prison at the time the riot started and great problems identifying who and how many were left in the prison until the final few days. Most prisoners were not going to admit who they were when involved in a disturbance. Many continued to wear face coverings to hinder identification.

I had some sympathy with the media as the Service had been unable to respond adequately in the first day or so of the disturbance. Dispatching an inexperienced press officer to the scene was insufficient. Fortunately one of my colleagues, Ian Lockwood, Governor of Haverigg Prison, stepped into the breach and we gradually started to provide a reasonable service of information to the media.

Day 4: Wednesday 4th April and beyond

A pattern began to emerge of staff trying to negotiate with prisoners and succeeding in whittling down the numbers behind the barricades by continuing to reassure potential surrendering prisoners about their future treatment. We continued to provide a strong management presence, together with a member of the independent Board of Visitors whenever a surrendering prisoner was being processed through reception and removed from the prison. There was an encouraging lack of complaints about the treatment of surrendering prisoners in sharp contrast to the lack of professional behaviour by staff on some previous occasions after riots such as at Hull.

There was one evening incident of bad behaviour by staff captured on watching TV cameras. Staff taunted prisoners with the term "Beasts", prison slang for sex offenders. This was entirely unacceptable. When I came in the next day, a number of staff came to see me to apologise for what had happened

Above: Forecourt damage.

– an encouraging development as they increasingly came to understand the need to restore order with a professional approach.

We were increasingly confident that no prisoner had escaped. On Day One when I arrived at the prison this seemed a real danger and for a number of days we were concerned to identify the whereabouts of those prisoners we regarded as being a serious security risk. We had particular concerns about some of the remaining rioters finding a way out through the maze of tunnels and passages under the prison about which we had limited information. Given that 7 of the rioters were to succeed in escaping from legal custody in 1992 and 1993 while awaiting trial for the riots, our concerns were thoroughly justified. Our success in preventing escapes, in the midst of all the many difficulties we faced throughout the disturbance, was something of which we could justifiably be proud.

By Day Four we were reasonably confident that Paul Taylor and Alan Lord had been and continued to be key leaders among the rioters. Their public performances on the roof on 4th April reinforced this assessment. I realised that I knew Paul Taylor. I spent time talking to him on the main prison centre some weeks earlier trying to persuade him to co-operate by going to work and pointing out the choices of activity we were now providing. It had been a vain effort but Paul Taylor has subsequently gone out of his way not to blame me for the conditions which contributed to the riot.

The prisoners increasingly tried to communicate with the media across the prison wall and we resorted to playing loud music to interrupt these attempted communications. This led to comparisons in the media with the siege in Panama involving General Noriega in which loud music was used. The media also had great fun commenting on our choice of music!

Another problem was how far we should use water to try and deny the rioters access to parts of the roof. Difficult negotiations took place with the Greater Manchester Fire Brigade, who quite reasonably did not see that task as part of their mission. The Fire Brigade were happy to use water to extinguish fires and on several occasions soaked areas of the prison where we suspected – or knew – that the rioters were preparing further arson attacks on the fabric of the buildings. But using water for controlling prisoners was not part of their brief.

By 8th April, I considered that we needed to have water available as a weapon against the remaining rioters. So I discussed with the acting Regional Director, Terry Bone, the possible use of help from the Army. I knew that during the Hull prison riot the Army had provided an armoured vehicle to move staff safely around the prison and I thought that the Army might be willing to help again.

On the 13th April, we received two "Green Goddesses" – without crew. These old fire engines released from central stores were soon manned by prison staff. Because the Goddesses were not very reliable, we ended up with a fleet of seven vehicles to ensure we had enough operational at any one time.

But using water against prisoners on the roof was a very difficult decision. The danger of knocking a prisoner off these very high roofs – 80 feet up and more – was considerable – and I knew very well that the person who gave an order resulting in a fatality would have to face a Coroners Court and probably a police investigation. These constraints were ignored by some of the public who advocated the riot should be ended by any means including lethal force.

On the evening of the 6th April, riots broke out in other prisons including Bristol, Cardiff and Dartmoor. This outbreak took some of the focus away from Strangeways – and meant that our staff resources were reduced to assist other prisons facing the need to control rioters and restore order. Quite a large group of our staff were also detached to Risley where some old accommodation had been rapidly reopened to help make up for the loss of accommodation at Strangeways.

I became especially worried about the situation as Holy Week began. Intelligence reached us that the prisoners were threatening all sorts of bizarre actions including trying to make a huge bonfire of the prison on Good Friday. We took practical precautions but I also gave Bishop Patrick Kelly – Bishop of Salford – a call to ask for special prayers at the Cathedral and elsewhere for a peaceful resolution to the crisis. The Bishop responded positively and I am sure that the power of prayer played a part in the eventual peaceful outcome.

We struggled on. The difficulties caused by the allegations of the possible existence of bodies in the wreckage of the prison was a constant source of irritation – we were almost certain that there were no bodies in the wreckage but we could not give a categorical assurance until we were able to account for the whereabouts of all our prisoners.

I set up a negotiating team containing both local and national staff resources, all with special negotiating skills and experience. The mixture worked well – but the real problem was that we lacked means to put pressure on the prisoners to negotiate. They could continue their protest in the knowledge that their actions were getting wide publicity. So we resorted to a whole variety of tactics from using food as a lure; warning that the SAS were around – they certainly were not – and using every opportunity to talk to individuals and groups to see if we would achieve a negotiated surrender. But the weakness of our position was that the prisoners believed we could not use force against them so they had little incentive to surrender.

Dialogue had been going on with prisoners from the first day of the riot. We had a number of very able staff who used every opportunity to talk with the rioters to try and reassure them about what would happen to them if they wanted to surrender and to evaluate the state of the rioters' resources and morale. The negotiating team allowed us to formalise this process and to organise what pressure we could put on them in order to achieve an end to the riot.

The negotiating team set up a telephone link to the rioters to facilitate negotiations. In the first phase of negotiations, from 4th to 8th April, the number of rioters reduced from 41 to 21. Some prisoners within the siege area decided that it was better to surrender. The negotiating team worked to reduce the number of rioters to the "hardcore". From the 9th to the 17th, the numbers were reduced from 20 to 7, again largely thanks to the quiet and persistent work of the negotiating team.

In parallel with the negotiating team, we used the remaining C&R teams to start to probe the barricades and defences built by the rioters and to mount limited incursions into what the negotiators dubbed "the stronghold" i.e. the area still held by the rioters. These incursions helped us build up a picture of the barriers we faced in retaking the prison; they tested the defences and reactions of the prisoners and they were one of the few ways we could put any pressure on the "hardcore" rioters left.

Fortunately, the staff did not lose that most valuable commodity – their sense of humour. A few days after the start of the riot as I walked into the prison I was greeted by one officer – who had been in front of me on a disciplinary charge only a few weeks previous – with the comment, "Look Governor, we know you wanted the prison rebuilt – but this is taking it a bit far!"

As the days became weeks, morale faltered. Officer Walter Scott died in hospital on the 5th, not directly from injuries, but his medical condition may have been worsened by the stress he had undergone in the early days of the disturbance. There was a huge staff turnout for the funeral on 11th April which was very emotional for us all.

I tried to keep in touch with staff by my usual technique of spending time around the prison talking to everyone I could. I also sent circular letters to staff families explaining what was going on and how we hoped to safeguard the future. There was growing concern that Strangeways might be closed and demolished at the end of the riot – with many anxieties about job security and the possibility of staff having to move.

The Woolf Inquiry is set up

On 5th April David Waddington, the Home Secretary, announced that Lord Justice Woolf would head an inquiry into the disturbance. Lord Woolf appointed a number of Assessors including Gordon Lakes, a recently retired Deputy Director General of the Service. Gordon Lakes arranged for Lord Justice Woolf to meet me at my home the following week to have some initial contact about the inquiry. This took place on the afternoon of the 12th April. The original terms of the Woolf Inquiry were extended as riots took place at a number of other prisons.

How the end was engineered

On Friday 20th April, the end suddenly came into sight. Ivor Serle, local POA Chairman, was holding his usual media briefing. He explained how frustrating it was for staff that the siege continued and added, "If the Governor had been allowed to have his way, the riot would have ended on 2nd April – Day 2 of the riot". The media, had been told about this by the POA at the time but had not followed it up. Now journalists pricked up their ears and began to ask questions.

Politicians and senior people in the Home Office had to field many questions that day – so many that it was decided that the Director General, Chris Train, should give an interview the next morning to the BBC Radio 4 Today programme about what happened on 2nd April.

This was the only public interview given by Chris Train during the disturbances. On Saturday 21st, I was at home, my first day off since the riot began. The first I knew of this interview was at about 08.10 when I heard Chris Train being interviewed by John Humphreys. In response to the question as to whether the Governor had been overruled, the Director General said, "The Governor's view was the one that prevailed. The Governor was the man on the ground who knew exactly what the situation was."

I was taken aback by this public statement. There had been no discussion since the 2nd April about the decision. It looked as if HQ were embarrassed by what they had decided and the Governor was a very convenient scapegoat. I felt that I was being hung out to dry.

I immediately sought a copy of the interview so that I could be sure that I had heard Chris Train's words correctly. I consulted my colleagues in the Prison Governors Association and prepared to set the record straight as opportunities permitted.

The PGA issued a statement on 21st April saying:

"The Prison Governors Association are deeply saddened that the senior management of the Prison Service has seen fit to make statements to the media concerning the decisions made at the height of the disturbances at HMP Manchester.

"The PGA would have expected the Director General of the Prison Service and his senior managers to have reserved their comments for the inquiry being led by Lord Justice Woolf.

"While we will not comment on the actual events at HMP Manchester except to the Woolf Inquiry, we must make it clear that in all major incidents the Governor of a prison is not allowed to make decisions in isolation. There are times when he will be given specific instructions by Headquarters which override his own personal inclinations.

"Finally the PGA expresses its full confidence in Mr O'Friel and in the professional and expert manner with which he has handled the riot at Manchester Prison".

Interestingly, on Saturday 21st April, Home Officer Minister David Mellor visited Liverpool Prison. I was later sent a copy of an official note about part of the visit which said:

"Mr Mellor referred to Ivor Serle's claim that Mr O'Friel's plan to storm Strangeways was stopped at a higher level, and Mr O'Friel's failure to refute immediately and publicly this inaccurate statement."

So Ministers had not been accurately briefed about events on 2nd April and who had taken decisions.

On Sunday 22nd April, I received a phone call around 09.00 that the Home Secretary, David Waddington, would be arriving at the prison shortly. He was only accompanied by his protection officers and he sat down in my office and asked to be told the whole story. I explained what happened on 2nd April – he made no comment but I formed the impression that he had not been aware on the 2nd April of the important and difficult decision that had been made close to his office.

He asked to be taken round the prison and spoke to many of the staff including the negotiating team. We took him into the Chapel where it had all started – accompanied by a strong contingent of C&R trained staff. After the tour, he made it clear that he accepted that we needed to end this sorry saga as quickly as possible and that he would be expecting early moves from HQ to support the necessary action at Manchester. We needed some of the C&R units back so that we could confront the remaining prisoners with overwhelming force.

On Sunday 22nd April came news of a further serious disturbance at Pucklechurch Remand Centre, near Bristol.

On 23rd April, Sir Clive Whitmore, Permanent Secretary at the Home Office, visited; Sir Clive had been Permanent Secretary previously in the Ministry of Defence. Through Sir Clive, we were given authority to retake the prison on Wednesday the 25th. More good news came in during the afternoon: the success of a planned ambush that allowed a C&R team to arrest Alan Lord, undoubtedly a key ringleader of the disturbance. I called a news conference at short notice to ensure we made the most of a rare success.

On the 24th we assembled the necessary C&R units and held a practice in one part of the remand prison away from the rioters. We were ready to bring the disturbance to an end.

On 25th, everything was in place by 09.00 and I gave the order to commence the attack. The operation went well without significant casualties and the remaining prisoners finally surrendered at about 18.00 hours. When the staff had cleared the main prison at around 13.00, I made an unfortunate mistake and visited the building. The extent of the damage affected me more than I realised; I quickly recognised that I was not making sound decisions so handed over to my deputy and went home about 16.00. I watched this end of the siege live on BBC Six O'Clock News that evening.

Above: Example of riot damage.

Questions remained about the decision not to attack on 2nd April. I concluded that this was for the Woolf Inquiry to examine, though I could not resist referring to the fact that after the decision I looked "poleaxed", an expression coined by a member of the Board of Visitors who had seen me on 2nd April immediately after my phone call with HQ.

At the Woolf Inquiry, responsibility for the decision was attributed to HQ and the Woolf Report includes the following about Chris Train's BBC Radio 4 interview on Saturday 21st April:

"Mr Emes however agreed that the interview was unfortunate in that it created the impression that the decision had been taken by the Governor and not by HQ."

The public account of the decision to cancel the planned assault on 2nd April leaves unresolved issues including:

- Mr Train did not give evidence to Part One of the Woolf Inquiry. Consequently he was not questioned about what he knew. Mr Train was in the same room as Mr Emes when the phone call took place at which Mr Emes cancelled the planned attack. So it is difficult to understand how Mr Train did not know that Mr Emes had taken the decision. So why did he say that the Governor took the decision when he was interviewed on the Today programme?

- Given that Brian Emes took the decision, what part did Chris Train play? If he played no part – why not? He was after all, as John Humphreys reminded him, "The Director General". He had a responsibility to see that his Deputy took the right decision. Brian Emes had been working continuously for over 24 hours – was he in a fit state to take the decision? Had he been given all the necessary information? Had he considered the impact on the rest of the Service of the riot continuing?

- After being briefed about the riot on 2nd April, did the Home Secretary, or any of his advisers, ask the question "How do we end it?" If he did, was he satisfied with the answer?

- How was the decision not to proceed with the planned assault explained to Ministers? The report from Mr Mellor's visit to Liverpool Prison on 21st April clearly indicates Mr Mellor did not know that the decision not to attack had been taken by Mr Emes. It appears that Ministers had not been properly informed of what took place.

These unanswered questions mean that some official Home Office documents for April 1990 may make interesting work for a future researcher.

Above: Green Goddess.

29. AFTERMATH

Coming in to Strangeways the day after the riot ended was a very odd experience. The rioters had gone; the danger had diminished, but as we rapidly discovered, the buildings were in a terrible state and in places very hazardous. The staff were great: recognising that I might be fairly depressed, a delegation came in to present me with a framed piece of slate from the roof inscribed with the words:

"Brendan O'Friel – Governor 1

Thank you for your leadership

Well Done!

From the Staff – H. M. Prison Manchester 1st April 1990"

That was a real "pick me up" and I felt better able to confront the huge task ahead.

We had to prepare for the public hearing of the Woolf Inquiry which was to take place in Manchester for 3 weeks in June. Reports had to be prepared; documents found; issues revisited; statistics drawn together – all in a wrecked prison. We were to discover many aspects of the lead-up to the riot and what happened during the riot as we examined the records and had the chance to properly debrief the staff. In particular, staff started to remember odd events from the day before the riot – but I suspected this was assisted by hindsight. Nobody had passed on these suspicions to me at the time and I had been on duty on 31st March.

The note was found that a prisoner had written predicting a riot starting in the Chapel. We had not acted on this as fully as perhaps we should – but we

Above: The Governor's Slate.

had had many warnings over many years which had not resulted in disorder. Extra precautions were taken – so the warning was not ignored. But it gave me food for thought – especially as I had rather cheerfully remarked some days into the riot – thinking at that stage there had been no warnings – "at least we didn't sail out of harbour with our bow doors open" – a reference to the Herald of Free Enterprise ferry disaster a year before. I had to eat my words!

We needed to restore to working order as much as we could. Our Works Department had an enormous task ahead. But we also knew that there might be pressure to abandon the Strangeways site and build a new prison elsewhere. We did not want that.

The staff was very battered and depressed after their experiences of the last 25 days and they needed clear leadership to recover.

We had retained a small number of prisoners throughout the disturbance – largely the party of prisoners who worked in the staff mess. We had found them temporary dormitory accommodation in one of the workshops and they were extremely helpful by their positive attitude. Our staff mess was outside the walls so had escaped the impact of the riot. It had been extremely busy for the duration of the riot so the contribution of prisoners was appreciated. Staff went to considerable trouble to see that the prisoners were able to get their visits and their other normal entitlements. Consequently Strangeways never closed – we retained a very small number of prisoners throughout the period of the riot and beyond.

Twenty years later, I heard of an incident involving our staff collecting prisoners from Winchester Prison shortly after the riot. The Manchester staff were having a meal with Winchester staff and a senior member of the Winchester staff was apparently very critical of the way I had handled the riot. One of my officers was outraged by this and she told the critic his fortune.

The next day, returning to Winchester to pick up the prisoners, the Manchester staff went into reception – and were surprised to find the critic there. He apologised profusely for what he had said – the Governor of Winchester then appeared and congratulated the Manchester staff on their loyalty. It was remarkable to hear of this incident so long afterwards and humbling to know how loyal the staff had been.

I held a final news conference to mark the end of the riot. When pressed about the decision not to attack on 2nd April, I made it clear that this was a matter for the Woolf inquiry.

I also held a separate conference with the religious press to reflect on the issue of "Evil" during the riot. The Strangeways riot was a testing time for us all. Reflecting on what had happened, I was conscious of the power of God as we struggled against appalling and mindless violence creating chaos and suffering. The riot felt – on occasions – as if a struggle between good and evil was being acted out. Staying grounded in my faith helped me through the longest siege in British penal history.

We heard that a decision about redeveloping the site was to be taken by ministers during the early part of May. An announcement was finally made on 17th May. I had an uncomfortable end to the day when Minister David Mellor complained about me saying things to the local media welcoming the decision – apparently pre-empting an interview he was to give in London. In fact I had cleared with the press office that I could talk to the local media at the time that I did – but I had an anxious Sir Clive Whitmore on the phone about the issue.

The decision was to refurbish all the cellular accommodation in the prison including installing integral sanitation. The gate was to be moved to the west side of the prison making use of the newly acquired land. Other supporting facilities would be provided including new visit rooms and a new administration block. This brought huge relief to the staff as the future became clearer. But many staff would not be required for some time so we encouraged anyone who wanted to apply for a transfer. Over 100 staff moved to other establishments during the summer of 1990.

Before the Woolf Inquiry, I took a week off in the Isle of Man. From the moment we drove on to the Steam Packet ferry, I was given tremendous support from crew members and later from the locals who knew us in Port St Mary. By the time I returned to face three weeks of Woolf hearings in Manchester, I was ready to deal with the challenges ahead.

When the Woolf Inquiry hearings were over, I had to decide what to do next. At Strangeways there was to be a period of recovery and reconstruction – the plan was to get the remand prison functioning as quickly as possible. Around 300 prisoners could be housed at Strangeways while a major building programme – taking a number of years – was delivered. A very senior Governor was not required – and I knew that I urgently needed a change from Strangeways – there were too many difficult memories associated with the establishment.

Pressure was applied for me to accept a post on promotion to Assistant Director of Prisons at HQ. A move to London, away from my wife and family, was not a sensible way to recover from what I had experienced. My colleague Ian Boon, Governor of Risley, accepted promotion to Assistant Director, creating a vacancy at Risley. This was much closer to my home in Warrington, so there were many advantages. The most important reason was that I wanted to recover my confidence by demonstrating that – after all the stress of Strangeways – I could continue to govern a prison effectively. When you have fallen off your bike, it can be sensible to get up and ride again as soon as possible! So I applied to transfer to Risley.

The Service should have done more to learn lessons from the riot. The reason for the failure to review was probably the looming Woolf Inquiry. Interesting operational lessons from the riot, consequently, were never fully explored. For the first three days the police helicopter, hovering over the prison, provided important information about what the prisoners on the roof were doing. The value of the helicopter, because we had communications with it from the prison control room, made a helpful difference. This was never evaluated. Given the possibility of using police helicopters or police drones in future serious disturbances to provide intelligence on rioting prisoners, this was an opportunity lost.

There was no evaluation of the siege from the decision to abort the attack on 2nd April until 25th April. This was a difficult and testing period and the lessons from the 3 weeks of "stalemate" should have been carefully examined to try to avoid any future repetition. Why did it take so long to obtain the "Green Goddess" fire engines to use within the prison? Fourteen years earlier, the staff at Hull obtained an Army vehicle to protect staff in two days! I am sure this delay was never properly reviewed. Exceptional challenges like Strangeways will occur very infrequently – the need for training and preparation for major emergencies is crucial – and that includes learning lessons from the past.

Over the next few years I was asked to talk about my experience of managing a major incident by a wide cross section of organisations. This gave me the chance to reflect on the riot. I also continued to read accounts of other unrelated disasters, looking for common themes and common lessons. Almost always there are huge problems with communications – the 2017 Manchester Arena Bomb Inquiry highlighted the complete failure of a critical helpline.

I was very surprised at the lack of official recognition for the gallantry of some of the staff who performed heroically, rescuing trapped staff and prisoners. On occasions the staff were exposed to acute and very serious risks but they carried on despite the dangers. It was their work that enabled us to evacuate the vulnerable prisoners who had been assaulted and the staff may well have saved lives by their actions. Despite numerous requests to HQ over a number of years, I was unsuccessful in gaining adequate recognition for staff bravery.

30. THE WOOLF REPORT

The Inquiry Report was published in February 1991. I had been heavily involved in both Part One and Part Two of the Inquiry. Part One, the inquiry into the disturbances, sat for 3 weeks in public in Manchester taking evidence and I attended every day. I gave evidence for some 10 hours, a difficult and demanding experience. The Home Office was represented by experienced QCs and I was grateful that the PGA also had a strong legal team to ensure that our Governors were treated fairly.

The conclusions of the Woolf Report include the following about the responsibility of the management and staff at Strangeways for the conditions that led to the riot:

"The conditions which contributed to the antagonism of the majority of the inmates towards the prison system in general was not the responsibility of the staff and management of the prison. Well led by the Governor, Mr O'Friel, the overwhelming majority had done their best to improve the position of the inmates. However in addition to the undermining of what they had achieved as a result of the additional pressures to which the prison was subjected in the period leading up to the disturbance, the management and staff at the prison were faced with immense problems due to the failure of Governments in the past to provide the resources to the Prison Service which were needed to enable the Service to provide for an increased population in a humane manner. The long overdue improvements in the prison which were recognised as being needed at the time of the riot should already have been implemented."

Above: Lord Justice Woolf with Gordon Lakes.

Woolf also commented on the handling of the riot:

"Especially after Mr O'Friel had taken command, the staff's behaviour was commendable."

Woolf addressed the question of decision taking between HQ and locally:

"The person in command at HQ ...should recognise that his role is primarily supportive and supervisory although in the final analysis he has the right of veto in relation to particular proposed action. He can also, if this is necessary, replace the commander at the establishment."

The Woolf Report was a remarkable document. In some 600 pages, Woolf set out a very careful balanced analysis of what was wrong with the Service and suggests in a series of key recommendations how things should be put right.

On the first page of the Report, Woolf began by asking two questions:

Why did the riots not happen earlier?

And

Why were the consequences of those riots not even more serious?

And then answers the questions as follows:

"Members of the Prison Service as a whole, against heavy odds, have managed over a number of years to contain an almost impossible situation by showing immense dedication, courage and professionalism."

His analysis of what was at the root of the problems of the service was:

"It is possible to identify one principal thread which links these cause and complaints and which draws together all our proposals and recommendations. It is that the Prison Service must set security control and justice in prisons at the right level and it must provide the right balance between them. The stability of the prison system depends on the Prison Service doing so."

Woolf continued:

"There is a fundamental lack of respect and a failure to give and require responsibility at all levels in the prison system."

The Woolf Report set out a set of recommendations to reduce the risk of further disturbances and to provide a way of radically improving the Service over future years. The Government responded to these recommendations by publishing a White Paper "Custody, Care and Justice" later in 1991 followed by a programme of improvements.

The Woolf Report has often been hailed as an important turning point for the Prison Service. Without the disturbances, the Woolf Report would not have happened. That is true, but it is also important to balance the benefits that flowed from the Woolf Report against the sufferings of so many in and after the prison disturbances of 1990. Staff were injured and many were subsequently displaced, having to move themselves and their families away from Manchester. The scars – mental and physical – of what took place remained with many staff for the rest of their lives. Prisoners suffered immensely as the lost prisoner places at Strangeways resulted in Manchester prisoners being dispersed across the country making it difficult to remain in touch with family and friends. The negative consequences of what happened are substantial and must be borne in mind when reviewing the significance, importance and benefits flowing from the Woolf Report.

The rioters' fate

Following the riot there was an extensive police investigation and prosecution of the rioters. Attempts were made to bring charges relating to the death of the vulnerable prisoner Derek White, but these failed because of the lack of reliable witnesses and the possibility that Mr White had died from a pre-existing condition.

There were a number of trials.

In April 1992, four of the rioters were sentenced. Paul Taylor received a 10 year sentence with the others given shorter sentences.

On 2nd March 1993, a further trial of more of the Strangeways rioters concluded. Eleven of them were jailed for a total of 88 years including 10 year sentences for Alan Lord, Kevin Gee and Glyn Williams.

Judge Michael Sachs is reported to have said to the rioters:

"It is only by the providence of God that worse injuries were not sustained by those trying to recover the jail. Your complaints about the regime real or imagined could not excuse any of you taking part in the longest, most expensive and most violent prison riot in the history of this country."

Another 26 rioters were dealt with, following plea bargaining, by pleading guilty to lesser charges. The last trial directly related to the riot took place in September 1993 involving one defendant. However, there were two escapes from custody involving 7 prisoners who had been rioters which resulted in their being returned to court to face justice after re-capture. Finally there was further court action against 2 defendants in 1994 for attempting to pervert the course of justice.

31. RISLEY PRISON 1990-1995

Background

In September 1990, I arrived at Risley ready for my own "Fresh Start". Risley had experienced a serious riot in 1989, the year before Strangeways, so the staff at Risley knew that I understood what they had been through. The Risley riot included an incident when two officers were trapped in a cell inside D wing over which the rioting prisoners had control. The prisoners attempted to break into the cell. Only swift action by other staff by breaking into the cell from outside saved the two officers from being taken hostage or worse. Many staff witnessed the incident. One officer, several years later, told me of his feelings during the incident with tears in his eyes, evidence of the lasting stress violent incidents often cause.

Above: Women's Governor Madeline Moulden briefing Lord Justice Woolf at Risley.

Risley was constructed on the site of a former Royal Naval shore base, HMS Ariel, built before 1939. Risley was part of the building programme of new purpose built remand centres envisaged in the 1959 White Paper "Penal Practice in a Changing Society" – and was opened in 1965. The design was flawed with very poor sight lines for staff supervision. There was no integral sanitation in the very small cells. Rising numbers resulted in cells becoming overcrowded with each small cell holding 2 prisoners. There were few activity facilities and what was available was totally inadequate for the population Risley was expected to contain. Consequently, Risley's staff and prisoners had endured a torrid existence for many years. Suicides, overcrowding, poor conditions and a lack of regime all contributed to the failure of the establishment. There had been one dreadful incident on 14th April 1978 in one of the young offenders' dormitories in D Wing when a prisoner, David Evans, was murdered by four of his fellow young offenders. What a legacy.

Physically Risley was very different from Strangeways, reflecting the fact that it was not in the centre of a built up area but rather on the site of a sprawling former naval facility. There was plenty of space within the perimeter wall; many of our buildings were single storey and none of the buildings were above 3 storeys high. The site had considerable potential.

The 1989 riot was followed by an inquiry by Ian Dunbar, a Regional Director. He recommended Risley's closure. After much debate at HQ, it was decided to retain the establishment but to change it into a training prison. The hope was to consign to history the grim nickname of "Grisly Risley", a reflection on the suicides and other incidents for which the establishment had become notorious. The change also meant a huge building programme – just what I had campaigned for at Strangeways! So there would be considerable opportunities to significantly improve Risley – an opportunity which I was keen to exploit.

The decision to change Risley into a training prison ignored the existence of the women's unit. Since Risley opened, the women's remand unit had crammed too many women into poor accommodation with few supporting facilities. I had not worked with women prisoners before so that was a new challenge.

Risley had another interesting dimension. One of the accommodation units housed vulnerable prisoners and the plan was to develop an integrated regime where both ordinary and vulnerable prisoners (VPs) shared the common facilities around the prison. After the savagery meted out to some of the VPs at Strangeways during the riot, I was keen to see if this could be made to work. I knew that one prison in the Midlands, Littlehey, had already launched a successful integrated regime.

Risley was built with 4 male wings, a female wing and a hospital. One of the male wings was severely damaged in the 1989 riot and had been demolished; the 3 remaining male wings were in poor condition. The plan was to replace all the accommodation with new "open" wings.

These were to be built on ground outside the existing perimeter wall and the existing wall then extended to bring the new accommodation within the perimeter. A total of three large accommodation blocks were planned – each subdivided to provide six living units for 96 prisoners each. No thought had been given to what was to be done about improving the women's accommodation – so I started to plan to use one of the new blocks under construction for the women. There was a point of principle here about equal treatment.

The female wing was much worse than the male accommodation – extremely cramped with much of the original classroom and activity space converted to dormitory use.

Establishing the integrated regime

When I took charge of Risley in September 1990, I was also Chair of the PGA. Trying to ensure I gave sufficient attention to both tasks was a considerable challenge. Inevitably there was an overlap between management and PGA issues, so parts of Chapter 34 (PGA 1990-1995) will include references to my management work at Risley.

On arrival, I found that all the prisoners were in poor accommodation. Building work was in progress but it would be over a year before staff and prisoners would benefit from the new accommodation with integral sanitation. We were committed to launching our integrated regime for ordinary prisoners and VPs. While they would live in separate accommodation blocks all activities would be open to all the male prisoners. The new integrated regime began just weeks after my arrival and worked remarkably well. By February 1991, we had 300 prisoners in the integrated regime in the training prison.

The success of the new integrated regime owed much to a programme of staff training for most staff before the new regime was launched. This was the work of one of my Governors, Paul Norbury, working closely with the Senior Probation Officer. It included explaining in detail what the plan was; it provided staff with the chance to question the practicalities of delivering the plan and exploring with management the challenges they faced. This did much to bring on board the less enthusiastic members of staff – something I had been unable to do at Strangeways before "Fresh Start" in 1987 because of the totally inadequate allowance of time for staff training.

The prisoners, while security-categorised as "C", were generally serving medium and long sentences, up to 15 years. The range of offences reflected the length of sentences imposed by the courts. Many of the VPs were sex offenders and some had committed very serious offences.

What were my hopes and plans for the Risley regime? To counteract the dangers of offenders leaving prison worse than when they entered, prison regimes need to have a number of features:

- Offending behaviour programmes
- Education – especially basic education
- Skill training to increase employability
- Opportunities to repay society through voluntary work
- Sufficient activity to keep prisoners fully occupied

I was determined that we would deliver positive regimes at Risley. What were the opportunities for delivering a positive regime in practice?

The hospital building offered new and interesting opportunities as it was no longer required for medical use. It was transformed into an "Activities Centre", including a number of CIT and Vocational Training Courses leading to NVQ qualifications. Courses in Tiling and Painting, Industrial Cleaning and Storekeeping, Hairdressing, Desk Top Publishing and Computing were all to be set up.

There was a newly converted Education Centre of 70 places, with art and craft rooms, a catering classroom and multi-purpose classrooms. Around this time, the Service made significant changes to the way education was delivered as groups of Further Education Colleges were invited to compete to provide the service we required. Implementing this change, especially when staff who had taught for many years at Risley found themselves under threat of redundancy, was challenging but the outcome was an improved service to prisoners. This was of huge importance in offering them opportunities to increase their basic skills of literacy and numeracy, factors that we knew would lessen the chance of their re-offending. In subsequent years after I had retired, the provision of health services was contracted out to local NHS Trusts so the trend to use specialist providers has continued. Associated with education was our library, run by Peter Creer, an experienced officer who originated from the Isle of Man. Peter was supported by library expertise provided by our local libraries and by prisoners who became proficient librarians.

Physical Education was in the hands of an enthusiastic staff team, but the facilities were very limited. The old and very small camp theatre from the wartime naval base served as a makeshift gym while the stage area was all we had available for visits for our women prisoners. We managed to get funding for a new sports hall and turned the old one into a proper visiting room for the women although that took three years to deliver.

Management structure and staff

On arrival, I was struck by the lack of positive staff feeling about the establishment. There was a lack of evidence of achievement and a striking lack of ownership. Not even a Governors' Board, listing the previous Governors, or a staff photograph, let alone certificates or trophies of achievement, were to be seen. I was told that the staff had been too busy taking prisoners to court to grapple with the task of improving the establishment. At least I inherited an excellent Governor's office – large and with decent views of the establishment. A great contrast to the office at Strangeways which was cramped and without any view at all.

I looked carefully at the existing management structure and tried to clarify responsibilities and ensure duties were properly shared around. I continued my usual approach of spending time around the prison talking to everyone and learning as much as I could about the establishment. In particular, as we had far less prisoners than at Strangeways, I took my share of dealing with the more difficult prisoners – spending more time than I had ever been able to at Strangeways listening and talking. This clearly signalled to the staff what was expected of them – and for many of the staff – having worked as remand centre officers for many years – building up relationships with prisoners was a new experience and required new skills. The staff had a good laugh at me one evening when I was cornered during my evening visit by a particularly talkative young man, Kevin, with quite severe learning difficulties – I walked around with him for half an hour to be shown where he had spotted birds nesting. But this showed the staff that I was prepared to be a listener and – as some of them put it afterwards – I had saved other staff from having their ears bent about the birds' nests! Kevin incidentally went on to gain an NVQ in industrial cleaning, a quite remarkable achievement given his disability.

Two of my former Strangeways staff joined me at Risley – Pat Nolan on promotion to Deputy Governor and Stan Plater, who had been a great co-ordinator of the prison workshops and quickly adapted to a wider range of prison activities including organising "working out" opportunities for suitable candidates. These two contributed considerably to making Risley a successful establishment.

On arrival at Risley I was rather appalled to find that the staff sickness rates were worse than Strangeways had been. I was told that this was partly the result of having a large contingent of women officers. However, investigation into the extent of the problem uncovered a fairly unpleasant truth – many of those who were taking excessive sick leave had been doing so for many years; there had been insufficient management action to address the problem – I found that I could not even rely on the statistics when I first arrived as they understated the problem. However in five years we reduced the average sick absence from 23 days a year to 15. We retired many staff that were no longer able to meet the requirements of the modern Prison Service.

Staff sickness absence was a national problem for the Service. As I set out in Chapter 26, the National Audit Office became interested in sickness absence in the Service and eventually in 1999 produced a report on "Managing Absence in the Prison Service". It was a critical report and revealed that the overall absence rate of the Service was around 14 days per prison officer. I was disappointed – but not surprised – that the Service had failed to adequately brief the NAO about the many years of effort that had already gone into trying to address the problem as set out in Chapters 22 and 26. Nor had the NAO picked up on the importance of recognising the efforts of staff with an excellent attendance record.

Much of what I introduced to change the culture towards sick absence was based on what I had found had worked at Strangeways. Absences were carefully monitored and recorded and middle managers were encouraged to have a "Return to Work" interview with staff that had been off sick. The Senior Management Team regularly reviewed the establishment's list of sick absentees and confirmed that action was being taken where appropriate. One area where we made some useful progress was in organising a phased return to work for those who had been off sick for a substantial period of time – staff had often lost confidence and felt out of touch. Coming straight back into supervising prisoners could be challenging at the best of times so after a period in hospital and ongoing concerns about health any staff member needed careful support. Phased return to work brought a number of staff back successfully enabling them to pick up their career and to contribute again to the work of the establishment. Letters of appreciation were introduced for those staff who had a full attendance record for the previous year. We published the sick absence statistics for the establishment to educate staff about the problem.

We also kept in touch with anyone off sick for more than a few weeks. Managers would visit to provide support and to ensure we were doing as much as we could. Some staff were off sick following assaults and needed help to rebuild their confidence. On occasions I became directly involved. In April 1995, I saw three staff and arranged a phased programme of gradual return to duty. Within a few months all three were undertaking their full range of duties.

Visits to those off sick also ensured that we were not being given inaccurate information. Some years previously, before managers paid regular visits, a Governor and Chief Officer decided to visit a member of staff off sick for weeks with a bad back. They went without prior warning. When they found the individual on the roof of his house replacing slates, the game was up and the Chief Officer told him to report for duty the next day. Abuse of sick leave by a small minority of staff was a feature of the Prison Service and it had to be actively discouraged.

Risley had well established computer systems for maintaining prisoner information. No card indexes and books such as I had found at Strangeways on arrival. It also had Fresh Start arrangements in place although there was plenty to do to ensure that the cultural changes needed to get full value from Fresh Start were developed effectively.

The POA had treated Risley as two establishments since it opened – a male and a separate female establishment. There were two POA committees representing the male and the female parts of the prison. Male staff had been deployed to the female prison but no women officers had been allowed to work with the men. I made it clear that this was going to change and although it took time and effort, we got there reasonably quickly by talking issues through and giving the male POA some time to adjust to the changing world. Unlike at Manchester, I had Principal and Senior Officers on the female prison who wanted experience of working with the men. This meant that the male staff had to adjust to having women managers as well as colleagues. We soon had about 15% female staff in the male prison and about 25% male staff in the female prison.

We had a similar reaction from the prisoners as at Manchester. Mixed staffing made a big difference; behaviour improved and the whole prison became more civilised. I was interested to find out how the male officers were faring in the women's wing and again we had clear evidence that mixed staffing produced better behaviour among women prisoners. We had to be particularly sensitive to the fact that a huge proportion of women offenders had suffered abuse from men in their lives before prison so male staff needed to be very aware and careful when working with women prisoners.

Opening new accommodation

We decided to utilise the first new accommodation blocks for the men in the training prison and to organise the accommodation into four "House" units, each with a name. I encouraged the use of well-known prison reformers. John Howard had written his seminal book on "The State of the Prisons" in Warrington with a plaque to prove it in the town centre! We decided to use Howard, Fox, the Chairman of the Commission after World War Two; Paterson, another Commissioner who also had connections with Cheshire; and Vidler, an interesting Governor from the 1950s whose book "If Freedom Fail" records the way prisons and borstals worked during his time.

When the new accommodation was ready for opening, I invited Lord Justice Woolf to visit and perform the ceremony. To our great delight, he accepted and spent much of the day going round the prison seeing the work that staff and prisoners were doing. This was a valuable boost to morale, one of a number of visits which helped Risley to change its culture.

As soon as these units came on stream we were able to build up the male population to 384 as we had more accommodation. In January 1993, we opened the fifth of the house units, named "Churchill", as a multipurpose unit with a segregation facility and a pre-release/resettlement unit for prisoners close to being discharged.

The move into the new accommodation blocks freed up the accommodation in the old A Wing which had previously been occupied by the VPs. We were soon under pressure to take more prisoners and in early 1993, we set up another separate prison within Risley to hold convicted men awaiting sentence. We were asked to accommodate 100 prisoners but within a short time we had to increase this to 180. Physical changes to achieve reasonable separation from the rest of the regime had to be made but we quickly delivered 180 additional places. We named the new unit the Transpennine Allocation Centre (the TAC) – and a Governor, David Brown, took charge and started to develop the regime.

Prisoner activities

One of the training courses that I had inherited at Featherstone was an excellent Industrial Cleaning Course leading to an NVQ. I was delighted to have another of these courses at Risley which catered for a wide range of academic abilities and an even wider range of people. The course built ownership of high standards – I was fascinated to watch the course working to restore part of the prison to a high standard of cleanliness with the course members telling off any passing member of staff who dared to walk on their recently cleaned floor! Perhaps just as importantly, the staff recognised the value of the prisoners having this commitment to their work and took the comments in good part.

Within months we were starting to see results from the Education and Skill Training Programmes as prisoners achieved academic success and NVQs. I tried to present certificates whenever I was available to mark the importance of what prisoners achieved. For some of them, this was the first time they had achieved any qualification and the improvement in confidence resulting from achievement was encouraging. We were slowly changing their expectations and this was another important step towards reducing re-offending.

Offending behaviour programmes included attempts to improve prisoners' ability to consider the consequences of their actions – "Think First". Many offences were committed under the influence of drugs and alcohol; many without any thought or evaluation of the risks and penalties of committing criminal acts.

Deterrence is a very uncertain policy with offenders – but there are plenty of other ways of reducing re-offending. It has always been thus – there are reports of thefts taking place among the crowds gathered for public executions of those sentenced to death for stealing.

Risley was one of the first prisons to run the Sex Offender Treatment Programme. Under the direction of our Principal Psychologist, nine trained prison officers delivered the programme with strong support from our multi-disciplinary back-up team. We also introduced programmes to address anger management and drug and alcohol offending. The anger management programme was particularly impressive as we were soon seeing results in the establishment. On the one hand some difficult prisoners noticeably improved their behaviour. On the other, the expertise of the course tutors was so respected by other staff that they would ask for assistance from their colleagues if dealing with a confrontation. Staff skills at defusing these occasional episodes were considerable.

Several years later in 1998/99, Professor Alison Liebling of Cambridge led a small team to study the work of staff at Whitemoor maximum security prison. The resulting description of critical officer skills in managing and defusing tensions is remarkably like the staff performance that I had observed at Risley, although we were working with a less challenging prisoner population. The talents of talk, peace keeping and discretion were usually described by staff as "common sense". Professor Liebling notes that if at the end of the day nothing had happened, this is due to the skills and abilities of staff in defusing and handling potentially difficult situations. There is an interesting echo here of the extract from the Woolf Report in Chapter 30 about why the disturbances had not occurred earlier and not been more serious. The staff skills that Professor Liebling observed and recorded take years of experience and training to develop. Inexperienced staff cannot be expected to deliver such good results.

Improving conditions for women prisoners

In my first annual report I noted that "the female accommodation was dreadful – I had never seen such overcrowded dormitories". This in turn had reduced the room for activities, making a rather spartan regime even worse.

Working with women offenders was a new challenge as I had very limited previous experience of women's establishments. The number of very young women was troubling; the extent to which drugs played a part in their offending and their lives was extraordinary. We occasionally found ourselves with three generations of offenders, as when one young woman came dashing down one of the corridors in the women's wing to announce to her friends "My Granny is in Reception"!

While there were far fewer women prisoners in the whole system – usually considerably less than 10% of the total prison population – the women who ended up in custody were generally much more damaged and disturbed than the male population. A huge proportion had been drug abusers; had been sexually or physically assaulted, and a very high proportion had significant mental health problems. They needed particular care and attention not because they were likely to riot; it was much more likely that they would self-harm. A positive active regime is vital for all prisoners but doubly so for women prisoners. Anything that helps improve their self-respect and gives them opportunities to achieve can make a huge difference to women prisoners.

I was fortunate that after a year, Governor Madeline Moulden arrived to run the women's prison and she quickly began the work of transforming both conditions and attitudes. One of her first projects was to convert one room into a decent common room for the women, with comfortable furniture. This was appreciated by both prisoners and staff and demonstrated in a small way how we could start to improve conditions for everyone. We allocated one of the new cell blocks to the women which they occupied in 1992 and this transformed their lives in many ways and eliminated overcrowding at a stroke. We consulted the staff about a name for the new wing and it became "Butler House" after RAB Butler and the Butler Trust.

Butler House freed up the rooms in the old women's prison from dormitories to be returned to classroom and activity use. We also realised that we had the opportunity to upgrade the old cellular accommodation in the women's prison and use it as an incentive for the better behaved prisoners with a more relaxed regime. This became Windsor House with room for 34 prisoners, and was very well looked after by prisoners. Together with the 30 places we had in Health Care, the women's prison could now take 160 without overcrowding.

We obtained portacabins next to the women's prison to increase the number and range of activities. I was delighted when the staff set up a pre-release course for women giving them experience of job interviews, and other practical skills.

There was a tradition in the women's prisons that the prisoners were often referred to as "girls". Madeline Moulden strongly challenged this use of "girls" – a legitimate approach as it made us all think more carefully about treating the women prisoners as individuals. There was a wide range of ages, although many of the women were teenagers.

The very high turnover of the unit was a constant problem as we were serving the courts. In a nine month period in 1994, we had around 3500 movements in and out. Some of these would be the same prisoners but the work of coping with an ever-changing group of prisoners was a considerable challenge to our staff.

After Madeline Moulden departed for other challenges, Katie Dawson joined us to take charge and continued to build up a more positive regime for the women. She also wrote and published novels.

There was a long history of prisons containing both male and female prisoners from the nineteenth century in quite separate accommodation. When the remand centre building programme started around 1960, several remand centres were built with both male and female accommodation. Some of these establishments had a small amount of combined activity facilities – for example at Low Newton education classes and chapel services were often combined.

We decided to try and integrate the women's prison rather more closely into the rest of the establishment in order to increase opportunities for the women prisoners to access good quality regime activities, especially within the Education Block. We allowed the women access to the well-equipped cookery classroom in the Education Block. We also allowed the occasional and very carefully selected woman to join other educational activities where the case for doing so was strong. We had occasional special events in the prison principally for the male prisoners but we also considered whether it was reasonable to allow selected women access to those activities. Visits from an organisation with large birds of prey is one example – this sort of activity was a way of broadening their experience and it helped break the sheer monotony of life for prisoners serving long sentences. The hairdressing NVQ course occasionally asked if a group of women would like to have their hair done and this happened from time to time – a benefit to both groups of offenders. I kept this development under very close scrutiny indeed, recognising that it was innovative but needed to be carefully managed to avoid problems.

Women's prisons – very properly – had separate security keys and in those establishments where both male and female prisoners were kept, separate suites of security keys were used so that any member of staff with male security keys could not access the female part of the prison. Among the changes we brought in was to combine the two different sets of security keys at the main gate of the prison; previously the female security keys were kept in the women's prison itself.

Some of our women prisoners appeared to be in prison for relatively minor offences. Jailing people for non-payment of TV licences and other "civil" offences such as non-payment of fines is a misuse of prison. Other means of collecting fines need to be developed so that anyone who genuinely cannot pay a fine is dealt with by a less costly and less damaging way than imprisonment.

In 1995, the Penal Affairs consortium published rather startling figures about fine defaulters. In 1994, 22,723 were imprisoned for non-payment of fines. This was a rise of 36% on the number imprisoned in 1990.

As Governor of Risley, I became aware, through the briefing by staff in our women's unit, of examples of the disgraceful imprisonment of women for non-payment of fines, especially non-payment of TV licences. We arranged for suitable cases to be quickly referred for legal advice. Did this have any impact? A solicitor, Richard Wise, wrote to me in August 1995 as follows:

"In three recent cases Lord Justice Balcolm and Mr Justice Buxton were highly complimentary of the systems invoked by HMP Risley to identify appropriate cases of potentially unlawful and unnecessary imprisonment, in particular among vulnerable women and how they could be avoided. In particular the Courts were impressed with the speed, training and commitment shown by the prison in seeking appropriate legal advice for the prisoner and avoiding further distress."

This demonstrates that local action can achieve much. This was a well-deserved compliment for our hard working staff.

Suicide prevention

As previously explained, the main reason Risley was known as "Grisly Risley" was the many deaths by suicide over the years it had been a remand centre. Changing the culture included doing everything we could to reduce the dangers of suicides. This was especially true of the women's unit in which we continued to hold remand prisoners who were especially vulnerable.

In trying to prevent suicides, good relationships with staff, active regimes and a readiness to be flexible in our approach all played a part. We introduced the use of trained inmate "listeners" under the auspices of the Samaritans;

we worked hard to ensure those at greatest risk were quickly identified and we actively developed the regime wherever we could. An example was that our nursing staff, who worked with very vulnerable women, brought in a large white rabbit and this animal attracted the attention and affection of a number of our most disturbed women and helped them to survive a really difficult period in their lives.

The results were encouraging. We had no suicides in the women's prison in the five years that I was there – although we had some "near misses" where only very prompt staff action prevented a tragedy. One male prisoner committed suicide during that period and when we reviewed all the circumstances we could find nothing that would have given us prior warning. The evidence was that Risley had changed for the better.

Visitors

I had kept in touch with the Isle of Man Prison Governor and the Island's Department of Home Affairs. In April 1991 I arranged a short visit to Risley for a Manx Committee of Inquiry set up to examine a serious incident at Victoria Road Prison. Gordon Lakes, who had been an Assessor to the Woolf Inquiry, came along to meet the Committee so that they had the opportunity to consider the Isle of Man Inquiry against the background of the Woolf Report. While at Risley, they were able to admire the Manx-made "Viking Boat" on my office wall!

Above: Governor's office at Risley with Manx Viking ship.

On 9th July 1992, we received a lengthy visit of over 2 hours from the Princess Royal, which was a splendid morale boost. We had a good number of staff nominated for Butler Trust Awards with several receiving awards from HRH at Buckingham Palace and at Holyrood. This was valuable evidence of the changing staff culture as more staff took up opportunities for improving the prison. Around the prison there was increasing evidence of achievement, a very welcome change from the lack of ownership I found on arrival in 1990.

Above: HRH Princess Anne with SOPEI Kate Hall and Instructor Mike Chidzey, Butler Trust Award winners.

Chaplaincies and other developments

We encouraged involving the prisoners in problem solving within the prison. A prisoner who had become a Buddhist – he was originally from Liverpool and had a familiar Liverpool name – approached me to explain that in his opinion what Risley needed was a "Buddha Statue". I asked him why and he provided a reasonable answer. I explained that if he wanted this change he must contribute to achieving it. This was a new idea to him and after a couple of weeks he came to see me again and asked what I was doing about the Buddha statue. I explained carefully that if he wanted it, he must help achieve this. We had a conversation about what he needed to do. He believed the Buddhist Minister could obtain a statue – but where should it go? Among trees outside, he thought. So I suggested he talk to the staff that organised the gardens to see if they might agree.

We got our Buddha statue – and interestingly it was never vandalised. Occasionally a hat would appear on it but because the idea for the statue was a prisoner initiative, it meant that it was accepted and in part respected.

The final part of this story was when Fr Aiden Kelly, our very able RC Chaplain, told me that the prisoner concerned was no longer a Buddhist – he had discovered that the Buddhist Minister did not agree that taking drugs was acceptable behaviour within Buddhism!

A newly arrived notorious Liverpool prisoner sought me out to register his support. "I am pleased we have a Catholic Governor," Delroy told me, "and one educated at Ampleforth!" Not all our villains were well briefed!

We had one of the best prison chapels I had seen. Well-furnished and fit

*Above: A remarkable handmade clock being presented to
Archbishop Worlock and Bishop Shepherd by the maker.*   © *Catholic Pictorial.*

for purpose, it was ecumenical and well supported. In my time we added a
prayer room for the use of non-Christian faiths. The chapel acquired stained
glass windows while I was there; the windows were made in our own stained
glass workshop and funded by charitable donations from a variety of sources.
The windows were blessed and dedicated by the Bishop of Lincoln who took
a special interest in matters penal for the Anglicans. Shortly after the windows
were installed, we had a visitation from Archbishop Derek Worlock and Bishop
David Shepherd from Liverpool. They spent the best part of a day at the prison
talking to staff and prisoners and left us all much strengthened and uplifted
by their interest and advice.

I continued my usual practice of often attending Mass in the prison. This was
always a great learning experience because prisoners constantly surprised
me by their approaches and attitudes. In November 1995, one of my last Mass
attendances was shortly after the birth of our first grandchild, Emily. Three
women prisoners approached Barbara and me after Mass to present an outfit
they had knitted for the new baby. Many prisoners care deeply about people as
this touching gesture showed. I had learned a great deal in the 30 years I had
worked with prisoners and the most important principle was that prisoners are
very like the rest of humankind – good and bad, but certainly not a race apart.
Each one needed to be treated individually, justly and with dignity. Prisoners
learned from us but we also learned from them as their faith and approach, on
occasions, was quite remarkable.

We organised a number of Conferences at Risley for interested groups of people and included prisoners among the Conference Speakers to ensure that the perspective of the prisoners was articulated to wider audiences. For example in 1991, I encouraged one of our long term prisoners at Risley to share his experiences with a Conference of Prison Visitors. Austin had this to say:

"Imprisonment reinforces the prisoner's criminal inclinations by introducing him to like-minded people.... it reinforces the prisoner's resentment and hostility towards anyone who attempts to discipline him and relieves him of all responsibility for his own existence. The prison environment exposes each prisoner to a high degree of criminal influences."

At another Conference, a woman prisoner was one of the speakers and her description of the impact of imprisonment was very telling:

"Among women prisoners and particularly those who are mothers thoughts of our children and families seldom leave our minds. We worry about our children – are they all right? Are they being well looked after – will they forget us? Will they forgive us for leaving them? But prisoners' families are about more than children, important though they are. It is also about husbands and wives, about mothers and fathers and grandparents, some of whom may be elderly and have very real fears that they may not live to see their son or daughter released."

One of the ways in which we were able to improve staff/prisoner relationships was by an increasing use of first names of prisoners. The women staff were especially good at this – an approach often used by staff dealing with women prisoners – and the women officers often used first names with the male prisoners. This probably encouraged some of the male staff who also used first names on occasions. We also encouraged the wearing by prisoners of their own clothes which was seen as much better by the prisoners – and removed the embarrassment for staff of trying to fit prisoners out in "institutional" clothing which was often ill-fitting.

Prisoners also benefitted from the introduction of pay phones as they could keep in touch with their relatives and friends. But this was not always a benefit. One prisoner had an especially difficult phone call with home and ended up smashing his fist into the wall with frustration – he had to be taken to hospital to have a broken bone set.

Much good work was done with individual cases. Occasionally I became directly involved in a difficult case – one of these involved a Nigerian sentenced for drug smuggling, who faced a very uncertain future if he was deported on release. The drugs cartel with whom he had been involved were out to kill him. I wrote to Doug Hoyle, Risley's local MP, about this case and eventually when the prisoner was released he was allowed to stay in the UK. Doug was very supportive and visited the establishment from time to time, showing great interest in the improvements we were delivering.

Prisoners were encouraged to take part in programmes where their efforts could help others, especially to assist people with disabilities. We developed a programme to bring people with severe disabilities to use some of our gymnasium facilities and a group of selected prisoners were trained to assist our visitors in using the gym equipment. Such experiences often had a profound effect on individual prisoners as they discovered how difficult and restricted life was for some other people – they would reflect afterwards about what they had learned and gained by helping others. We also developed a project for a number of prisoners to assist with riding for those with disabilities.

A range of activities developed through staff initiatives including a music group "Temporary Accommodation", the musicians a mix of staff and prisoners; allotments; occasional charity initiatives such as a sponsored bike ride by staff and prisoners.

Another unusual initiative was to use the experience of prisoners as a way of deterring young offenders from further offending. We developed and ran one such programme at Risley. There were two prisoners serving sentences from the Toxteth area of Liverpool at the time that two young children were killed by so-called "Joy Riders". Locally mothers set up an action group including temporarily blocking roads where they saw dangers from joy riders for their children.

The two prisoners approached me to ask if they could have some access to potential joy riders to warn them of the dangers – I suggested they talk to a couple of our officers who agreed to be involved in trying to set up a programme. With co-operation from the Police, Probation Service, Children's Services, the Toxteth Mothers and others, we established a programme which ran for several years and appeared to be having a positive impact – along with many other measures.

I was involved in trying to improve the behaviour of one of our very troubled young women. At the time there was growing evidence that diet influenced behaviour including some interesting work on this developed at Aylesbury Young Offenders Establishment. A balanced diet with fruit and vegetables had some beneficial impact on some prisoners' behaviour. This young woman wouldn't eat vegetables but would eat apples. I spent some time persuading our caterer that some exceptional treatment was in order and we arranged for her to get an increased amount of fruit. Her behaviour did improve – but that might have been as a result of the attention she was getting or some other apparently unrelated cause! We were ready to innovate; to individualise the approach of the staff to difficult prisoners and we saw some encouraging improvements in some difficult individuals.

My daughter Helen visited Risley. She was in her late twenties, and having spent some seven years travelling had seen a great deal of life. Returning to England, she was staying with us so I asked her if she would like to visit the prison. She agreed enthusiastically and spent the day with me walking around the prison, seeing the range of activities and gaining some idea of the culture of the establishment, especially the interaction between staff and prisoners. One of the older women prisoners spotted a family likeness and inquired if Helen was my daughter.

Another challenging issue emerged as restrictions on unlimited cigarette smoking started to come in – especially for visits. We introduced the change with some trepidation but prisoners coped and those who found it very difficult were allowed to use a small smoking room during a break in their visits. It was important to educate the prisoners not just to the dangers of smoking but also to encourage them to understand that the world was changing while they served their sentences. The tragic fire on the London Underground at King's Cross brought a smoking ban on the Underground and I made much of the changing attitude of society towards smoking in my daily contacts with prisoners. They were always ready to let me know of their concerns and grumbles about changes! Prisoners could be very conservative – with a small "C"!

We continued to look for ways to utilise our good facilities for the benefit of the wider service. Our new accommodation, although not specifically designed for this purpose, was ideal for prisoners with disabilities. Prisoners in wheelchairs or with artificial limbs needed special arrangements. I knew from my years at Strangeways how difficult life could be for such prisoners in a busy local prison full of stairs and different levels, totally unsuitable for anyone with serious mobility problems. We offered to take prisoners from other establishments – especially Victorian prisons – who had disabilities and started to build up staff expertise in managing these individuals.

The Prisons Inspectorate commented on the approach of our staff to the challenge of coping with prisoners with disabilities:

"The overall approach to the care of people with disabilities typified the attitude of Risley staff. They were responding to an issue in a positive and practical manner and at the same time promoting the independence and supporting the dignity of those involved."

The Inspectorate team reported speaking to one nearly blind prisoner who felt he had been considered a liability at other prisons: a person to be moved on because his needs were too demanding for the Prison Service to cope with. He was content at Risley. He had been found a job, felt that he was well looked after and was grateful because as his nearest relative lived at Exeter, he was allowed a 10 minute phone call in lieu of a visit. Small changes often made all the difference.

The Inspectorate team also praised some pioneering work we introduced to prepare prisoners for any home leave they might be granted. A pre-home leave course had been introduced in January 1994 and appeared to be making a difference. Of the 115 prisoners granted temporary release in 1993, 11 had failed to return; 108 had completed the course since then and only 3 had failed to return. The course was the result of discussions with staff and was organised and led by prison officers.

Costs

The figures for Risley for 1993/94 reveal that our total net budget was just over £13 million and our cost per prisoner per year was just under £20,000. Given that Risley's population included around 130 women remand prisoners, that figure was encouraging – as the average cost of women's prisons was just over £28,000.

Integrated regime under threat

The riot at Wymott in 1993 brought unwelcome and difficult consequences. The destruction and damage to accommodation at Wymott provoked a further population crisis especially as the impact of Michael Howard's "Prison Works" approach brought about an increase in prisoners. The Prison Service devised a plan to move more VPs into Wymott as soon as it could be repaired on the basis that this class of prisoner presented fewest risks of rioting. The VPs at Risley were seen as part of the population that could be transferred to Wymott. The implications for the integrated regime and the expertise we had developed in delivering the Sex Offender Treatment programme were largely ignored.

There was a determined attempt by the whole Risley community to resist this change. Prisoners wrote to their MPs; the Board of Visitors lobbied to retain the progress we had made; everyone played their part. It was a difficult time and I was highly unpopular at HQ for not being co-operative. Derek Lewis visited to see for himself what we had achieved and clearly was impressed as the Risley integrated regime got a positive mention in his book "Hidden Agendas". I remember the visit particularly well as it took place on my birthday 30th March and one of my colleagues organised a birthday cake when we were having a working lunch!

Inspection Report and departure

When the Prison Inspection Team visited in 1994 they had this to say about the integrated regime and the Sex Offenders Treatment Programme:

"Risley was one of the Establishments taking part in the Prison Service's national initiative on the treatment of sex offenders. At the time of our inspection, programmes for sex offenders had been running in the training prison for over 2 years.

"We were concerned that population pressures in the northwest might also cause the redistribution of vulnerable prisoners from Risley. We recommend that this is kept to a minimum because the integrated regime appears to be very successful and the sex offender treatment programme was the best we had seen during our inspections."

The integrated regime survived but it was a narrow escape. We did what we could to boost our numbers and play as full a part as possible in coping with the rising prison population. Consequently Risley housed well over 800 prisoners by the time I left.

The Report of the Inspection was published in April 1995 and concluded:

"The decision, following the riot, in 1990 to redevelop the site at Risley and to change the function of the male side of the prison from that of a Remand Centre to that of a Category C Training Prison was grasped with vision and enthusiasm by the Governor and staff. The ethos Risley had has been transformed from the 'Grisly Risley' image of the 1980s to one of a positive and innovative prison where staff and prisoners are encouraged to develop and participate in constructive programmes. The role of the women's prison has remained largely the same but the regime there has also been developed.

"Risley is well resourced but can boast of being a centre of excellence in its delivery of education, training courses, sex offender treatment programmes, offending behaviour groups, community work and pre-release training. An integrated regime for vulnerable and other prisoners has been developed successfully in the training prison and some gender mixing has been introduced. These innovations have been managed and monitored carefully.

"We left Risley with a feeling of optimism that the significant progress that had been made since the disturbances can continue. The Prison Service should foster that progress and should not allow it to be jeopardised by measures purely to cope with short operational and population pressures."

Looking back at some five years at Risley, I was encouraged by the great response from both staff and prisoners to opportunities for improvement and change. While it is always sensible to be cautious about achievement, I considered that much had changed for the better in the way prisoners responded to each other, especially the success of the integrated regime in developing positive relationships between ordinary offenders and sex offenders. The number of initiatives shown by staff in leading positive programmes of many kinds appeared to be making a real difference to prisoners' prospects after release.

We had documented and researched the impact of our programmes wherever we could and the research – conducted through our excellent Psychology Department – reinforced that we were making progress. But we did not have the follow-up research to study how prisoners survived after release. That is needed urgently in the future so that Governors can benefit from reliable feedback about what appears to be making a difference in reducing re-offending.

In September 1995, at the invitation of the Adullam Homes Housing Association, I delivered the first Walter Moore Memorial Lecture to an invited audience. Adullam worked effectively with discharged prisoners, one of the important voluntary organisations providing essential services to reduce offending.

In November 1995, I left Risley on promotion to Assistant Director at Headquarters. I left with considerable sadness as my years at Risley had been rewarding.

In early 1996, the opportunity was given to older senior prison staff – under a special scheme to help balance the Prison Service's budget – to retire early. Thirty-three years working in the Service, and especially the stresses and strains of the Strangeways riot, had taken their toll. I was very grateful to be able to depart in September 1996 and still be fit enough to take up other opportunities and interests.

Just before I retired I became an Honorary Fellow at Liverpool John Moores University. This was a remarkable experience, held at Liverpool's Anglican Cathedral in the presence of a large family gathering and many colleagues from the Service.

"I Wish"

Above: Manchester's senior team summer 1990 before dispersing.

Above: Risley's senior team 1995.

Above: PGA National Executive at Newbold Revel College 1989.

Above: John Moores Honorary Fellowship 1996. Front row – Pat Nolan, Arthur de Frisching, Brendan and Barbara, Robin Halward and back row – Tim Hewins, Gordon Hutchinson and Terry Bone.

RISLEY ACTIVITIES

Above: Sponsored cycling.

Above: Temporary Accommodation Group.

Above: Hairdressing NVQ.

Above: Word processing NVQ.

Above: Buddha statue.

Above: Great, great grandparents
Robert and Jane Cowley,
Sulby, Isle of Man. Taken around 1895.
© Manx National Heritage (PG/13554).

Right: Miss May O'Friel,
Dr Arthur O'Friel and
Mrs Phyllis Margaret O'Friel,
October 1964.

Left: Brendan,
Annie, Barbara
and Francis,
Seated – Helen,
Michael and Mary.

32. PRISON SERVICE LEADERSHIP

Background

Crucial to the success of large public organisations is leadership. This chapter considers aspects of leadership in the Service, both individual contributions and the structures within which leadership was exercised.

Until the 1877 Prisons Act, prisons were a local responsibility; when nationalised they were placed under the control of the "Prison Commission" which came under the jurisdiction of the Home Secretary. The Chairman of the Commission was a significant public figure: several served for many years and made substantial contributions to the Service. Chairmen generally came from military or civil service backgrounds. Sir Edmund Du Cane (1878–1895) was the first; Sir Lionel Fox (1942–1960) acquired a considerable reputation internationally for his knowledge of prisons, but as suggested in Chapter 17, may have failed to commit uniformed staff to the task of rehabilitating prisoners. Fox's address of 10th April 1959 to "Prison Commission and Home Office Staff" includes only passing reference to uniform staff and to overcrowding.

Visible leadership

From Mountbatten in 1966, a succession of reports criticised the lack of "visible leadership" in the Service. In response to Mountbatten, the top person became "Director General". Sir William Pile (1969–1970) was the first appointment and I found he was highly visible when visiting establishments.

Soon after the Mountbatten Report, a new "Inspector General" was also appointed. Brigadier Mark Maunsell (1967–1971), who had both military and commercial experience, arrived to improve "visible leadership". The Inspector General was a member of the Prisons Board and most Governors welcomed his interest and his regular visits to establishments. When the Brigadier retired, the post of Chief Inspector was given to an experienced Governor, Stanley Clarke 1971-1974.

Sir William Pile's successor as Director General, Mr WR Cox (1971–1973), was much less visible; he was followed by Eric Wright (1973–1977) and Denis Trevelyan (1977–1981) both of whom provided more visible leadership.

Policy and operations

Leadership and structural issues were complicated by divisions between "operations" and "policy". "Operations" was broadly described as "doing the business" – "Policy" as "thinking about the business".

Largely the preserve of civil servants, policy was about deciding the framework within which prisons should operate. It included advising the Minister, questions and statements to Parliament, developing new legislation and taking legislation through Parliament. Policy was regarded by some as of greater importance than operations: for civil servants seeking to further their career, experience of policy work was said to be crucial.

There was rarely a sensible integration of policy and operations. When an issue was being decided or reviewed, both operations and policy needed to be taken fully into account. For example, HQ decided, as a new priority, that staff needed more race relations training. But that decision was only deliverable if staff were able to undertake the training. Very often the resources for staff training were not there and HQ was not willing to face up to consequent difficult decisions. Could Governors close down activities to free up staff for training? Preferably not, would be the response from HQ! And when an incident occurred where a lack of staff training had been a cause of what had gone wrong, HQ would demand to know why training had not been delivered! Governors quickly learned they could not win!

So in practice, many issues could only be sensibly addressed by considering policy and operations together. But the emphasis for decades at HQ was on policy at the expense of operations. Yet the Service depended, as I have described in Chapter 15, on staff performing the basics well – but this was neither properly understood nor accepted at HQ. Managing routine work and encouraging the basics to be done well is a continuing challenge in any penal establishment. The PGA regularly raised this problem with HQ and it was highlighted in the 1994 Woodcock Report into the escapes from Whitemoor Prison:

"The more senior the manager the more necessary it is for him or her to concentrate on the change agenda. There was no space for senior people to spend time checking compliance with basic procedures."

This was a crucial structural weakness in the leadership and management of the Service.

The autonomy of the Service

The 1964 experiment of integrating the Prison Service into the Home Office failed and from 1980, following the May Report, the Service was gradually given greater autonomy – a development which eventually led to it becoming an "Executive Agency" in 1993.

In April 1980, following the May Inquiry, the post of Deputy Director General (DDG) was created as the professional or operational Head of the Service. Gordon Fowler, a very experienced Governor, was the first DDG. At the same time, the four

Above: Gordon Fowler, Deputy Director General 1980-1982.

Regional Directors joined the Prisons Board which gave it a more operational focus.

Other appointments included John Chilcott becoming Director of Personnel and Finance. This was a crucial change as the Service became responsible for its own staff. John Chilcott was succeeded by Eric Caines who played an important part in the negotiations to introduce Fresh Start.

Chapter 15 sets out the crucial importance of staff and how the period from the mid-1960s until Fresh Start in 1987 was bedevilled by dysfunctional shift systems and unsatisfactory and complex agreements which destroyed continuity and severely diminished job satisfaction. The 1980 changes to HQ structures marked the start of work to address the staffing problems and that eventually led to Fresh Start.

"Visible Leadership" was reduced when Chris Train was Director General from 1983 to 1991. While spending a good deal of time visiting establishments, Train did not undertake media appearances and the Service's public image suffered. Behind the scenes, however, Train enabled others to take forward the work on Fresh Start, including Gordon Lakes, DDG from 1985 to 1988. Gordon, working closely with Eric Caines, deserves much of the credit for ensuring Fresh Start was accepted and introduced.

Train encouraged another review of the structure of Prison Service HQ published in 1989 which recommended abolishing regions and introducing 15 "Areas". HQ was to be moved out of London to Derby, the move being expected around 1995. The question of the Service becoming a stand-alone Executive Agency would be further re-examined and more power would be delegated to Governors. The regional organisation was abolished in 1990, but the move to Derby was soon abandoned. It was too expensive – and money had to be saved from the Prisons Budget.

An Executive Agency

To take forward the suggestion of the Service becoming an Executive Agency, in 1991 Admiral Sir Raymond Lygo was asked to conduct a review of the management of the Service with the following terms of reference:

"To review the management effectiveness of the Prison Service both at HQ and at establishments, with particular reference to its management structures and personnel policies and to make recommendations."

Lygo reported in December 1991. His report begins by setting the scene:

"The Prison Service is the most complex organisation I have encountered and its problems some of the most intractable."

Lygo recommended many changes including:

- Prison Service should become an Agency
- Post of Director General to be filled by open competition

- The Agency should have a Management and a Supervisory Board
- Improved communications and more backing for Governors
- If no improvement in Industrial Relations, legislation should bring the Service into line with the police
- More devolution to Governors
- Governors to wear uniform
- Governors in charge should have longer in post

In March 1992 it was announced that the Prison Service would become an Agency from 1st April 1993 and that the Director General would be appointed by open competition.

Joe Pilling (1991–1992), who followed Train as Director General, made strenuous attempts to improve the Service's public image, but his term was very short as the next Home Secretary, Ken Clarke, was determined to bring in an outsider to lead the Service.

A radical appointment as Director General

Derek Lewis's arrival from a career in industry in late 1992 certainly brought a new broom to the Service. Many of us knew all too well the difficulties Derek Lewis would have to confront. Working long hours, he impressed many Governors by his approach. Some found him lacking awareness of the importance of emotions – one senior Governor told me how he had been to see the Director General just because he had to get things off his chest – but didn't need anything doing – just to be listened to. He came out feeling that Derek didn't really understand the emotional dimension to our work. Perhaps Derek's biggest weakness was his lack of understanding of the long stressful time that many of us had been through. Years of dealing with overcrowding, the threat and reality of prisoner disturbances and the constant grind of dealing with the POA had left many of us wary of how quickly change could be introduced.

Derek Lewis was extremely unfortunate to be confronted with a change of Home Secretary so soon after he had taken up post. Governors knew that a change of Minister could make a substantial difference – and in Michael Howard there was such a change of emphasis, a lack of understanding of the problems of the Service and a determination to push ahead with his own political agenda, that a crisis was almost inevitable.

The Learmont Report of 1995, following the escapes from Whitemoor and Parkhurst, included a summary of the way HQ worked:

"At present the Prison Service is led by a Director General recruited from industry, supported by mainstream civil servants and a few Governors promoted into the Civil Service Structure. The management style and culture at the top of the Prison Service, not surprisingly, reflects that of the senior civil service, which is trained to support Ministers rather than to manage a people-orientated organisation."

A Director General with operational experience

In evidence to the May Inquiry of 1978, the Governors Branch had proposed a radical approach to filling the post of Director General:

"There is a strong feeling in the Service at all levels that the post of Director General should be filled by someone who has had direct operational experience of work in the field."

It took two decades to achieve, but the successor to Derek Lewis was Richard Tilt, a career Governor with considerable experience of governing difficult prisons as well as working at HQ. Since then most Director Generals have come from those with some experience of being an operational Governor, a major change from the past.

Prisons Board

The title "Prisons Board" can give a misleading impression of the Service being a "stand-alone" public sector organisation. Not so; the Board ran a Service which was part of the Home Office. The Permanent Secretary at the Home Office had considerable influence on decisions. So too did other parts of the Home Office including Finance and Staffing. This continued until the Service moved to the Ministry of Justice the following century.

Prison Service top leadership and management structures; therefore, need to be seen in a Home Office context. Derek Lewis's account "Hidden Agendas" of his time as Director General exposes the way the Home Office worked from 1992 to 1995, including after the Prison Service had become an "Executive Agency", and the constraints imposed on the Service. Another account of the way the Home Office worked – from a different perspective – is given in David Faulkner's book "Servant of the Crown". The Prisons Board was more of a "cog in a machine" rather than a "free-standing" leadership team.

33. POSITIVE POLITICIANS

Resolving the deep rooted crisis of prison overcrowding has been and continues to be primarily a task for our politicians. Politicians legislate, defining offences and punishments. Politicians decide prison budgets.

Many politicians have avoided involvement in the crisis of prison overcrowding. Is it seen as too difficult? Some politicians may regard any involvement with prison issues – especially advocating reduced use of prison – as damaging to their re-election prospects.

But there have been exceptions. Some politicians have contributed to developing a principled, evidence-based approach to offenders and prisons.

More than a century ago, Winston Churchill served as Home Secretary and delivered this thought provoking analysis of how we should approach crime and criminals:

"We must not forget that when every material improvement has been effected in prison, when the temperature has been rightly adjusted, when the proper food to maintain health and strength has been given, when the doctors, chaplains and prison visitors have come and gone, the convict stands deprived of everything that a free man calls life.

"The mood and temper of the public in regard to the treatment of crime and criminals is one of the most unfailing tests of the civilisation of any country. A calm and dispassionate recognition of the rights of the accused against the state, a constant heart searching by all charged with the duty of punishment, a desire and eagerness to rehabilitate in the world of industry all those who paid their dues in the hard coinage of punishment, tireless efforts towards the discovery of curative and regenerative processes, and an unfaltering faith that there is a treasure, if you can only find it in the heart of every man – these are the symbols which in the treatment of crime and criminals mark and measure the stored up strength of a nation and are sign and proof of the living virtue in it."

In more recent times, several remarkable politicians have worked to develop a positive, evidence-based approach to the problems of crime and criminals.

In the 1970s, while in opposition, Willie Whitelaw MP developed an interest in and understanding of prisons. In Government he proved very effective. Governors learned that when Whitelaw became Home Secretary in 1979, he told his officials to write to the Treasury for more resources for the prisons. When a negative reply came back from Treasury, unlike his predecessors, Whitelaw simply refused to take no for an answer and he quickly obtained important extra resources to start to make a difference.

Above: Home Secretary Douglas Hurd visiting Manchester.

The years that he was Home Secretary saw the implementation of parts of the May Report and the first steps towards the Fresh Start initiative which hugely improved the Service later in the decade.

Douglas Hurd MP was another Home Secretary (1985–1989) who did much for the Service. He provided substantial political support in the fraught years when Fresh Start was being negotiated. In his memoirs Hurd recognises the importance of the Service among his many Home Office responsibilities – even if he notes that it was the most exasperating.

Hurd visited Strangeways while I was Governor and showed a genuine interest – as Willie Whitelaw had done – in improving our prisons. A decade later, after leaving Government, Hurd agreed to chair the Prison Reform Trust, illustrating his lasting commitment to penal reform.

Tony Blair MP served as Shadow Home Secretary before becoming Prime Minister. One of his lasting improvements was to set up the Social Exclusion Unit (SEU). This produced evidence based reports on major social problems. Chapter 40 sets out how one of these reports demonstrates a clear pathway to reduce re-offending.

I have used the heading "Positive Politicians" to underline that some politicians have laid foundations on which others can build. Positive Politicians are all people who have achieved great things in their lives. Their example in signposting a way ahead could be crucial for achieving future improvements to the Service. What that might involve I shall consider in Chapter 43.

34. THE PRISON GOVERNORS ASSOCIATION 1990-1995

Early in 1990, following the resignation of Terry Bone, I was elected Chair of the PGA. My colleagues were immensely supportive during the Strangeways riot and during the long months that followed, as the Woolf Inquiry held public hearings. I was Chairman until the autumn of 1995 when Chris Scott succeeded me. In this chapter and the three following, I will review the work of the PGA and the main issues we had to confront.

For almost all the time I was Chairman, I combined it with being Governor of Risley. This meant a very heavy workload as there was always a great deal to do at Risley to take advantage of the opportunities that existed and to meet the issues that inevitably arose. Simultaneously, I faced huge challenges leading the PGA. The Government developed a privatisation agenda; there was a continuing drive towards improving efficiency and to greater delegation to establishments. Overcrowding; security issues, Industrial Relations and control problems continued. Fortunately, I was supported by an active and talented National Executive Committee.

Throughout the period, I had to respond to regular media inquiries and was involved with many live interviews on current prison issues to give a perspective on behalf of the PGA. An example of the wide range of such activities was when I took part in the first Butler Trust Symposium held on 13th October 1992 at Wormwood Scrubs Prison. Introduced by the Princess Royal, the Symposium included a debate on questions of prison policy with a platform which included Home Secretary Ken Clarke, Lord Woolf, Professor Simon Lee, a prisoner from Wormwood Scrubs, and me.

Prison privatisation

A new challenge had arisen in the late 1980s. The Government, partly in response to the difficulties it had experienced with the POA, started to examine the question of allowing the private sector to run prisons. The Government was in favour of competition. The first step was in 1988: a Government Green Paper "Private Sector Involvement in the Remand System". The PGA became increasingly concerned at the implications of privatisation.

But the Government was committed to privatisation. Their next move was to set up two initiatives. First they decided to "contract out" the new prison at the Wolds. Group 4 won the contract and opened the prison successfully in 1992. I paid a visit to the Wolds and was fascinated to see the strengths and weaknesses of the private sector in operation. In 1993, Blakenhurst Prison opened, another new prison run by the private sector, followed by Doncaster in 1994.

"Contracting out" Court Escort Work to the private sector was the second initiative. Group 4 won the first contract for the area covering Humberside and the East Midlands. This took effect in April 1993. There were considerable problems as the contractor, Group 4, and their newly recruited staff had to find out how to manage prisoners and run a complex system to transport prisoners to Court when required. There were escapes; prisoners arrived late for Court; and then there was the tragic loss of a prisoner in a secure vehicle whose death was not discovered for a considerable time. Perhaps the only immediate benefit in the early days of the privatised Court Escort Service was that a splendid series of cartoons appeared in the national press about the woes of Group 4.

The Government pressed ahead with "market testing", holding a competition for who was to run prisons between the private and public sectors. Some of us in the public sector responded energetically. At Risley I held a series of briefings with groups of staff following my visit to the Wolds to explain the implications of competition for us all. Staff responded pretty well when the situation was carefully and fully explained. We might not like it – but we had to change and learn to live with the new realities. "More for less" became the watchword together with efforts to drive up standards, achieve increased efficiency and reduce waste.

In 1993, a further move to extend the influence of the private sector was to "market test" the "new" Strangeways. The public sector bid, led by the admirable Robin Halward, eventually won and Strangeways remained in the public sector. But it was a steep learning curve for everyone. Governors increasingly challenged the way prisons had traditionally organised work and whether there were better and more economic ways of achieving results.

The PGA continued to criticise the rush to privatisation. We requested proper monitoring of the experiment and the publication of any evaluations undertaken. Our members were generally opposed to what was happening but, for a small minority, the move to the private sector opened up new job opportunities as public sector Governors were "poached" by the new private operators.

We developed some ideas on "Charter" or "Trust" prisons to see if there was any scope for experimenting in a similar way to the development of NHS Trust organisations. Alas, there was little sign of interest by the Government as they implemented their programme of prison privatisation.

Michael Howard appointed Home Secretary

The appointment of Michael Howard as Home Secretary in May 1993 began a period of extreme difficulty. Over the next two years, I had a number of meetings with him leading a delegation from the PGA.

Michael Howard's lasting legacy is the prison population explosion that followed his new policies. He effectively reversed the steps towards ending overcrowding following the Woolf Report.

His new mantra "Prison Works", delivered in a speech to the 1993 Conservative Party Conference, was a complete reversal of previous policies. Howard had this to say:

"Prison works. It ensures that we are protected from murderers, muggers and rapists and it makes many who are tempted to commit crime think twice.

"This may mean that more people go to prison. I do not flinch from that. We shall no longer judge the success of our system of criminal justice by a fall in our prison population."

For decades, successive Home Secretaries had put the emphasis on reducing the use of imprisonment where possible. Michael Howard, having ramped up the rhetoric, then failed to deliver the resources the rhetoric demanded. As the prison population rose in response to the Home Secretary's new approach, we urgently needed more places and therefore more resources. These were not forthcoming. It was as if a return to greater overcrowding was part of his plan – if indeed he had a long-term plan.

The change was dramatic. By the spring of 1994, I had this to report to the PGA's Annual Conference:

"In March 1993, the prison population was starting to rise from a low of 40,000. At the beginning of 1994 it was over 45,000 – the latest figures indicate that it is now well over 48,000. Hundreds of prisoners are being held in police cells and many establishments are under acute pressure."

Governors were dismayed by Michael Howard's approach. To see the chance of an end to overcrowding swept away for party political reasons was tragic. Governors were also increasingly concerned about other approaches that he took.

Howard rarely visited prisons. He had little previous experience of large organisations and the need to relate to people. He was under the illusion that it was enough to give an instruction to make changes. If only life was that simple! He did not give time and attention to understanding the complexity of the Service, something every outsider who had examined the Service since Mountbatten, had commented on.

Governors gathered that the Home Secretary was concerned at the conditions for prisoners in prisons. He regarded the standard of comfort difficult to justify. He thought regimes were lax and that prisoners should spend more time working. There followed a series of rather disconnected initiatives to reduce the use of TVs in cell and to reduce access to Home Leave. The combination of increased numbers without extra resources, the reduction in the regimes and the rhetoric all concerned Governors, as we knew that there could be unpredictable prisoner reaction.

The Learmont Report published figures for the amount of work senior Prison Service people had to do for Ministers. In a period of 83 days in late 1994 to early 1995, over 1000 documents had been submitted to ministers. The Learmont Inquiry noted that when the Director General was giving evidence to them, he was interrupted on a number of occasions to speak to Ministers.

My final letter to Michael Howard as PGA Chairman was immediately after the publication of the Learmont Report and the sacking of Derek Lewis. We noted the extent to which Learmont had revealed that senior people were spending time on ministerial papers and briefing. Among a number of suggestions we made about reducing the pressure on the Service was "that there is substantial scope for immediately reducing ministerial oversight of minor operational matters".

Unsurprisingly I received a reply that included "I do not accept that there is or has been ministerial oversight of minor operational matters".

Just before I handed over the Chair of the PGA to Chris Scott in the autumn of 1995, I was involved with the launch of a "Manifesto for Change", the most comprehensive statement of PGA policy that we had put together since the PGA was formed in 1987.

There were three other major issues confronting the PGA during this time in addition to privatisation. Overcrowding, the legality of strike action and a greater emphasis on trying to scapegoat Governors. I will consider each of these in the following chapters.

35. OVERCROWDING 1981-1996

Police cells

Upward pressure of numbers continued throughout the nineteen eighties. Industrial action by the POA often made the situation worse as a refusal to accept prisoners in one prison often led to overcrowding elsewhere. So bad was the situation that prisons were unable to take all the prisoners being sent by the courts. An overflow population in police cells again became a regular complication for prison management as previously reviewed in Chapter 24.

Police cells provided much worse conditions for prisoners as they were only designed for overnight stays rather than lengthy periods of incarceration. They had one advantage that in many cases they were much nearer for relatives and friends to visit – but whether visits could be arranged due to lack of space and staff was another matter.

To counter the impact of rising numbers and industrial action, the Service turned once more to the military for assistance. Rolleston Camp was opened again in 1988; and Alma Dettingen barracks near Camberley were used for most of the year. The camps were staffed by the military, but managed by Governor Grades.

The Woolf Report gave the cost as being £25 million for police cell use during the period April to August 1990.

Woolf recommendations on overcrowding

The Woolf Report recommended a new device for avoiding gross overcrowding reoccurring. The Inquiry was assured that there was every prospect of substantially reducing and possibly eliminating overcrowding by the end of 1992. Woolf recommended a procedure to allow limited overcrowding but with fresh safeguards. A new Prison Rule was proposed requiring the Home Secretary to have to issue a certificate allowing an establishment to exceed its Certified Normal Accommodation (CNA) for a period longer than 7 days or in excess of 3%. The certificate – which could be renewed – would be for a maximum of 3 months. The certificate and the reason it was needed would have to be laid before Parliament.

Regrettably, while many of the Woolf recommendations were implemented, this one was too radical and too difficult for the politicians.

In 1990 and for the two years following, the prison population dropped to around 40,000. Alas – this relief was not to last.

PGA proposals to tackle overcrowding

In 1992, the PGA renewed our attempts to persuade the Government to tackle overcrowding. We had long been concerned that the cell certification process took no account of all the other facilities needed to support the care and custody of prisoners. Accordingly in 1993, we wrote to Headquarters with a number of suggestions to improve the certification process for cells and related issues. We said:

"The present practice, unchanged for some decades, is to link the certification of sleeping accommodation to the capacity of establishments. This was entirely understandable at the time when prisoners worked and slept in their cells. But this process of establishing capacity figures has been seriously weakened by the growth of out-of-cell activities. No equivalent machinery has been developed to certify that all the necessary facilities are in place to support the population for which a penal establishment has certified sleeping accommodation. For several decades, very overcrowded older prisons have suffered totally impoverished regimes as a direct result of linking the capacity of an establishment only to its sleeping accommodation without sufficient regard to supporting facilities.

"We propose that this serious procedural weakness should be remedied immediately. The steps to establish the capacity of a penal establishment should include two separate exercises. First, the present process of certifying cells should continue. A parallel exercise should be conducted to assess the number of prisoners the facilities within the establishment could provide for. This should result in a second certificate being issued specifying the number of prisoners. Facilities should at least include catering, bathing, sanitation, visiting, exercise, reception, medical and spiritual. An assessment should also be made of the number of prisoners who can be given out-of-cell activities for a specified minimum period: we propose a minimum of 10 hours. Certification should be the responsibility of a senior member of Headquarters, perhaps the Area Manager."

We also raised the fundamental question about whether it was right to compel prisoners to share cells; we advocated that staff should always be able to keep prisoners apart in single cells so that cells certified for multiple occupation gave flexibility but no guarantee of additional accommodation. Further we proposed that an "operating margin" of perhaps 10% was needed. This was to take account of cells out of use for repairs and maintenance.

We also made it clear what was the position of the PGA on overcrowding. On 9th March 1993, I addressed the PGA Annual Conference as follows:

"Let me say clearly and precisely where this Association stands on the matter of overcrowding. We condemn it; we oppose it; we believe that it is intrinsically wrong. The Prison System should not be overcrowded. It brings no benefits to prisoners; it brings no benefits to staff. Most importantly of all it brings no benefit at all to the public. Overcrowded prisons are unhealthy places, far more likely to turn out embittered hardened and contaminated individuals. Overcrowding reduces the opportunities to combat contamination. It makes it very difficult for staff to put in place positive programmes to encourage prisoners to face up to their offending."

I went on to describe another highly undesirable consequence of overcrowding – the need to move prisoners around the system often far away from their homes.

"In my view what we have been compelled to do has been to impose a form of internal exile on many of our prisoners."

On 19th September 1995, not long before he was sacked, Derek Lewis, Director General, wrote to the PGA as follows:

"It was accepted that the current definition of operational capacity requires an assessment of regime facilities by the Prison Service Area Manager. This assessment must take account of the risks to good order, security and the proper running of the planned regime. It requires an operational judgement based on experience."

Derek Lewis then addressed the question of changing the Prison Rules and concluded:

"Now is probably not the best time to take forward any radical changes".

Prison Service Journal on Overcrowding

In March 1994, the PSJ (Number 92) focussed on "Overcrowding", reproducing my article first published in 1971. I was also asked to contribute an introduction to the article. I summed up the situation 22 years on as "Nothing changes". I suggested that there was a serious lack of research into the effects of overcrowding, especially the way prisoners could be damaged and contaminated by their experience. There was a need to define overcrowding. I included evidence to the Woolf Report (Annex 2E) which described the experience of overcrowding:

"When I discovered that 3 men had to share a cell of only 8 x 12 feet or thereabouts I was astounded. A remand prisoner has no work, therefore he has to stay in a cramped stuffy cell with two other men who he probably hates the sight of for 14 hours a day. Many cells have only one chair or two chairs, or maybe no tables, so that the inmates are forced to eat sitting on the bed. Try sitting on the lower bunk of a double bunk and eating a meal. You too would become frustrated and angry. Meal time over he has to lie on the bed. Just for a change he could maybe sit on the bed. If he walks up and down the floor, he is told to sit down or be put down. He has a head full of worries and problems about the forthcoming court case. One of the other inmates has a radio on full blast driving him crazy. He needs to use the toilet but the staff won't let him and he daren't use the bucket or he gets beaten by the others. Wouldn't anyone get depressed?"

I included suggestions about mechanisms which could be adopted to control overcrowding:

(a) A considerable surplus of accommodation that can be brought into use when numbers rise

(b) Machinery whereby selected prisoners can be released by administrative action to balance the inflow of prisoners from the Courts

(c) A limit on the places provided within the prison system by which the Courts have to abide.

None of these options are easy or palatable."

THE PRIME MINISTER ATTEMPTS TO HELP WITH OVERCROWDING

36. LEGALITY OF INDUSTRIAL ACTION?

As part of his Inquiry into the Prison Disturbances of April 1990, Lord Justice Woolf examined Industrial Relations in the Service.

In his Report – Paragraph 13.244 – he states:

"There is a body of opinion which is firmly of the view that Industrial Relations can only be improved if Industrial Action by prison officers is made unlawful..... the position should be the same as that with the police....this is not a contention that was advanced by the Prison Service....

"We accept that there may come a time when this will have to be re-examined."

What did not appear in the Woolf Report or in the earlier report of Mr Justice May in 1979, which was primarily concerned with Industrial Relations, was any hint that the POA did not have the legal right to take industrial action. In 1991 Admiral Lygo included the possibility of banning industrial action in his recommendations so he too clearly was unaware of the true position. This did not emerge until 1993 when Derek Lewis was faced with POA industrial action.

Above: Director General Derek Lewis arriving at Risley.

Derek Lewis has published an account of his experiences as Director General under the title "Hidden Agendas". In it he reveals that he was told in 1993 by the Director of Personnel, Tony Butler, that the Home Office was well aware that the POA was not a proper trade union under the law because prison officers had the powers of a constable. This startling admission was apparently known for years by politicians and senior civil servants. Derek Lewis was given the impression that both the POA and the PGA "probably knew the real position". The PGA certainly did not know. Indeed, we had campaigned on a number of occasions from the May Report onwards to have industrial action by prison officers outlawed but with proper safeguards for staff as compensation.

When the POA threatened further industrial action in November 1993, Derek Lewis worked to use legal means to defeat the POA. After meetings with the Prime Minister, legal action was authorised and the Service sought an injunction against the POA. On 18th November 1993, the matter went to the High Court and an injunction was granted.

The essence of the argument was that prison officers – and prison Governors – under Section 8 of the Prison Act 1952 had "the powers, authority, protection and privileges of a constable". This meant they could not take industrial action. There had been an interesting case in 1982 – Home Office v Robinson – when the Courts had held that the Employment Tribunals had no jurisdiction to hear a claim from a prison officer.

The POA made a further attempt at Preston Prison to test the validity of the injunction. Governor Grades were again put on standby to assist if necessary at Preston and HQ sought a second injunction. This was granted and the industrial action was averted.

There were damaging consequences for the PGA as it was clear that we also were covered by the ruling. We sought to find a path through the legal minefield in which Governors, too, were trapped. On 15th June 1995, after considerable delay, we had a meeting with the Home Secretary. We set out the delays we had experienced in restoring our bargaining rights following the court case in November 1994 aimed at the POA. The PGA – while covered by the ruling – were trying to keep prisons running despite the behaviour of the POA. Yet we had been penalised by the failure to put in place alternative arrangements for dealing with terms and conditions of service! Michael Howard had little to offer us.

There are interesting questions about the POA's right to strike and the knowledge in HQ for many years that strike action was illegal. If this was so, why was the chaos Governors had to face for years not addressed much earlier? The Governors Branch had specifically raised the right to strike with the May Inquiry in 1979 and the May Inquiry had examined the issue. (See pages 106-107)

Chapter 24 recounts the serious disturbances at the end of April 1986 following the POA overtime ban. We know from Douglas Hurd's memoirs that Mrs Thatcher was most concerned about the 1986 prison disturbances and even advocated bringing in the military. It seems very strange that the Prime Minister who took on the miners and won would not be prepared to take on the POA. Did she know about the legal position?

Reflecting on the years of difficulties with the POA, I find it extraordinary that the ability to ban strikes by prison officers was not activated years earlier. This surprising lack of action should be researched and the motives revealed of those who allowed the POA to continue to use illegal industrial action when it could have been prevented under the law.

The question of the legality of industrial action by the POA was to rumble on for a number of years after I had retired. After the Labour Government experimented with an agreement to replace the ban, the POA broke the agreement in 2007 and Jack Straw – who was then the responsible Minister – succeeded in passing legislation to reintroduce the ban.

37. PRISON GOVERNORS: CONVENIENT SCAPEGOATS?

Background

When disasters struck, Governors were convenient scapegoats for both senior people in the Service and for politicians. While Governors should take responsibility for matters within their control, on many occasions the causes of disasters were multiple and the responsibility should have been apportioned carefully. That did not always happen.

Early examples of scapegoating

At the time of the Mountbatten Report, triggered by the escape from Wormwood Scrubs of George Blake, the Governor retired. It was widely believed that he was pressurised into doing so. This was despite the lack of criticism of the Governor in the Mountbatten Report which instead highlighted that HQ had failed – without explanation – to grant the Governor's request to move Blake to more secure accommodation (Mountbatten Report Paragraph 70).

Pressure on Governors involved in disasters continued with an especially distasteful attempt to blame a relatively junior governor at Hull Prison following the 1976 riot. After the riot, staff did not treat prisoners properly and in July 1978, the charge of "Malfeasance in Public Office" was targeted at an Assistant Governor as he was technically in charge at the time. The weaknesses in the management structure, discussed in Chapter 13, were not recognised. The Assistant Governor had a torrid time for many months as the case came to court but he was acquitted. The experience left the Assistant Governor scarred. It damaged the morale of other Governor Grades. As described in Chapter 16, the strains between Governors and their trade union were also increased.

The escape of three high security prisoners from Brixton in 1980 resulted in the Governor in charge being moved. The statement of Willie Whitelaw, Home Secretary, about this decision said:

"The failure to prevent these escapes arose from human errors in the establishment. The Governor Mr Selby himself must accept and very properly does accept the principal responsibility. Mr Selby has been moved to a post in the Prison Service's Regional Office structure."

Governors generally regarded Willie Whitelaw with respect and thought he had behaved in a reasonable way in handling the aftermath of the 1980 Brixton escape.

More recent examples

From 1990, unfortunately, there was a marked change for the worse in the behaviour of politicians. Governing Governors found themselves increasingly in the firing line as politicians sought ways of distancing themselves from prison disasters.

Governors required support when they faced the inevitable inquiries following any disaster. The media needed to be briefed – often about very complex situations. Representations to the Director General or Ministers were required. The PGA rapidly discovered how much there was to do.

A further escape from Brixton in July 1991 involving a firearm was followed by an inquiry by the Chief Inspector of Prisons and an interim Security Audit by Gordon Lakes and Ron Hadfield. The Home Secretary, Kenneth Baker, made a statement accepting the recommendations and noting that the Chief Inspector had found a number of causes. He concluded that "The Governor of Brixton, Mr Withers, who is due to retire in October, has been asked to take pre-retirement leave immediately."

The PGA was so concerned at the way this decision was reported in the media, that we issued the following statement:

"The Governor of Brixton, Mr Withers, has neither resigned nor has been given early retirement. He has been sent on extended leave pending his retirement on 3rd October. The new Governor of Brixton, Dr Coyle, had been appointed in June and the decision to bring forward the previous Governor's annual leave was to allow Dr Coyle to take up post immediately."

On September 6th 1993, a serious riot broke out at Wymott Prison near Preston. The contingency plans, improved since Strangeways, worked pretty well; no prisoner escaped and order was restored quite quickly. But the damage to the prison was considerable – Wymott had been built for prisoners expected to behave – and had always been vulnerable to severe damage if a serious disturbance broke out. Michael Howard considered the calling in of the army as Mrs Thatcher had suggested during the 1986 disturbances. But significantly, it soon got round that Michael Howard was looking for someone to blame for the riot – a scapegoat to avoid any blame landing on him. Governors started to realise that this Home Secretary appeared less interested in the good of the Service than his own political future.

Whitemoor

The next crisis, involving the scapegoating of Governors, was in September 1994. The escape from Whitemoor High Security Prison caused considerable shock as a number of IRA prisoners breached the perimeter of a top security prison. Their speedy capture was a relief, but the fact they got as far as they did was a huge setback for the Service. What was worse, they were in the Special Security Unit in Whitemoor, meant to be the most secure part of the prison.

There had been other escape attempts from Special Security Units decades earlier, so we had had warning of the vulnerability of even the most secure prisons.

HQ had to recommend who was to lead the inquiry into the Whitemoor escape. This was an important decision and one that would have far reaching consequences. One obvious person was the Chief Inspector, but Judge Tumin was not a popular figure with the Home Secretary and he was partially compromised as there was a recent inspection report on Whitemoor conducted by his team. The PGA was surprised to learn that a retired policeman was chosen – and assumed that this was another Michael Howard move. However, Derek Lewis's account indicates that it was a Home Office official who first suggested Sir John Woodcock, retired Chief Inspector of Constabulary.

Senior policemen had been utilised in three previous prison inquiries. At the time of the Mountbatten Report, Mr R Mark, Chief Constable of Leicester, acted as one of a number of Assessors to the Inquiry. Sir John Nightingale was a member of the May Inquiry of 1979. Ron Hadfield, Chief Constable of the West Midlands, jointly conducted the interim Security Audit of 1991 – with Gordon Lakes, retired DDG of the Prison Service, into the arrangements for holding and managing Category A prisoners following the 1991 escape from Brixton. However, there had been no previous occasion when someone from the police services had been asked to lead an inquiry into events in prisons.

There are significant cultural differences between the police and the Service. There is, moreover, a history of difficult relations dating back at least to the Birmingham Bombers and their treatment at Winson Green. The Service's view was that at least part of the blame for any mistreatment of the suspected Birmingham Bombers lay with the police – but in the end the investigation into the alleged mistreatment of the Bombers was conducted by the police and it was prison staff that faced criminal charges. The fact the staff were eventually acquitted did not reduce the Prison Service's concerns about the interface between the two services.

But that is only part of the story. In practice there is much co-operation between the police and prison services. There is a police adviser appointed to the Service and I worked closely with him during 1982-84 at HQ when I was in P5 division as described in Chapter 21. Each prison has a police liaison officer who works closely with the establishment's security officer.

The Woodcock Inquiry also made use of a former Police Adviser to the Service as part of the inquiry team. The approach was – as might be expected – very much like a criminal investigation. Prison staff who were interviewed started feeding back their concerns – especially those with experience of other sorts of inquiries. The PGA provided a "friend" to accompany our members when being interviewed – I sat in with the interviews with the present and former Governors as I did with the following Learmont Inquiry.

By the time a draft report was prepared, the Inquiry found it had to send out

"Salmon Letters" to those who were criticised in the Inquiry report. This gave the PGA a clear signal that the process was probably flawed. At the end of November, I wrote to the Permanent Secretary of the Home Office:

"We wish to express our concern about aspects of the Woodcock Inquiry into the escapes from Whitemoor Prison. Some of our members received letters from the Enquiry described by the Enquiry team as "Salmon Letters" giving extracts from the draft report for PGA members' comments. Members sought the advice of the Association which our lawyers have provided. Our Lawyers made the following comment about the language in the draft report:

"The language of the report is wholly inappropriate for a matter of this nature. The hyperbolic language used seems to emphasise the subjective and indeed pejorative description applied to much of what has taken place."

The language of the draft report contrasts sharply with the measured and considered text of Lord Justice Woolf's Report "Prison Disturbances April 1990", the last major Enquiry into incidents in prisons.

The reference to Salmon led us to look at the Salmon Report of 1966. Paragraph 43 of the Report describes Departmental Enquiries:

"A Departmental Enquiry is usually appointed by the responsible Minister to be conducted by an eminent lawyer alone or as Chairman with others.

"The PGA is surprised that a legally qualified person is not part of the Enquiry team. Such an appointment should have prevented the inappropriate language used in the draft report."

This sorry saga demonstrates the lack of professionalism in selecting an Enquiry team by both Home Office officials and the politicians. While the mistakes made at Whitemoor needed thorough investigation and appropriate remedial action, the Woodcock Report stands as an example of how not to conduct a Departmental Enquiry.

The Report was published in December 1994 with Home Secretary Michael Howard making a statement to the House of Commons. The Whitemoor Report had been highly critical of a number of staff including Governor Grade. But the decision was taken to refer the question of disciplinary action to an independent person Sir David Yardley, a former local Government ombudsman and lawyer. He was to conduct a disciplinary investigation. That seemed a more reasonable way to proceed. Yardley concluded his disciplinary investigation and recommended no disciplinary action against anyone.

Parkhurst

But worse was to follow. On 3rd January 1995, three prisoners escaped from Parkhurst Prison. This set in motion a sequence of events which led to the sacking of Director General Derek Lewis. An immediate inquiry led by the Service's Director of Security, Richard Tilt, was ordered by Derek Lewis. The results of that revealed a whole series of failures. The Director General decided that the Governor should be moved to other duties so that a new Governor could focus exclusively on putting matters right at Parkhurst. However, the Director General's approach was challenged by Michael Howard who on 10th January 1995 made a statement to the House of Commons in the following terms:

"The present Governor is today being removed from his duties at Parkhurst. Pending the outcome of a disciplinary inquiry and any subsequent proceedings he will not run any other prison in the Prison Service."

The way the statement was delivered and received made it sound as if Governor John Marriott had been sacked. And that was the way it was reported the next day in the media.

The next day the PGA had a scheduled meeting with the Director General. He had written a letter which went some way to clarifying the disgraceful way in which John Marriott had been publicly treated. His letter included:

"John Marriott is rightly noted and appreciated for his dedication, humanity, courage and innovation. I am therefore appalled by the misleading and inaccurate reporting there has subsequently been in the media. John Marriott has not been sacked or suspended. There is no prejudgement of any disciplinary proceedings which may follow the disciplinary investigation and there is no ban on John governing prisons subsequently."

The PGA considered this was a rather more helpful statement than Michael Howard's Parliamentary statement. It went some way to reducing the anger felt by members all around the country over the treatment of John Marriott.

What was entirely missing from the consideration of how to treat John Marriott was any proper understanding of his background. Over the 20 years up to the Parkhurst disaster, John had successfully managed a succession of difficult and challenging tasks. Such considerations did not appear to register with Michael Howard as he attempted to safeguard his own position.

John died on 11th June 1998 aged 51. We shall never know what part his treatment by Michael Howard contributed to his premature death.

When I reported all this to members in a PGA circular dated 17th January 1995, I was so concerned that I included the following advice to all members:

"Because it appears that the Home Secretary is seeking scapegoats for anything that goes wrong in prison establishments it is vital all our members fully understand the dangers for individuals in the present situation.

"Members are therefore advised to take the following action:

A. If it is not possible to carry out any important instructions, particularly security instructions, this fact should be reported in writing to your line manager. You should keep a copy.

B. In the event of an Enquiry into an incident taking place, you should not be prepared to be interviewed without first seeking the advice of the PGA. If necessary interviews should be delayed until a colleague can accompany you. This advice is especially important in the light of the action that was taken following Richard Tilt's inquiry at Parkhurst, which was not of course a disciplinary inquiry."

On 29th March 1995, I addressed the Annual Conference of the PGA with feelings running very high over the way Governors, and especially John Marriott, were being treated by Michael Howard.

I said:

"The PGA know that our members feel highly accountable for what they do. This is especially true of Governing Governors. I say clearly and publicly that we are prepared to be fully accountable for our decisions and for our establishments. There have been suggestions that Governors face no penalties when things go wrong. What rubbish. The way John Marriott was treated earlier this year is only the latest example of Governors who have been convenient scapegoats for major prison disasters. Many of us have had to face inquiries where our accountability was publicly examined. Many of us have had to give evidence in Coroners Courts. Some of us have had to face legal action. But above all Governors have had to face the unremitting glare of publicity when disasters, scandals or industrial disputes struck their establishments. I doubt very much whether any other group of public servants are as publicly accountable as we Prison Governors find ourselves."

"In order to protect our members, I propose that the certification of establishments should include certification of security systems. No longer should Governors have to bear the sole responsibility for holding maximum security prisoners when the perimeter of their prison is insecure. The purpose of my proposed certification is not to remove accountability from Governors but to see that matters that are not within the Governors' powers are made properly the responsibility of those who take the decisions."

The PGA met Michael Howard in June 1995. We drew his attention to the way Governors had been treated in recent months. We particularly underlined the treatment of John Marriott and the way an impression was given by the Home Secretary that was inaccurate – John Marriott had been moved not sacked and was not barred from being given charge of other prisons. We contrasted the treatment of John Marriott, with the much more balanced treatment of the Governor of Brixton in 1981 by Home Secretary Willie Whitelaw after other serious escapes.

There was no adequate response from Michael Howard.

Loss of a Director General

The final act in the drama around the sacking of John Marriott was the sequence of events leading up to the sacking of Derek Lewis by Michael Howard. The crisis resulted from a highly critical report from General Sir John Learmont into the Service, a report that Michael Howard had commissioned in December 1994 into Prison Security. On Monday 16th October 1995, Michael Howard made a statement on the Learmont Report noting that:

"Sir John has not found that any policy decision of mine, directly or indirectly caused the escape."

Above: General Learmont visiting Risley.

But someone had to be a scapegoat. He went on:

"Sir John Learmont has found a great deal that needs to be put right within the Prison Service, spanning leadership, structure, the management chain and the ethos of the service. He says that responsibilities ultimately reach Prisons Board level – and that the criticisms stop there.

"I have come to the conclusion that this requires a change of leadership at the top of the Service. The Director General has accordingly ceased to hold his post from today."

Michael Howard had succeeded in sacking an official at last.

The damage to Michael Howard's reputation was considerable following his extraordinary performance in failing to answer questions from Jeremy Paxman on a BBC TV "Newsnight" programme and the description of him by Ann Widdecombe MP as having "something of the night" about him.

Complex causes of disasters

General Learmont's Report also dealt with a crucial element in the Parkhurst escapes. The Report describes in some detail the perimeter deficiencies at Parkhurst which contributed to the successful escape in January 1995. Among these deficiencies was a failure to instal geophones on the perimeter, a requirement for top security prisons dating back to the Mountbatten Report of 1966. The organisational and management deficiencies that led to the failure to have this vital equipment installed over twenty years is recorded in Appendix F to the Learmont Report.

Operational disasters are rarely the sole responsibility of one person – so inquiries into disasters seeking to attribute responsibility need to fully explore the complexities that often lie behind serious failures. Governors have been prepared to accept responsibility but not for failures by others in other parts of the organisation. Public recognition of the complexity of many prison failures would be welcome. Politicians and the senior leadership of the Service should ensure future disasters are thoroughly investigated and that responsibility is fairly apportioned. That is the least that can be done for the present and future generations of Governors.

38. NORTHERN IRELAND LINKS

This chapter covers the considerable links there have been with the Northern Ireland Service.

In Chapter 13 I explained the co-operation between the English, Scottish and Northern Ireland Governors representative bodies at the time of the May Inquiry in 1978/79. The links between the Service in England and Wales and Northern Ireland had been strengthened during the early days of the "Troubles" when English Governors and staff had been asked to go for periods of "detached duty" to support colleagues in Northern Ireland.

Senior English Governors were asked to act as Advisers to the Northern Ireland Administration from 1971. Bill Brister – later the Deputy Director General in England and Wales – was the first; Captain WI Davies followed him. Over twenty years later, Robin Halward – who was my Deputy at Strangeways – was appointed Director General of the Northern Ireland Service from 1998 to 2001.

My first contact with the Northern Ireland Service was through one of the younger Northern Irish Governors, Billy McConnell. Billy had worked with my staff inspection team in 1976 in order to study our methods of working. He was subsequently murdered by the IRA outside his home, an event which brought home to me the seriousness of the threats faced by our Northern Irish colleagues.

The Northern Ireland Governors applied to join the PGA soon after it was established. Endorsed by the PGA Conference in 1989, the Northern Ireland Governors joined and two of their members became part of the National Executive Committee of the PGA.

I visited Northern Ireland several times as Chairman of the PGA. On one occasion, I met with the Permanent Secretary in Northern Ireland – the senior Civil Servant – at Stormont Castle. This was John Chilcott whom I had worked with when he was Director of Personnel and Finance for the Prison Service.

Northern Ireland Governors occasionally referred to ODCs – an abbreviation for "Ordinary Decent Criminals" to distinguish them from the terrorists and para militaries that provided such a high proportion of the prison population and most of the problems.

On one occasion, when visiting the Maze Prison, I was asked if I wished to see inside one of the H Blocks. After discussions between staff and the IRA – it was an IRA H Block – I was asked to meet a number of the senior IRA people during the visit. Their interest was to achieve the repatriation of prisoners from England to Northern Ireland – a policy we were broadly in favour of – so it was quite an amicable exchange. Afterwards I spoke to the Assistant Governor in

charge of the H Block and hoped that my visit had not disturbed the equilibrium he was trying to preserve. He was quite cheerful and said he thought the visit had gone well, adding "your name helped – though it wouldn't have done in some of the other H Blocks!"

Above: PGA NEC members at Stormont.

PART THREE – HOPE FOR THE FUTURE?

39. UNANSWERED QUESTIONS

On page 6, I set out "unanswered questions". What have we uncovered?

Why has prison overcrowding lasted so long and what damage has it done?

Research by Terry Weiler (Chapter 14) into the beginnings of overcrowding reveals extraordinary failures by the Prisons Board, Ministers and Parliament to appreciate the seriousness of the problem engulfing the Service. For such an important deterioration to occur without formal consideration by the Prisons Board, without Ministerial statement and with so little Parliamentary and Press interest or scrutiny, is almost beyond belief.

Was it ignorance or neglect that neither the Prisons Board nor politicians tackled overcrowding before it became a chronic condition? Why did Governments which delivered substantial domestic achievements during the period – the establishment of the NHS under Labour and the house building programmes under the Conservatives – fail to tackle prison overcrowding?

Abolishing overcrowding is the responsibility of our politicians. Some Home Secretaries started to try and balance the Service's tasks and resources. Willie Whitelaw and Douglas Hurd stand out as making a substantial difference.

Building on my articles on "Overcrowding" in the PSJ, I have argued that overcrowding increases the risk of contamination making overcrowded prisons "an expensive way of making bad people worse". The consequences of overcrowding deserve much more research. Is overcrowding a cause of our very high re-offending rates?

Some prisoners suffered violence and a few were murdered in overcrowded prison accommodation. The death of Zahid Mubarek at Feltham on 21st March 2000 is a dreadful reminder that overcrowding continues to cost lives.

There are serious issues arising from combining in-cell sanitation with compelling prisoners to eat meals in cells, very probably in breach of modern hygiene rules. Has this had any impact on prisoners' health?

So far more research is needed into many aspects of overcrowding.

Why did the Prison Service suffer disaster after disaster?

While many prison services suffer disasters from time to time, the number and variety suffered in England and Wales between 1964 and 1996 appears exceptional. Further serious disturbances and industrial disputes have continued since 1996. These disasters, while each has proximate causes, have, in my opinion, their roots in overcrowding which diverted efforts away from dealing adequately with other issues.

Why were the acute staffing and Industrial Relations problems not tackled earlier?

Modernising staff management was seriously neglected. Service leadership failed to address staffing issues. The long history of poor Industrial Relations is the result of a failure to prioritise staffing. Senior politicians also failed to grasp the importance of staffing and Industrial Relations.

The failure to achieve staff ownership of rehabilitation before 1963 probably contributed to the acute staffing problems of the following decades. The Prisons Board loss of control over its staff – "managed" by a division of the Home Office Establishment Department – almost certainly led to the serious deterioration in control, continuity and accountability of the 1970s.

If Ministers and senior officials knew that prison officers did not have the right to strike, why wasn't action taken earlier?

The revelation, described in Chapter 36, that prison officers and governors did not have the right to strike requires much more research. When did that become known to senior officials and Ministers? Did the May Committee know the real position? At the time of the 1986 riots, did the Prime Minister know that the POA were acting illegally?

Much more research is required.

Are there any undisclosed factors around the decision not to try and retake Strangeways on 2nd April 1990?

The events of 2nd April 1990 were probably more about "muddle than Machiavelli".

I have set out some unanswered questions around the handling of the Strangeways riot in pages 175-176.

I remain astonished that on 2nd April, the politicians did not appear to have asked how quickly the Service planned to restore order at Strangeways. Such a question would have led to a discussion about whether to use the assembled force to try and regain control quickly. If that had happened – while there were considerable risks involved – the wave of riots that followed the continuing Strangeways disturbance might have been prevented – including the loss of life.

Why is the prison population in the UK so high when many of our European neighbours have much lower prison populations?

Some European countries, with proportionately lower prison populations, demonstrate that a high prison population is not essential to maintain law and order. Much depends on defining what conduct is criminal within each country, on sentencing policy and on public and political attitudes.

"The Times" in January 2018 backed the need to revisit sentencing guidelines noting "England and Wales have some of the highest rates of imprisonment in Western Europe which is expensive and does little to keep less serious criminals from re-offending. It might be incendiary to use prison less but it is a good idea".

Similarly in October 2018, the Catholic Bishops published "A Journey of Hope: A Catholic Approach to Sentencing Reform" seeking a change in sentencing practice to reduce sentence lengths.

THIS NEW TITAN PRISON WILL SOON EXPAND TO HOLD ANOTHER TEN THOUSAND PRISONERS

40. REDUCING RE-OFFENDING

The 1997 Labour Government set up the "Social Exclusion Unit" (SEU). This unit tackled a variety of important issues from "Truanting" to "Rough Sleepers". One of the best reports was published in 2002 entitled "Reducing Re-Offending".

This report drew together research findings over many years on what reduced re-offending by ex- prisoners. The research findings included:

• Employment available on release reduces the risk of re-offending by between one third and a half.

• Having accommodation to go to on release reduces the risk of re-offending by at least 20%.

• Existence and maintenance of good family relationships reduces the risk of re-offending on release.

The report also lists factors that contribute to individuals re-offending. These include lack of education, social skills, mental and physical health problems, and alcohol and drug dependency.

The SEU's report concluded that there is much we can do to reduce re-offending **if that is made a priority**. Because of the overuse of imprisonment by our society, resources are wasted on incarceration which should be used on reducing re-offending.

In discussing re-offending, it is not possible to accurately predict the future behaviour of any individual. But the research shows clearly that groups of offenders have a significantly lower reconviction rate if they have employment following release, have accommodation and have family support.

The implications are clear. If the SEU's report recommendations are followed, the public will be safer.

Above: Prisoner working for an NVQ to improve employment prospects on release.

41. DEVELOPMENTS TO 2020

This chapter outlines some of the changes and pressures impacting on the Service in England and Wales over the last two decades. My knowledge of these events is indirect – it will be for others to write a full account of events from the perspective of Governors and of the PGA.

In 1996, the possibility of major and lasting improvements to the Service, through implementing all the Woolf Report recommendations, was vanishing fast.

In 1997, just after I had retired, the Service took over a USA prison ship. It was moored at Weymouth harbour and became HMP Weare, something of a return to the "Prison Hulks" of former centuries, although with considerably better conditions. Prisoners were kept on the Weare until 2006.

Prisoner numbers

Numbers of prisoners have exceeded 80,000 for some years.

By 2011, there were nearly 9,000 prisoners aged over 50, 42 were aged over 80 and one was 92. These figures have increased further in recent years. Some 40% of older prisoners have been convicted of a sex offence.

PAPERS SAY PRISON COSTS SOAR

NEVER FORGET, DEAR BOY,
PRISONS ARE THE CHEAP OPTIONS,
FAR CHEAPER THAN PUTTING IN
PLACE PROPER CRIME CONTROL

Government reorganisations

To abolish overcrowding, prisoner numbers must be limited to the available accommodation.

To achieve this, "joined up" thinking and agreement is needed between the Home Departments about the size of the prison population. Have recent Government re-organisations helped or hindered that process?

In 2004, the Prison and Probation Services were combined into the National Offenders Management Service (NOMS).

In 2017, NOMS was renamed the National Prison and Probation Service.

In 2007, a major Government reorganisation removed responsibility for the Prison Service from the Home Office to the Ministry of Justice. The police remained the responsibility of the Home Office. Has that change increased the difficulties of developing an effective and affordable criminal justice policy for England and Wales?

Since 2010, the Government has severely cut the Prison Service's budget resulting in a substantial reduction of prison staff, especially experienced staff. Although new prison officers are being recruited, the loss of experienced staff combined with high prisoner numbers is one of the major underlying causes of current difficulties in the prisons.

Too many prisoners, not enough accommodation and insufficient staff – the same combination of problems confronts another generation of Governors and staff.

From 2010, the Service's difficulties have been exacerbated by a rise in the number of prisoners described as "bizarre and deranged", often suffering from the effects of new psychoactive substances. These offenders – because of their behaviour – are an obvious target for the police to arrest and charge. Within the prisoner population, the balance appears to have shifted, leaving staff trying to manage a higher proportion of very unstable individuals. Assaults and self-harm statistics continue to rise alarmingly.

Police arresting more bizarre and deranged offenders may also be influenced by the establishment in 2012 of Police and Crime Commissioners (PCCs). Early in 2019, the Director General of the National Crime Agency claimed that insufficient attention and police resources were being committed by PCCs to combatting serious organised crime. While there is a national interest in targeting serious organised crime, such decisions also have profound consequences for the composition of the prison population and for the stability that the Service urgently needs to achieve.

In 2018, as the sixth Justice Secretary since 2010 took up post, the PGA called for a Public Inquiry into the state of the prisons. "The Times" described the situation in prisons as "dire". Meanwhile, the Service reported the highest ever statistics on self-harm, violence and suicide.

Towards the end of 2018, Phil Wheatley, former Governor and Director General from 2004 to 2010, analysed what had gone wrong. He identified the following key causes of the current crisis:

- Government's austerity policies of 2010–18.
- Lack of continuity of political leadership with six different Justice Secretaries introducing six different and often unhelpful initiatives.
- Continuing high prison population.
- The police arresting and charging a greater proportion of bizarre and deranged offenders, often under the influence of new psychoactive substances, making the prison population, especially in the local prisons, much more unstable and consequently extremely difficult to control.

Towards the end of 2018, the latest Justice Secretary, as justification for installing pay phones in the cells of more prisoners, referred to the evidence that helping prisoners maintain good family relationships reduced the risk of re-offending.

Yet in July 2020, the Chief Inspector of Probation reported that thousands of prisoners had been released over 2019 without homes to go to. Given the importance of accommodation in preventing re-offending, this is exceptionally concerning. Worse, the Chief Inspector of Prisons reported, that in the year 2019 to 2020, only 4% of prisons met their target for prisoners employed after release, another key indicator of preventing re-offending.

The problem of finding accommodation and work for discharged prisoners may partly result from the chaotic Government changes to the Probation Service over the last few years. Finding accommodation and work for discharged prisoners will be much more difficult in 2020 and beyond as prisoners are released from prison into the changed world caused by the Covid 19 Pandemic.

Covid 19 Pandemic

In March 2020, the Covid 19 Pandemic created an unprecedented additional crisis for the Service in England and Wales. Across the world many countries decided to grant early release to many prisoners. In England and Wales an early release scheme was announced but very few prisoners were actually released. The Service went into "lockdown" with prisoners largely confined to their cells with little contact with their families and friends.

Remarkably, and to everyone's great credit, the Service succeeded in preventing many Covid 19 deaths among prisoners and staff. The levels of violence, including self-harm, were also much lower than many expected. Longer term impacts on prisoners are very difficult to predict – especially as regards mental health. The effects of the "lockdown", from anecdotal information emerging, suggest that removing opportunities for prisoners to intimidate their peers has been a significant factor in the lower than expected levels of self-harm and suicide reported so far.

Emerging from the Pandemic, any easing of "lockdown" within prisons offers an opportunity to focus resources on regime activities rather than just "time out of cell". This has potential to maintain reduced prisoner violence and to reduce re-offending.

An unexpected opportunity for enhanced public understanding

An unexpected opportunity may be emerging as a result of "lockdowns" and related restrictions. Countless members of the public have found themselves, with little notice, deprived for months of some of their liberties. Most have found ways of coping but many have found this a difficult experience to endure. The inability to visit close relatives for months has been especially painful.

Many members of the public have previously dismissed the loss of liberty experienced by prisoners as of little consequence. Personal experience of "lockdown" has increased public awareness of the realities of loss of liberty. Uncertainty over the future, especially how long restrictions will last; the likelihood of restrictions being re-imposed; these experiences have combined to change public understanding about loss of liberty. Not everyone will agree, but many may be prepared to revisit attitudes to imprisonment, providing a window of opportunity for change.

The Pandemic may also bring public understanding that institutions can be overwhelmed by sheer weight of numbers. Hospitals have been full to capacity with bed occupation over 90%.

Concerns about further "spikes" in infections has led to suggestions of running hospitals only 80% full to ensure spare capacity to deal with future pressures.

The Prison Service has suffered exceptionally high occupancy rates, far above original design capacity, for seven decades. The case for reducing and abolishing prison overcrowding may now be better understood by the wider public.

The impact of the Pandemic could provide an exceptional opportunity for a new "Fresh Start" for the Service in England and Wales, a change much more fundamental than was achieved in 1987.

Looking ahead

In my final chapters, I set out conclusions emerging from many decades of troubled prison history.

To stimulate debate about improvement, I offer suggestions to move towards a Service fit for the twenty-first century, able to focus on reducing re-offending to keep the public safe.

42. CONCLUSIONS

What conclusions emerge from the Service's history over the last 100 years?

First – The size of the prison population has been very variable: it has ranged from over 30,000 in the 1870s; 10,000 between 1920 and 1940 to over 80,000 in the last 20 years. Is a population of 80,000 – or more – to become the norm?

Second – Many offenders suffer significant mental health issues, endure poor physical health, and display very low education attainment. Drug and alcohol dependency contributes greatly to re-offending.

Third – Re-offending can be reduced by training programmes during sentences.

Fourth – Ensuring accommodation, employment and ongoing support reduces re-offending on release. Providing such support requires a well-resourced Probation and Aftercare Service.

Fifth – To benefit from positive regimes, prisoners require stability not constant relocation.

Sixth – To be fully effective, staff need continuity of work, especially supervising and organising the same group of prisoners.

Seventh – To deliver effective programmes to reduce re-offending, Governors should be in post for some years.

Eighth – Because delivery of improvements depends on effective local management, Prison Headquarters should focus on Subsidiarity – leaving Governors in establishments with as much discretion as possible to deliver programmes to reduce re-offending.

Ninth – Research should focus on the effectiveness of offending reduction programmes and what experiences are most damaging to prisoners.

Above: Prisoner developing skills with his instructor.

43. EMERGING SOLUTIONS?

What is required to enable the Prison Service to contribute far more to keeping the public safe?

Following the shock of the Covid 19 Pandemic, Pope Francis challenged everyone to rethink our priorities. He emphasised our special responsibilities towards our fellow human beings who are suffering and in need.

For prisoners, an opportunity exists for change and improvement to make prisons "places of redemption", reducing re-offending and increasing public safety.

How might this be achieved?

Leadership – have we the positive politicians to take the lead?

Change will begin through outstanding leadership from positive politicians who are farsighted, principled and brave from all and any of the political parties.

How do we respond to Winston Churchill's challenge?

"The mood and temper of the public in regard to the treatment of crime and criminals is one of the most unfailing tests of the civilisation of any country."

Has the experience of the Pandemic changed "the mood and temper" of the public? Does it offer a unique opportunity for wise reflection about our use of imprisonment and to search for the best way to reduce re-offending?

The first step may be for positive politicians to work together to reform our present failed policy for prisons. A fresh

Above: Bishop Shepherd talking to prisoner.

© Catholic Pictorial.

"evidence based" initiative should be the foundation for developing new prison policies. Changing prisons is a long process; there is no "quick fix".

Changing prison policy will require a very wide coalition of organisations within society to support positive politicians. Existing prison reform groups, religious leaders, trade unions, business leaders, and many more, will be needed to deliver energetic and full-hearted support for change.

This presents an opportunity, but also a huge challenge, to us all.

Public encouragement and support is needed to encourage potential political leaders to take up this difficult challenge. John Hume in Ireland is an example of how determined individuals can make a remarkable and lasting difference, even in the face of intractable difficulties.

Critical to achieving change is for the media to develop a much more balanced and informed approach to prison issues. This is a huge challenge which will require very brave editors and journalists.

Overcrowding – *the prison population must be reduced.*

Prisons will continue to be needed and dangerous individuals will have to be imprisoned, some for long periods.

BUT

The size of the prison population must be reduced. Developing a solution which brings the size of the population in line with the resources available is the foundation for successfully reducing re-offending and increasing public safety.

The ways to achieve a reduction in the prison population include:

- Shorter sentences
- Greater use of alternatives to prison
- Diversion of the mentally ill
- Diversion of those with learning difficulties
- Reviewing the length of sentences for those committing lesser offences
- Diversion of chronic alcoholics
- Diversion of chronic drug users
- Greater use of Restorative Justice
- Introducing deferred sentences – in selected cases.

Keeping so many older prisoners in custody should be reviewed. The level of security needed for the incarcerated elderly should also be examined: greater use of lower security accommodation may be feasible.

Laws and regulations controlling the size of the prison population should be developed and incorporated into a new Act governing the operation of prisons. The Woolf Report's proposals to control overcrowding should be reconsidered. Reducing re-offending should become a new prison priority, enshrined in law.

Other difficult options should be explored where clear public benefits can be achieved.

Those sentenced to custody for the first time have a remarkable success rate in not re-offending. Should new mechanisms be developed to allow early release to some of these offenders? Imposition of alternative non-custodial penalties as a condition of release could be an option.

Requiring prisoners to eat meals in cells containing toilets, in apparent breach of hygiene regulations, may prove another compelling reason for change. Overcoming these difficulties will require a reduction in the prison population, coupled with a significant reorganisation of prison regimes and facilities.

Such measures may be even more urgent because of the Covid 19 Pandemic. Single cell provision for each prisoner may now be critical to reducing the spread of Covid 19 and to counter the threat of future pandemics.

The rise in the number of bizarre and deranged offenders could provide a catalyst for more radical change, perhaps a new class of institution designed for the treatment of these increasing numbers of bizarre and deranged individuals? They present too great a problem for many existing mental health facilities. Is there scope for bringing together the experience and skills of the Prison Service and the Health Service, and perhaps others, to cope with these new challenges – preferably locally based and serving local areas? Such a change, if properly resourced and adequately staffed, could provide a solution. It would require a new legal framework with a strong emphasis on reducing re-offending.

Adequate numbers of carefully selected, well trained staff are vital.

Alex Paterson's analysis, referred to in Chapter 15, that "the foremost task of a prison administration is the choice of staff suited to the needs of the establishment" remains true today.

Initial and regular refresher training is vital – something sadly lacking for staff over many years.

Governors must be given the opportunity to run good effective prisons.

Governors must be given sufficient time to bring about change and improvement. Delegation of responsibility and power to Governors should be encouraged as improvement is best delivered by local action by strong and committed local management teams. Subsidiarity should be the new watchword of HQ. Governors should be held to account for failures, but only for matters for which they are responsible – twentieth-century scapegoating should be consigned to the history books.

Governors must have scope to experiment with regimes.

To improve regimes, Governors should be encouraged to challenge existing traditions and constraints but in a well-planned way with proper evaluation. The objective being to test what regime options reduce re-offending to protect the public.

The tradition of always keeping certain classes of offenders apart should be revisited – to see if the benefits mentioned in Chapter 8 of adults and young offenders working together has validity. Running programmes for both male and female prisoners as described in Chapter 31 should be very carefully considered – and if implemented, very carefully monitored and evaluated.

Before 1966, the Service made greater use of prisoners to assist staff – the "Blue Band" and "Red Band" system. Much of that was lost during the implementation of the Mountbatten Report. Some prisoners still assist their peers by teaching – Adult Literacy work is an example. Others, under the "Listeners" scheme, have reduced the risk of suicide. Carefully enlarging the use made of selected prisoners to assist with some duties currently or traditionally performed by staff should be considered.

All developments should be carefully monitored, evaluated and researched to ensure that any potential benefits are identified and that failed experiments are quickly discontinued.

Release preparations and aftercare are essential.

Schemes for prisoners to be gradually prepared for release is at the heart of reducing re-offending and keeping the public safe. Pre-release courses, opportunities to work in the community and Home leave should be developed widely to prepare prisoners better for release and reduce the risk of re-offending.

To prevent re-offending, adequate investment in the Probation and Aftercare Service is vital especially after the disastrous experiments of the last decade. Support from the public is also needed for the many charitable organisations working with released prisoners who often make an important difference in preventing recently released offenders returning to crime.

Memories

Memories of childhood
Memories of pain
Memories of long nights
Locked up again.

Memories of dreams
The future I see
Memories yet knowing
One day I'll be free.

"What hope for his future?"
HMP Pentonville – © Andy Aitchison.

APPENDIX A – WORKING WITH THE IRISH PRISON SERVICE

In 1998 I was asked by the Irish Prison Service to assist my colleague Gordon Lakes with the Irish Prison Service's staffing problems. I was involved with the Irish Service until 2002. I also returned to Ireland after 2002 to provide "Expert Witness" advice about issues arising from incidents in Irish prisons – and other secure accommodation – over the following few years.

What was the staffing issue within the Irish Service? For a number of years, the costs of the Irish Prison Service had been rising sharply, so the Irish Minister for Justice, responsible for the Irish Prison Service, established a Committee, named the "Prison Service Operating Cost Review Group", to review the costs of the Irish Service. The Committee quickly discovered that the cost of operating the Irish Prison Service in 1996 was about £IR 102 million and that the average costs of keeping an offender in custody in Ireland were £IR 43,000, considerably more expensive than in other countries. Costs in Scotland and in Denmark, which had comparably sized services, were 40% and 47% lower. There was an absence of financial accountability within the Irish Service and no machinery existed for delivering financial accountability at local level. The Committee sought a way of improving matters. They sought expert advice from Gordon Lakes, former DDG of the Service in England and Wales. Gordon Lakes had spent the previous ten years since his retirement working on international prison issues and had a broad knowledge of penal issues across Europe and beyond. Gordon wrote a report for the Committee recommending ways of addressing the problems. The Committee incorporated Gordon's report into their own final document which was published in August 1997. A programme of work to address the staffing difficulties in the Irish Service was proposed. Among the problems to be addressed were the staff/prisoner ratios which appeared very high; the methods of rostering staff for duty; and the complexity of the existing staffing system.

In response to this report, the Irish Service set up the Staffing and Operations Review Team (SORT). Gordon Lakes and I were asked to provide consultancy support to their work. The SORT team consisted of four members, all with experience of working as Governors, Chief Officers or Administrators in the Irish Service. Initially we arranged some training for the team including a visit to Lancaster Farms Young Offenders Establishment in England. We supported their visits to each of the Irish establishments as an assessment was made of the staffing needs. The team visited 14 establishments. Gordon and I visited Dublin for about two days a month for team meetings to review the draft reports. We visited each of the establishments being reviewed by the team to ensure we had sufficient knowledge of the differing layout and characteristics of each prison to assess the quality and accuracy of the reports. The visits helped us to understand the culture and methods of operation in Ireland which differed significantly from those in other jurisdictions.

After the first year's work, with some six reports completed on the smaller establishments, we arranged additional training visits for the team including one to Scotland where the scale of the Service was closer to that in Ireland.

Most Irish prisons were very small, housing less than 200 prisoners. Mountjoy Prison was much the largest with some 700 prisoners. They included a few open establishments and a few dealing with young offenders. Several of the older establishments had originally been built for housing military offenders before Irish independence. There was a remarkable new women's prison built on the Mountjoy site, a real "market leader" in design and in regime delivery.

We found some marked similarities both in architecture and in working practice with the Services in Northern Ireland, Scotland and England and Wales. But there were also significant differences and Gordon Lakes and I found ourselves often having to check that we understood the meaning of terms used in the Irish Service. "Chief Officers" in Ireland were closer to the "Principal Officer" grade in England and Wales; "Assistant Chief Officers" to the Senior Officer grade. The "canteen", the prison shop in England and Wales, was known as the "Tuck Shop" in Ireland. "Night duties" were known as "Night Guard duties" – interestingly both in Northern Ireland and in the Republic. Before 1921, the Irish Prison Service included all the prisons in the 32 counties of Ireland so it was hardly surprising to find historical similarities in language and practices between the prisons in Northern Ireland and in the Republic.

Irish prisons had been starved of investment for years and the arrival of terrorist prisoners in such a small Service placed huge strain on resources. The staffing arrangements were very traditional and relied heavily on overtime. Apparent abuse of sick leave was a significant problem; Industrial Relations between the Prison Officers Association and management were often difficult. There were around 2,500 staff – for less than 4,000 prisoners. Prison staff were used to escort prisoners to Court and to staff the Courts cell areas and docks. This took staff away from internal duties. Irish prison officers were also employed on office work, a common feature in other services from decades earlier, but hardly an economical or appropriate use of trained staff.

At Portlaoise Prison, which housed many of the top security prisoners in the State, the Irish army was used to provide outer perimeter security because of the threat in earlier years of armed attacks by terrorist groups. There had also been a helicopter escape from Mountjoy Prison in 1973 organised by the IRA.

One of our first tasks as consultants was to make it clear that we were not advocating using solutions such as "Fresh Start" in Ireland. Our mantra became to develop an Irish solution to what was an Irish problem – quite different in many ways from the situation in England and Wales or in Scotland. However, encouraging the review team of the possibility of different approaches was important and the visits we arranged to prisons in other jurisdictions gave team members the chance to see for themselves the range of different ways of approaching staffing issues in prisons.

Relationships between staff and prisoners in the Irish prisons were usually good, helped by the small size of many establishments. We saw a wide variety of physical conditions ranging from excellent to very poor. This reflected the lack of investment in some of the older prisons. It also reflected the continuing pressure of numbers of prisoners being sent to prison by the Irish Courts.

The Irish Service was building new establishments and we were involved in assessing the staffing requirement for the new prisons at Cloverhill near Dublin and the new "Midlands" prison near Portlaoise.

Over the four years, we found very considerable scope for improving the use of staff and delivering a better service. The team produced a report on the staffing of every Irish prison and a summary or "Global" Report at the end of the project. Gordon and I provided further advice about how the Irish Service might consider implementing change and concluded our work in 2002.

Implementing change in the Irish Service was always going to be difficult and challenging but substantial progress was made over the next few years as overtime was reduced and working practices became more efficient.

The Irish Service was, in places, very overcrowded but methods had been devised for keeping the prison population from growing further. An early release programme for some offenders appeared to prevent the Irish prison system being overwhelmed by numbers. This illustrates that solutions to controlling overcrowding can be found if politicians and senior administrators are prepared to act.

APPENDIX B – AUTHOR'S PRISON ARTICLES AND LECTURES

1970 (April) – *Living with the Job* – Prison Service Journal

1971 – *Overcrowding (past, present and future)* – Prison Service Journal April

1978 – *Prison Problems* – The Tablet 22nd July

1988 – *Strangeways makes a Fresh Start* – Prison Service Journal 71

1991 – *Christians, Crime and the Penal System* – Annual Debrabant Lecture
LSU College, Southampton 2nd May 1991

1991 – *Improving Leadership in the Prison Service* – CORE Conference
2nd July 1991

1992 – *Crime: a Challenge to Lawyers and Prison Governors* – 1992 Liverpool Law Review – public lecture as part of the events marking the centenary of the Faculty of Law at Liverpool University

1994 – *Overcrowding* – Prison Service Journal 92

1995 – *Crime: A challenge to us all* – First Walter Moore Memorial Lecture

1996 – *PGA – The First Eight Years* – PGA Magazine Issue 39 November 1996

1997 – Peter Heery Memorial Peace Lecture

1997 – *Sentencing and Penal Policy* – Inaugural lecture for the Criminal Justice Unit at the Faculty of Law at Liverpool University

1997 – *Prison isn't Working* – The Tablet 8th November 1997

1997 – *Letter to a Prisoner* – The Tablet 20th December 1997

2018 – *From Stonyhurst to Strangeways* – Stonyhurst Record 2018

APPENDIX C – FURTHER READING

- *State of the Prisons* – John Howard 1777
- *Paterson on Prisons* – Frederick Muller Ltd 1951
- *Wynn-Parry Report into Prison Staff Pay* – published 11th August 1958
- *Penal Practice in a Changing Society* – Cmnd 645 February 1959
- *Prison Commission* – Sir Lionel Fox 10th April 1959
- *Anatomy of Prison* – Hugh Klare 1960 – Penguin Books
- *Pentonville: A Sociological Study of an English Prison* – Terence and Pauline Morris – Routledge & Kegan 1963
- *If Freedom Fail* – John Vidler Macmillan and Co Ltd 1964
- *Mountbatten Report* – 1966 Cm 3175 HMSO
- *Eleventh Report from the Estimates Committee* – 1966-1967 published July 1967 HMSO – *Prisons, Borstals and Detention Centres*
- *The Regime for Long-term Prisoners in conditions of maximum security* – Report of the Advisory Council on the Penal System 1968 HMSO
- *Report of an Inquiry into the Escape of WT Hughes from a Leicester Prison Escort on 12th January 1977* – published March 1977 HMSO
- *Report of an Inquiry into the Hull Prison Riot 1976* – published 13th July 1977 HMSO
- *Her Majesty's Commissioners 1878-1978 A Centenary Essay* – by Kenneth Neale – printed by the Home Office for private circulation
- *5th Report from the Expenditure Committee session 1977-1978 – The Reduction of pressure on the Prison System* – ordered by House of Commons to be printed 27th July 1978 (662-1)

- *May Report* – 1979 Cm 7673
- House of Commons Fourth Report from the Home Affairs Committee session 1980-1981 *The Prison Service* 20th July 1981 (HC 412–1)
- *Report and Statement on 1979 Wormwood Scrubs Disturbance* – HoC published 23rd February 1982
- *A Time for Justice* – Catholic Social Welfare Commission 1982
- *Island of Barbed Wire* – Connery Chappell Robert Hale 1984
- *Summons to Serve* – Rev Richard Atherton 1987 Geoffrey Chapman
- *Woolf Report* – February 1991 Cm 1456 HMSO
- *Custody Care and Justice* Cm 1647 – Government response to the Woolf Report – 1991
- *Coping with a Crisis: the introduction of Two and Three in a cell* – T.G. Weiler printed by Home Office 1992. A shorter version of this article was published in the Prison Service Journal 92 of March 1994.
- *The Prisons We Deserve* – Andrew Coyle – Harper Collins 1994
- *Learmont Report* – October 1995 Cm 3020
- *HM Prison Featherstone* – Report by HM Chief Inspector of Prisons published in June 1981
- *HM Prison Manchester* – Report by HM Chief Inspector of Prisons published on 29th March 1990
- *HM Prison Risley* – Report by HM Chief Inspector of Prisons – published 5th April 1995
- *Prison Policy and Practice* – published by Prison Service Journal 1996
- *Hidden Agendas* – Derek Lewis 1997 Hamish Hamilton
- *The Prison Governor* D Wilson and S Bryan 1998 – published by the Prison Service Journal
- *Managing Sickness Absence in the Prison Service* – National Audit Office April 1999. HC 372
- *Appreciative Inquiry and relationships in prisons* – Liebling A, Elliot C, Price D 1999 – The International Journal of Penology
- *Reducing Re-offending* – 2002 – Social Exclusion Unit HMSO
- *Modernising the Management of the Prison Service* – Lord Laming 2000
- *Bromley Briefings* – Prison Factfile – published by Prison Reform Trust
- *Keys and Cuffs* – History of the Isle of Man Prisons – ND Quilliam 2009
- *Servant of the Crown* – David Faulkner Waterside Press 2014
- *Lowdham Grange Borstal* – Jeremy Lodge 2017
- *Calling Time on a Broken System* – Phil Wheatley The Tablet October 2018

- *A Journey of Hope* – Catholic Bishops of England and Wales 2018
- *Friend or Foe?* – Women's internment in the Isle of Man during World War Two – Rushen Heritage Trust – 2018
- *Major H – the Life and Times of a Victorian Convict Prison Governor* – Prison Service Journal 249 – May 2020
- *Immigration Service Union* – David Evans, University of Strathclyde, 2020

APPENDIX D – RETIRED GOVERNORS NEWSLETTER AS A RESOURCE

PERENNIS

The Retired Governors Newsletter (RGN) was founded in 1980 and has been produced continuously for 40 years. By 1988 RGN was printed rather than duplicated and was published twice a year; in 1991 the current format was adopted. Photographs were included.

For several years the RGN was printed in the Isle of Man by Quine and Cubbon.

A key element of the RGN has been the publication of letters from its readers giving much information of their previous experiences in the service. The RGN has also published tributes and obituaries on former colleagues. The material includes valuable accounts of Prison Service history probably unrecorded elsewhere.

Examples of unusual information:

- Portland Borstal regime in 1950 – RGN 50
- Reopening of Lancaster Prison in 1955 – RGN 65/65
- The Lowdham March in 1930 – RGN 83

Above: Harry Brett, an outstanding worker for both the PGA and the RPGA.

ACKNOWLEDGEMENTS

My deepest gratitude goes to Barbara and my children for giving me sustained inspiration and support throughout the writing of this book. A particular thanks to daughter Annie for creating a promotional website and to granddaughter Katie for her drawing.

Thanks to all my older grand-children who, by their curiosity and encouragement, spurred me on to complete the project. Relatives and friends also helped with advice, contributions and encouragement.

Thanks to my amazing Manx support team: Marion Hughston of Artstream Graphic Design, Andrew Kerr-Phillips for proof reading, to Ricky and Callum at Quine & Cubbon Printers and to Moira at Lexicon Bookshop.

To countless members of the Service who helped with information and their stories.

To the committees and members of the Prison Governors Association and the Retired Governors Association – who provided a rich source of material. The cartoons mostly first appeared in the RGN.

To the many prisoners who contributed their stories, especially to the women at Risley, around 1990, examples of whose work are included on this page and throughout the book.

Any mistakes, misjudgements and inadequacies in the book are unintentional and may reflect the passing of the years. Developments commented on after retirement lack my direct knowledge of events.

Many of the photographs and illustrations are from the author's collection supplemented by material from:

Andy Aitchison, Warrington Guardian, Catholic Pictorial, Prison Governors Association, Retired Governors Association and the Prison Reform Trust. Manx sources include: Stan Basnett, Manx National Heritage and Culture Vannin.

My grateful thanks to all the above.

INDEX

Prison related Establishments, People and Topics

ILLUSTRATIONS

Above: Former Victoria Road Prison, Douglas, Isle of Man.   *© Culture Vannin.*

The Key Tower

Above: Milner's Tower, a landmark in the south of the Island shaped as a key.

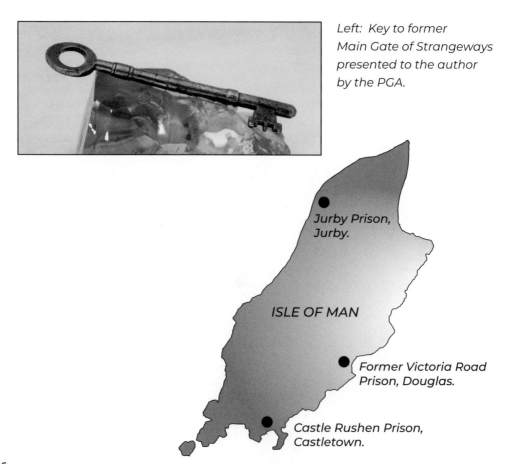

Left: Key to former Main Gate of Strangeways presented to the author by the PGA.

Jurby Prison, Jurby.

ISLE OF MAN

Former Victoria Road Prison, Douglas.

Castle Rushen Prison, Castletown.